■ *The Collected Lyric Poems of* LU

THE LOCKERT LIBRARY OF POETRY IN TRANSLATION

EDITORIAL ADVISOR: Richard Howard

For other titles in the Lockert Library, see p. 369

The Collected Lyric Poems of
LUÍS DE CAMÕES

<small>TRANSLATED BY</small> Landeg White

PRINCETON UNIVERSITY PRESS   *Princeton and Oxford*

Published by Princeton University Press, 41 William Street, Princeton, New Jersey 08540

In the United Kingdom: Princeton University Press, 3 Market Place, Woodstock, Oxfordshire OX20 1SY

Library of Congress Cataloging-in-Publication Data

Camões, Luís de, 1524?–1580.
  [Poems]
  The collected lyric poems of Luís de Camões / translated by Landeg White.
    p. cm.
  Includes bibliographical references and index.
  ISBN 978-0-691-13656-1 (cloth: alk. paper)—ISBN 978-0-691-13662-2 (pbk.: alk. paper) 1. Camões, Luís de, 1524?–1580—Translations into English. I. White, Landeg. II. Title.
  PQ9199.A5W54 2007
  869.1'2—dc22   2007033549

British Library Cataloging-in-Publication Data is available

This book has been composed in Dante
Printed on acid-free paper. ∞

press.princeton.edu

Printed in the United States of America

10 9 8 7 6 5 4 3 2 1

As always,

for MARIA ALICE...

My first encounter with Camões was through her in Beira, Moçambique, in July 1970, when I bought *Os Lusíadas* (in the Sá Costa edition) and she bought Jane Austen's *Orgulho e Preconceito* (trans. Lúcio Cardoso, Editorial Bruguela).

My prayer is this book is worthy.

✱ CONTENTS ✱

▣ ACKNOWLEDGMENTS ▣

These translations were made possible by a substantial grant over three years from the Calouste Gulbenkian Foundation. I am grateful to Paula Ridley, director of the United Kingdom branch, and to Miguel Santos, programme director in Anglo-Portuguese Cultural Relations, both of whom advised upon and monitored the grant.

I am indebted to my colleagues at Portugal's Universidade Aberta, in particular Maria do Céu Marques, Maria de Jesus Relvas, and Ricardo Prata for responding patiently to constant questions on antique vocabulary and points of grammar, and to Jeffrey Childs for help with Camões's Spanish poems. Hélio J. S. Alves of the Universidade de Évora provided expert bibliographical advice and drastically improved my introduction. The faults and failings that remain are, of course, my own.

The Camões collection at Lisbon's Biblioteca Nacional is an indispensable source, and the staff were unfailingly helpful in locating books, articles, and former translations.

Earlier versions of some of these translations were published in *O Lago de todos Recursos: Homenagem a Hélio Osvaldo Alves* (Centro de Estudos Anglísticos da Universidade de Lisboa, 2004), and in Joanne Paisana, ed., *Hélio Osvaldo Alves: o Guardador de Rios* (Centro de Estudos Humanísticos, Universidade do Minho, 2005). Earlier versions of "Aquela cativa" appeared in Landeg White, *Where the Angolans are Playing Football: Selected and New Poetry* (Parthian, 2003), and in the *Times Literary Supplement*, 9 June 2006.

Portuguese spelling was rationalized in 1911. The spellings used throughout this book, though occasionally inconsistent, reflect accurately the standard editions of Camões's lyric poems.

INTRODUCTION ⊞

But I who have criss-crossed the globe
being, as it were, doubly cognizant,
remain at heart a deluded peasant
whom my sufferings have not ennobled.

—From "Julga-me a gente toda por perdido"

Of all Renaissance poets, Luís de Camões was the most widely trav-
elled. Born in Portugal, he served in his twenties as a soldier in North
Africa, losing an eye in fighting with the Berbers. Between 1553 and
1567, he served in India and beyond, joining expeditions to the Red Sea,
along the Malabar Coast, and to islands further east, and holding ad-
ministrative posts in India and Macau. So far as the English-speaking
world is concerned, the best-known product of these journeys was
The Lusiads (1572), Camões's epic account of Vasco da Gama's pioneer
voyage to India. Beginning with Sir Richard Fanshawe's superb trans-
lation of 1655, there have been at least eighteen versions in English,
culminating in the Oxford World's Classics translation of 1997. But in
Portugal, Camões is equally loved for his lyric poems—sonnets, songs
(redondilhas), elegies, hymns (canções), odes, eclogues, and others—
that have never been translated in full and are virtually unknown out-
side his home country.[1]

Approximately half of this lyric poetry, including examples of all
the main forms, was written during his years of travel. There are ele-
gies written in Morocco in the late 1540s. There is a hymn, written circa

[1] Camões's lyric poems are in the forms of redondilhas, sonetas, canções, elegias, odes,
eclogues, oitavas, and a single sestina. "Redondilhas" means, literally, "rounds." I have
called them "songs," the closest English equivalent. "Canções" is the Portuguese trans-
lation of the Italian "canzone"; rather than call such elaborately constructed poems
"songs," I have chosen the term "hymn." "Oitavas," or "eights," are, of course, poems
in ottava rima, while the form of the sestina is explained in the note to that poem.

1555, at Cape Guardafui on the northern tip of Somalia at the entrance to the Gulf of Aden, and other hymns, elegies, sonnets, odes, and an eclogue written in India and further east. What makes this poetry unique is that Camões was the first great European artist to cross the equator and face the challenges to language and form in describing the unfamiliar people and places he encountered. An ode, "Aquele moço fero" (p. 196), and the song "Aquela cativa" (p. 253) are the first poems by a modern European poet about love for a non-European woman. It seems anomalous, to put it no more strongly, that such profoundly cosmopolitan work remains virtually unknown outside Portugal.

This volume collects these poems in English translation. But the question at once arises, collects from where? Apart from *The Lusíads*, Camões published only three poems in his lifetime. The first edition of the *Rimas* appeared in 1595, fifteen years after the poet's death. It contained 58 sonnets, 75 songs, 8 eclogues, 4 elegies, 5 odes, 10 hymns, and 3 poems in ottava rima. Expanded collections followed, in 1598 and 1616, the latter including for the first time poems retrieved from India. But even this early, poems were being published under Camões's name that are no longer believed to be his. Two editors, living two centuries apart, were crucial to this process: namely, Faria e Sousa, the many-sided Renaissance humanist, and the Visconde de Juromenha. In their respective editions of 1685 and 1860–1869, they attributed to Camões pretty well any poems they admired from the period. The fat tomes that resulted not only obscured his own genius, but made his relationship with contemporary poets virtually invisible. Diogo Bernardes, for example, published his own lyrics in 1595, only to have his better poems attributed to the master. By the time Teófilo Braga came to coordinate the tercentenary celebrations of his death, Camões was being credited with no less than 380 Sonnets, 21 hymns, 27 elegies, 11 oitavas, 13 odes, 15 eclogues, and 5 sestinas.[2]

Much scholarship was expended during the early twentieth century in cutting these attributions by roughly half, not least by recognizing the achievements of Camões's fellow poets. These included such figures as Sá de Miranda and his pupil António Ferreira, Jorge

---

[2] Theophilo Braga, *Parnaso de Luíz de Camões: edição dos poemas líricos consagada do centenário de Camões*, 3 vols. (Porto: Imprensa Internacional, 1880). Curiously and without explanation, this attempted reconstruction of Camões's stolen *Parnassus* (p. 6) excludes all but 7 of the redondilhas.

de Montemor, Andrade de Caminha, Frei Agostinho da Cruz, and Manuel de Portugal, to whom Camões addressed a fine ode (p. 291). It is a significant historical fact that the process of paring down the Camões canon was accomplished at a time when other Portuguese heroes were being puffed beyond recognition as founding fathers of Salazar's Estado Novo. While Camões was being celebrated as the original and ultimate spokesman of the regime, Camões scholarship was quietly revealing his true dimensions as a poet committed to no politician's cause. Given it was *The Lusíads* that first created the concept of Portugal as a nation greater than its actual kings, a concept that took wing after the Restoration of 1640, any dispute about the Camões canon becomes implicitly a dispute about the national inheritance. Did Camões really write those poems (included in this selection) about his youth beside the Mondego River, the only sizeable Portuguese river in which no Spanish water flows? Or should they be attributed to Diogo Bernardes? Did he really write those ultra-orthodox Catholic sonnets (not included in the present volume)? Or were they foisted upon him by Faria e Sousa? Even today, in Portugal's liberal democracy, there is no firm agreement on exactly what Camões wrote or did not write, and among the bewildering variety of editions of the *Rimas* on sale in Lisbon bookshops, there are none whose contents are identical.

In preparing this translation, I have followed Álvaro J. da Costa Pimpão's pruned edition of 1944 (reissued 1994). I have omitted a handful of poems: namely juvenilia, poems with flawed texts, or (rarely) poems that are just a little dull.

Equally, there are few certainties in Camões's biography. An entry in the register of Lisbon's India House for 1550 reads as follows: "Luís de Camões, son of Simão Vaz de Camões and Ana de Sá, residents of Lisbon, in Mouraria, squire, aged 25 years. Accepted on the guarantee of his father, travelling by the man-of-war S. Pedro dos Burgalese." This tells us, far from conclusively, he was born in 1524–25, that his rank was that of escudeiro, literally "shield-bearer" or squire, belonging to the lower orders of the nobility, and that his father's name carried weight with the India House. Perhaps he was born in Mouraria, where his parents were living in 1550. Mouraria, over-looked by Castelo São Jorge on its rocky summit, was in those days the Arab district of

Lisbon. Later it was where Portuguese Africa slaves, liberated in 1761, made their home, and where in the 1840s Fado, that most distinctive sound of Portugal, was born. Artistically, it would feel right if Camões were born in Mouraria, but no proof exists.

For some reason, possibly because he was still in Africa, Camões failed to sail on the S. Pedro dos Burgales. A further entry in the India House register, this time for 1553, refers to one Fernando Casado, a squire resident in Lisbon, and continues: "in his place was Luís de Camões, son of Simão Vaz de Camões and Ana de Sá, squire, receiving 2,400 reis like the others." This time, he was sailing under compulsion. In the previous year at Corpus Christi, one of Lisbon's biggest festivals, he had brawled with Gonçalo Borges, keeper of the King's harness, and wounded him with a sword-thrust. Initially jailed in the Tronco Prison, he was released on payment of a fine of 4,000 *reis* and an undertaking to proceed to India as a common soldier.

It was not the first time he had been so sentenced. Willingly or otherwise, he may have spent some months in Punhete, an exquisite town in the Tagus valley, now called Constância. The evidence for this is some lines from the elegy "O Sulmonense Ovídio, desterrado" (p. 80) describing a type of river-craft found there. The elegy itself was written in Morocco, where he was dispatched in 1547 to the garrison at Ceuta, originally captured by the Portuguese in 1415 as the first step in their acquisition of a sea-borne empire. Legend and all Camões's biographers claim that both these "exiles" were consequences of the court's disapproval of his pursuit of an heiress, Caterina de Ataide. There are several poems referring to "Natercia," and several more about a love condemned by differences in rank.

Camões spent up to three years in Ceuta. Then in 1553, after his spell in the Tronco prison, he sailed to India on the *São Bento*, the only ship of four to survive the outward voyage that year. He was twenty-nine years old when he arrived in Goa, and had three years of military service before him. Almost immediately, he took part in Vice-Roy Afonso de Noronha's expedition against the Sultan of Chembe, dubbed the "Pepper King," describing this action at the climax to his elegy "O Poeta Simónides, falando" (p. 148). Then, between February and November 1554, he sailed with the huge armada commanded by D. Fernando de Meneses to the Persian Gulf. Later, this "Ilustre e dino ramo dos Meneses" (p. 285) was flattered with a sonnet ("so the Red

Sea, from that time on / became so only with the blood of Turks"). At the time, writing his "Junto um seco, fero e estéril monte" (p. 192), he was overwhelmed with the futility of his existence in "the most tedious place in all nature," where he "whiled away wretched days . . . toilsome, full of grief and resentment."

By 1556, however, he was released from "having to pursue dreadful Mars" and was appointed to the post of "Trustee for the Property of the Deceased and Absent in Macau," which the Portuguese had captured just two years earlier. It was his first ever opportunity to prosper. Long afterwards, in a personal intervention in *The Lusíads*, he complained bitterly of the injustice of his summary dismissal from this position. We cannot know for sure what went wrong, but it is hard to imagine Camões as a trustee, or indeed as a businessman of any kind. He was careless even with his manuscripts, and perhaps the charges of embezzlement arose from the haphazard nature of his bookkeeping. The same stanza of *The Lusíads* describes being shipwrecked in the mouth of the Mekong River:

Gently, compassionately, he will receive
On his broad bosom these Cantos, snatched
Soaking from sad, wretched shipwreck,
Surviving treacherous shoals, and hunger
And countless other dangers, when
An unjust mandate is imposed on him
Whose lyre, played with such sweet dexterity,
Will bring him fame, but not prosperity.[3]

Once again he was jailed ("Em prisões baixas fui um tempo atado" [p. 224]) and, when finally he was cleared of any financial irregularities, he was jailed yet again for being unable to pay his debts.

Given that most of the meager records of Camões's life refer to episodes when he was in desperate trouble, the absence of records for the succeeding years is probably a good sign. In a letter home, he summed up Goa as "the mother of evil villains and wicked stepmother of honest men."[4] Yet this cannot be the whole story. Though

[3] Luís Vaz de Camões, *The Lusíads*, translated by Landeg White (Oxford: Oxford University Press, 1997), 10.128.

[4] Clive Willis, ed., "The Correspondence of Camões (with introduction, commentaries, translation and notes)," *Portuguese Studies* (London: Kings College, 1995), 2:59.

the Portuguese Empire was already overextended, leading Camões to draw contrasts between his own times and former glory, Goa was no colonial backwater. Among his friends, acquaintances, and rivals were some of the most distinguished men of the day. Much of his greatest poetry was written in "India and Beyond," including the bulk of *The Lusíads* and many of his finest sonnets. It also includes the genial banter of "Se não queries padecer" (p. 260), in which five friends are invited to a dinner party, promising "roasted crumbs of nothing / with zero as a piquant sauce," along with other teasing verse addressed to various ladies, and the deeply felt stanzas addressed to Barbara. When he left Goa in 1567, however, he was still destitute, getting only as far as Moçambique Island on the East African coast, unable to afford to travel further. In 1569, the historian Diogo do Couto (1542–1616) found him stranded there, surviving on the charity of friends. He coordinated a fund to pay the older man's outstanding debts and for a passage to Lisbon on the *Santa Clara*. Couto makes a tantalizing reference to *O Parnaso de Luís de Camões*, a book "de muita erudição, doutrina e filosofia," which was stolen from him and has disappeared.

Lisbon in the spring of 1570 was plague-bound, and the sixteen-year-old King Sebastião, who had succeeded to the throne two years earlier, was widely regarded as mad. Camões's mother was still alive, perhaps still living in Mouraria, but legend has the poet living in poverty at Alcântara on the Tagus, along with one black servant. *The Lusíads* (1572) brought him a small pension from the king "for the adequacy of the book he wrote on Indian matters." The evidence of his final poems, with their eulogy of possible patrons, is that he longed for greater recognition and suitable employment.

Six years after *The Lusíads* appeared, with its closing appeal for the imperial adventure to be rekindled, Sebastião led an army of over 20,000 of Portugal's finest men to catastrophic defeat at Alcácer-Kebir in Morocco. The outcome was that the Portuguese throne passed to Philip II of Spain. Legend declares Camões's last words to have been, "All will see that so dear to me was my country I was content to die not only in it but with it." But even the date of his death is uncertain, perhaps 10 June 1580, perhaps exactly one year earlier. According to Josepe Índio, the Dominican priest who was at his bedside, he was laid to rest in a borrowed shroud. The church of Santa Ana, his final home, was destroyed in the earthquake of 1755. For the tercentenary celebrations of 1880, what were assumed to be his remains were re-buried in the monastery of the Jerónimos at Belém.

✦

So much for the facts. Evidently, they tell us little for sure about far the most important aspect of Camões's life, his poetry. *The Lusíads* did not take contemporaries by surprise. His friends and acquaintances were well aware of the verse circulating in manuscript, and one of his odes, "Aquele único exemplo" (p. 266), had been published in 1563 as preface to Garçia de Orta's *Colóquio dos Simples e Drogas da India*, a pioneer study of India's medicinal plants. But court records, together with the odd glimpse in the memoirs of his contemporaries, throw little light on the sources of Camões's poetry.

Somewhere in his youth, perhaps at Coimbra University, he acquired a profound and extensive knowledge of Latin literature. Virgil and Ovid, in particular, left lasting imprints. So broad was his knowledge that some of his classical references effectively function as riddles. How many of his readers back in the 1570s would have been able to identify "the bright lover of the adulterous Larissen" mentioned at the start of canto 10 of *The Lusíads*? The reference is to the sun god, Apollo, who had an affair with Coronis of Larissa, in the course of which she was unfaithful to him, so that Camões is describing, with appropriate wit, dawn rising over the Island of Loves.

More is involved here than university-educated men showing off. Camões lived at a time when the established classics still provided a sure guide to life. To imitate classical writers, demonstrating their continuing relevance by giving familiar passages a modern twist, was to offer contemporary readers both instruction and delight. *The Lusíads* is a Christian epic, but Virgil's *Aeneid* provided much of its framework. Ovid's *Metamorphoses* supplied a number of myths involving Arabia, the Indian Ocean, and India itself, giving Camões a "tradition" on which to build, and simultaneously allowing him to claim these places had been colonized by European imaginations long before the arrival of the "Moors," the arch-enemy of *The Lusíads*. This method has its origins in the lyric poems, though, once Camões's travels began, it was the Ovid of the *Tristia*, those poems of banishment to the barren coast of the Black Sea, that nourished the fertility of the *Elegies*.

Latin literature from another source came through the filter of his favorite renaissance poets. Camões's older contemporary Sá de Miranda spent the years 1521–26 in Italy, and wrote the first Portuguese sonnets, as well as introducing the hymn, the elegy, the tercet, the oitava, the eclogue, and the decasyllabic line, all forms Camões was to make his own. As Sá de Miranda was returning to Portugal, he spent time in Spain, where he made the acquaintance of Juan Boscán and Garcilaso de la Vega, who were themselves the first to introduce Italian verse forms to Spanish readers. Whether Camões first encountered Petrarch and the Italian pastoralist Jacopo Sanazzaro through Sá de Miranda, or through their Spanish imitators, is not clear. But his admiration for these poets is attested not just by the number of times he imitates or borrows from them, but by unqualified eulogy:

> Petrarch will sing to us of that laurel
> he burned for, Daphne's tree, and his own Laura,
> the same who with his rare, grand style
> halted in full flow the crystaline river:
> Sanazzaro would play his flute awhile
> on the mountain, in the village, or wherever,
> and Castilian Garcilaso would serenade us,
> repeating his praise of the proud Tagus.[5]

The greatest of these debts to Renaissance poets is transparently to Petrarch. What Petrarch knew as his *Rerum Vulgarium Fragmenta* (Fragments in the Vernacular) was published after his death as the *Canzoniere*, or Song Book. The majority were sonnets, and though the collection also included hymns (canzone), sestinas, ballads, and madrigals, it was the sonnets that swept Europe in a literary craze that took two centuries to exhaust itself, moving through Italy, Spain, and France, and washing up on the shores of Elizabethan England in Sidney's *Astrophel and Stella*, Spenser's *Amoretti*, and Shakespeare's *Sonnets*.[6]

---

[5] "Quem pode ser no mundo tão quieto" (p. 141), 1.193–200.

[6] Petrarch's sonnets are divided into an octave, rhyming *abbaabba*, and a sestet, rhyming *cedcde*, but with variations. It was Henry Howard, Earl of Surrey (1517–1547) who modified this form, inventing what is now called the Shakespearean sonnet, rhyming *abab cdcd efef gg*.

But there was a third, important ingredient to the fashioning of Camões's mature style, namely, his deep love of Portuguese folksong. This knowledge is freely on display in the epigraphs to many of his songs, such as "To this old song," "On this common song," or "On this theme," followed by three or four lines of quotation before his own poem begins. It is a striking feature of Portuguese literary history that Camões did not have to scour the countryside collecting this material. He would have encountered the taste for folksong at court. Some of the oldest poetry produced at the Castilian and Portuguese courts between 1200 and 1350 was in imitation of Provençal troubadours. Some 1,680 cantigas have come down to the present day, written not in Castilian, the normal language of the court, but in Galician-Portuguese, the dialect of northwestern Iberia. There are cantigas d'amigo, or songs about a friend, usually a lover, and cantigas d'escarnho, or songs of scorn, directed at landowners, hypocritical priests, exorbitant prostitutes, cowardly soldiers, and rival poets, and including some five hundred examples where the singer is assumed to be a woman. Among the poets of the cantigas are Kings Sancho I and Dinis of Portugal, both hero figures in *The Lusíads*. This courtly appreciation of vernacular folksong was continued in such influential Portuguese anthologies as Garcia de Resende's *Cancioneiro Geral* (1516), which, alongside poems inspired by Dante and Petrarch, printed vilancetes and madrigals much in the manner of the older cantigas.

Camões's songs may be seen as continuing this tradition. No less than three-quarters are in the forms used in the cantigas, with lines of five to seven syllables in stanzas of seven or eight lines, rhyming *abbaacc*, with variations. Songs like "Caterina é mais Formosa," (p. 128) or "Por cousa tão pouco" (p. 190), a girl's complaint about "dumb John" in love with "a turban," would have been instantly recognizable to the troubadours. Camões did not need to turn to his Petrarch to appreciate what could be done in vernacular styles. He had models much closer at hand.

Virgil and Ovid, Petrarch and Boscán, together with Portuguese folksong: these were the principal poetic resources he took with him when he sailed to Ceuta in 1547 and to India in 1553.

In the elegy, "O Poeta Simónides, falando" (p. 148), Camões describes his voyage to India via the Cape of Good Hope. As he leaves the estuary of the Tagus, the nymphs Galateia, Panopeia, and Melanto accompany him, scattering spray from their scallop shells, and he chats with them companionably. They had been the heroines of the eclogues of his juvenilia. But they cannot face the Atlantic. They have to turn back, promising to convey his farewells to the shepherds of the Tagus valley, and inscribe his name on the gold-bearing sands. Within three tercets, he is in a new hemisphere under constellations he does not recognize, as "the waves became vertiginous," "the rigging whistled in the uproar," and "the blaspheming of the shocked / mariners curdled the atmosphere." Ovid's *Tristia* (especially 1.10) may have been partly in his mind here, but he had never written anything remotely similar. Though he vows, in true Petrarchan fashion, to be eternally faithful to his lady, and though he concludes the elegy with lines evoking lives of pastoral simplicity, both courtly love and rural peace have to be redefined. For "love is never truly courtly / while in the presence of its cure," while no "happy peasant" could be expected to grasp the exigencies of his new "muscular verse." Later, in canto 5 of *The Lusíads*, this same storm was to be worked up into the epic encounter with Adamastor.

He had not previously tinkered with the epic manner, but he had faced the challenge of difference. His first two elegies, "O Sulmonense Ovídio" (p. 80) and "Aquela que de amore" (p. 86), were written in Ceuta, drawing directly for both form and content on Ovid's *Tristia*. From the very beginning of his travels, Camões contrasts "this exiled life of pain / with the good I knew in another time." But he was not unresponsive:

> Pacing out my life of pain,
> and declaring its unremitting sadness
> to the burning sands of this African
>
> beach, I study the sea's relentless
> motion, as with its thunderous booming
> it reverberates in the greater emptiness,
>
> and with its furious white spume
> it takes sorrowful hold
> of the earth where it disperses foaming,
>
> and earth in turn appears to yield
> her beckoning womb helplessly
> to the penetrating, saltodorous tide.

In all such matters I feel such empathy
I scarcely know if I'm seeing what's out there
or whether it's determining me.

If I'm tempted by such misfortune to despair
I cannot, because love and the heart's
affections do not accommodate self-murder.

I meditate at times on the newness
and oddity of things, such as change,
if only I could direct its course,

and my mind struck by this foreign
land, these new ways of being human,
a different people with customs I find strange,

I climb the mountain Hercules the Theban
divided from Gibraltar's Rock,
giving entrance to the Mediterranean,

and I try to imagine where he picked
the apple of the Hesperides . . .

These extraordinarily rich lines contain so much of what is to
follow—the lonely pacing of the beach, the interrogation of the sea,
the deep curiosity about "this foreign / land, these new ways of being
human," the obscure sense he is himself changing in response to this
new geography, and the recourse to classical myth to get his bearings
in a new poetic language. The elegy ends with the vow that no matter
how far his travels take him, even as far as the "black waters / of Co-
cytus," he "will sing what is written in my heart," celebrating "though
tired and cold, the shining face / of Fancy, of whom I never lost sight."
His dedication is to his poetry, and that poetry is sustained by love that
"is never forfeit in exile":

still less is it cancelled by dying obscurely,
for in the end the soul lives eternally
and love is the effect of soul and endures.

Evidently, Camões did not travel for travel's sake. He left Portugal
to avoid jail, and he presents his years abroad as a sustained banish-
ment, imposed on him by an implacable destiny. He experienced the

exile's idealization of home, the nostalgia for past pleasures, the sense of time passing to little purpose, the longing for and the fear of death. He did not like being stranded at Cape Guardafui, "a place the sun blazes / on so ferociously it vanishes." The description was accurate, and he must have taken a craftsman's pleasure in evoking such an unfamiliar landscape. But only the sight of migrating birds gave him a sense of distant contact with all he valued. He rarely says anything complimentary about Goa, which a savage sonnet categorises as "source of the pus / that gathers around the world's disease" (p. 234). The hymn "Com força desusada" (p. 263), acknowledging plants on which "both cattle and one's eyes feast," may be about Goa, though Ternate and Ambon are also candidates. He praises the "palm groves" that "keep the peasant on his farm / contented for ever / with various fruits from the one trunk." But there is otherwise very little in these lyrics to prepare us for the luxuriant description of trees and flowers in canto 9 of *The Lusíads*, or the celebration of the earth's wealth and its multitude of peoples in canto 10.

There are twenty-first-century readers who will take him to task for this. Where are the commemorations of the richness and variety of African, Indian, and Chinese culture that are supposed to be the endgame of such travelling? Camões lived in a different world, and if we are to recognize his achievement we must be prepared to travel mentally. After the major European powers had seized control of three-fifths of the earth's surface, the age of the discoveries seemed in retrospect a confident assertion of Europe's imperial destiny. In the sixteenth century, however, the first impact of those voyages to the Americas and to India was a profound questioning of all that had appeared fixed and secure. As Bartolomé de Las Casas wrote, hoping to catch the ear of Charles V of Spain, "Everything that has happened . . . has been so extraordinary . . . it seems indeed to overshadow all the deeds of famous men of the past and to silence all talk of other wonders of the world."[7] Wonder at what had happened, in this case at the scale of the atrocities committed in Spanish America, extended to uncertainty about the very foundations of human knowledge, and is reflected across the age as one element in those vast movements we

---

[7] Bartolomé de Las Casas, *A Short Account of the Destruction of the Indies* (London: Penguin, 1992), 3.

encompass metaphorically as the "Renaissance," the "Reformation," and the "Enlightenment."

From this perspective, pacing that beach in North Africa, Camões is a poet of questioning, reinterpreting the poetic idioms of the day in terms of those new lands and unprecedented encounters. Each poem, no matter how brief, has a point to make, in the metaphysical manner, and behind most of them one senses the pressure of lived experience. He brings to his travels a creative literal-mindedness, so that all inherited metaphor is tested against his own "truths," a word he invariably employs in the plural. How ridiculous, for example, and yet how marvellous, that he should be searching in Morocco for the exact location where Hercules picked the apple of the Hesperides and fought with the giant Antheus! Later, in *The Lusiads*, Vasco da Gama is made to boast to the Sultan of Malindi that his pioneer voyage to India puts those of the ancients in the shade. He vents his professional scorn for Odysseus for abandoning half his crew on the island of the lotus eaters, and for Aeneas for losing even his helmsman on a calm night, and we are brought face to face with a practical navigator's reading of the *Odyssey* and the *Aeneid*. The words are da Gama's, of course, but Camões never distances himself from them.

Camões's editors are fond of identifying which of his sonnets derive from which Petrarchan originals. "Tanto de meu estado" (p. 26) is patently a rewriting of Petrarch's "Pace non trovo". Similarly, "Lindo e sutil trançado" (p. 32), about ribbons that have fallen into the lover's hands, is based on Petrarch's "O bello man," where the adored object is a glove, while Camões, too, has a sonnet "O culto divino" (p. 34) that describes falling in love during divine worship when his thoughts should have been elsewhere. What appear to be the earlier sonnets contain much that is more generally reminiscent of the *Canzonieri*: snow that burns, happiness that hurts, eyes that kill and restore to life, together with the constant play of antithesis as Love wars against Reason and both war against Destiny. Love is the principal actor, personified in a variety of roles, ranging from the grinning Cupid of "Num jardim adornado" (p. 31) to the capricious tyrant of "Bem sei, Amor" (p. 99) or "Quando, Senhora, quis Amor" (p. 103). As in Petrarch, language itself is a central theme, for while both poets insist on the absolute primacy

personal experience, both poets recognize their dependence on
se idioms to understand love, and to reproduce the same feelings in
r readers. In two early sonnets, Camões promises,

> Once you experience love, I'm persuaded
> you'll know what I'm on about in my verses,

while the contrary of this delicate balancing act declares,

> I'll sing of love in a manner so svelte
> with theme and style perfectly matched
> two thousand amorous parts of speech
> will make hearts feel what they never felt.[8]

But all this is before Africa and India. What is striking about the
poetry of Camões's travels is the way the derived features of his style
are transformed to serve utterly contrasting ends.

Consider the song "Aquela cativa" (p. 253), known to generations
of Portuguese readers as "Stanzas to the Slave Barbara." It is a poem in
the Petrarchan manner, the poet praising his mistress for being lovelier
than the rose, brighter than meadow flowers or the stars in the heav-
ens, a heartless, unattainable beauty, whom the enslaved lover can wor-
ship only from afar. Yet this Barbara is dark-skinned, with black hair
and non-European features. She is his "captive," a female prisoner
whom the soldier poet has made his apparently reluctant concubine. It
is this situation of gross sexual exploitation, reflecting the cruel reali-
ties of early colonial conquest, to which the Petrarchan conventions
are applied, providing Camões with the astonishing opening lines,
"That slave I own / who holds me captive," and the equally astonishing
conclusion, "This is the vassal / who makes me her slave." Having
turned both poetic and social conventions upside down, he continues
by subverting other modes: the assumptions that white skin, an al-
abaster neck, a bosom like snow, and hair like gold are the marks of the
desirable mistress. So Barbara becomes "distinct in feature / eyes dark
and at rest," her "hair is raven / and the fashion responds / forgetting
its given / preference for blonde," and finally "Love being Negro, / at
so sweet a figure / the blanketing snow / vows to change colour."

---

[8] "Enquanto quis Fortuna que tivesse" (p. 25) and "Eu cantarei do amor tão doce-
mente" (p. 25).

Perhaps the poem's most disturbing line is the fourth, "who scorns I should live." This sounds like the cruel mistress of Petrarchan courtly love, despising her adorer. Or is it instead the smouldering resentment of a slave, hating her exploiter? A generation later, Shakespeare and Donne would take pleasure in upsetting the conventions ("My mistress' eyes are nothing like the sun"), but it is hard to feel that anyone travelled so far as Camões in taking Petrarch apart.

It is not an easy poem to translate. The doctrine of "types," the convention that different styles were necessary for representing different social levels, has been obsolete for over two centuries. Those opening images of rose and starlight seem merely hackneyed, and we no longer feel, as Camões's first readers would have felt, that it is precisely their application to a slave girl that is startling. The effect could so easily have been mock-heroic, diminishing Barbara by the extravagance of the language applied to her. Instead, we have a poem of such tender authority that, although there is no evidence Barbara ever existed, most readers are instantly persuaded not only that she was a real person, much as described, and open to erotic fantasy, but that Camões was deeply in love with her.

Something similar happens in the mature sonnets, as the familiar Petrarchan tropes are turned inside out under the sheer pressure of "pure truth / living experience my teacher."[9] Several are based explicitly on the contrast between "those days when love was a fine game" and his present existence as "a galley slave."[10] The contrast is not just between past and present, Jerusalem and Babylon. In "Eu cantei já, e agora vou chorando" (p. 231), one of his subtlest, most poignant sonnets, he acknowledges, about the very act of writing, that "so wretched is my present condition / I was judging the past to be free of pain":

> What drove me to sing so cunningly?
> Fulfilment? No! It was the future's map
> I sang, but even then to the clanking of chains.

Evidently, the love of paradox and oxymoron remains, but the old Petrarchan gap between humble lover and exalted mistress has become the actual width of the Atlantic and Indian Oceans, as "fidelity" is

---

[9] "Conversação doméstica afeiçoa," p. 226.
[10] "No tempo que de Amor viver soia," p. 228.

"put to the ultimate test."[11] Those metaphors of pursuit and conquest and killing are suddenly serious as he fights in real wars, carrying "in the front line, in an echoing / strident voice," his mistress's name into battle.[12] Like an "adroit mariner" who has survived shipwreck and swears he will never again venture on the ocean, he swears to avoid his lady's sight, only to be drawn back inevitably to "that fatal coast."[13] He has been fettered "in vile prisons," sacrificing his life "as a warning / that love demands more than lambs or heifers."[14] Yet Cupid all but disappears as an actor. The poet's constancy in love established, perhaps not altogether convincingly, it is "time's project in me" and "the implacable fates" he struggles with, as "fortune, accident, time and luck / rule over this world's confusion."[15]

In the guise of the fisherman Aónio, he paces the tropical beach longing for the loved one's voice but hearing only the wind in the casuarinas.[16] Then there is the short cycle of sonnets addressed to the woman he calls Dinamene. No one has convincingly identified this lady, apparently drowned at sea—perhaps another local lover, possibly the Chinese mistress drowned, according to Diogo do Couto, when Camões was shipwrecked in the Mekong Delta on being summoned back from Macau, and who in turn was possibly Barbara. Originally, Dinamene had been one of the Tagus nymphs waving to him from her scallop shell as he set out for India, the name itself borrowed from a poem by Garcilaso de la Vega. As applied in these sonnets, it both undermines any sense of difference between Europe and the East, and emphasizes the cruel irony of his new situation: that in the real world of India and beyond, nymphs do not survive their submersion.

The main themes of these later sonnets are contradiction, no longer relished as paradox, along with stoic endurance, bereavement, and heroic death. In a manner that owes less to Petrarch than to the cantigas, he takes, as his heroes and heroines, peasants caught in the tangle of love and fate. Nise and Montano, for example, divided by

---

[11] "Quem quiser ver d'Amor ua exceléncia," p. 159.
[12] "Senhora minha, se a Fortuna imiga," p. 160.
[13] "Como quando do mar tempestuoso," p. 161.
[14] "Em prisões baixas fui um tempo atado," p. 224.
[15] "No mundo quis um tempo que se achasse," p. 220; "Verdade, Amor, Razão, Merecimento," p. 288.
[16] "O céu, a terra, o vento sossegado," p. 173.

circumstance, she "tired of herself, of fate and the years," lamenting his departure freshly each dawn while he, once again pacing "the beaches of the Indian Ocean" and perhaps echoing Dinamene, mourns her "who preferred to leave me."[17] Or Daliana, betrayed by the shepherd she loved, and taking revenge by marrying cowman Gil, only to wither away in her lifelong misery.[18] Or a second Daliana, married to Laurénio but desiring Sílvio, a case of "nature's discord" that pity for her husband, nor his genuine compassion for her, can resolve.[19]

These tales of love's contradictions and of time and fate to be endured are continued in sonnets on biblical and classical themes: Jacob, cheated on his wedding day after working seven years to earn Rachel, and at once embarking on seven more years' labor;[20] Cephalus, "under the power of misplaced passion," begging forgiveness from the wife who betrayed him;[21] Telephus, wounded by Achilles, and told by the oracle the only cure was to be wounded a second time:[22]

> such is your beauty, my prognosis
> is that of a patient swollen with dropsy:
> the more I drink in, the greater my thirst.

The sonnets celebrating heroic deaths follow naturally on such themes: Leander's dying wish that his body should not be exposed for Hero to discover,[23] and Portia's preferred method of suicide by swallowing hot coals, "for I don't want any death without pain."[24]

His oeuvre also includes sonnets, not all appearing in the present volume, of heroic death in colonial battles. These are rather less to modern taste, not least because such extravagant praise of figures so obscure they cannot always be identified rings a little false. It raises the question that hovers over the poems of Camões's final period: to what extent he was struggling finally to conform, religiously and socially, in the hope of gaining preferment. *The Lusíads* closes with an appeal to King Sebastião to find some use for his talents, and the

---

[17] "Apartava-se Nise de Montano," p. 166.
[18] "Tomava Daliana por vingança," p. 167.
[19] "Quantas vezes do fuso s'esquecia," p. 167.
[20] "Sete anos de pastor Jacob servia," p. 219.
[21] "Sentindo-se tomada a bela esposa," p. 164.
[22] "Ferido sem ter cura perecia," p. 165.
[23] "Seguia aquele fogo, que o guiava," p. 163.
[24] "Como fizeste, Porcia, tal ferida?," p. 279.

frustrations of his last years may be reflected in, for example, the extravagant flattery of the Duke of Aveiro in "A Rústica Contenda" (p. 307), or the self-repudiating orthodoxy of the second part of "Sóbolos os Rios" (p. 317). As Helder Macedo, one of Camões's most acute critics, has noted, the last line of the sonnet "Verdade, Amor, Razão, Merecimento" (p. 288), which runs "but best of all is to have faith in Christ," though perhaps intended as "simply an orthodox profession of Christian faith," seems "a non sequitur, an absurdity comparable to the absurdity of human existence."[25]

Apart from a handful of late sonnets, along with the sensuous eclogue "Arde por Galateia" (p. 328), and the stark sestina "Foge-me pouco a pouco" (p. 330), with its unrepentant devotion to "those lovely, gentle and lucid eyes," the greatest poem of Camões final period is the hymn "Vinde cá, meu tão certo secretário" (p. 297), which looks back on a lifetime to rehearse all his old themes—the reasons for writing; his audience of "the desperate"; his devotion to love imbibed at birth; the mistress worshipped for her flawless eyes; his exile; the "lawless fury of Mars"; the "friendly people" he first took to be hostile in a land that "seemed lethal"; his continuing ill-fortune; the irrepressible memories—until he cuts himself off with the cry that brought *The Lusiads* to an end, "No more, song, no more!" It is a poem that resonates throughout with all he has previously written, and it ends with a personal epitaph:

> Nor do I sing for courtesy's sake
> with a taste for praising, but to make
> pure truths known about my former times.
> Would to God they were mere dreams.

All translation involves compromise, literary translation most of all. In Camões's case, the principal trade-off is between the economy and simplicity of his nouns and verbs and the prolixity of his epithets.

Unlike *The Lusiads*, Camões's lyrics have found few English translators. Only Richard Burton has attempted what I have attempted

---

[25] Helder Macedo, "Conceptual oppositions in the poetry of Camões," in *Post-Imperial Camões: Portuguese Literary and Cultural Studies* 9 (University of Massachusetts/ Dartmouth) 66 (2003): 63–77.

here, and he suffered from two handicaps he never overcame. First, he was working with what were assumed in the late nineteenth century to be Camões's complete lyric poems. Though he never got round to doing the eclogues and elegies, he did translate 360 sonnets, 21 hymns, 14 odes, and 5 sestinas—considerably more than the present collection and more than half of it *not* by Camões. This handicap was compounded by his ambition to write as Camões would have written had he been born an Englishman in 1524: that is, pre-Shakespeare, pre-Spenser, a language he has to cobble together from such sources as Wyatt and Surrey. This, for example, is his version of the octave of one of Camões's most subtle sonnets, "Transforma-se o amador na cousa amada" (p. 93):

Becomes the Lover to the Loved transmèwed,
By thoughts and reveries the Fancies fire:
Then have I nothing left to desire,
For the Desir'd is in me embùed.
If my transmèwed soul in her be viewed,
What can my formal body look for higher?
Only in self for Rest it can desire,
Since that same Spirit has my form Imbrùed.

Nothing could be further from the grace and economy of the original. J. J. Aubertin, who translated 70 sonnets, just over half by Camões, in 1884, compared it to the music of Handel, and one has just that sense of fragile but robust perfection, reinforced by a steely wit.

This particular sonnet is unusual, though, in that over half the rhyming words are nouns or verbs. Far more commonly, Camões's rhymes are adjectives or adverbs, or verbs in participle form and hence functioning as adjectives. He could do this without sacrificing the natural word order because, of course, in Portuguese the adjective normally follows the noun and the adverb the verb it modifies, increasing exponentially the number of rhymes available. The translator's choice is whether to imitate Camões's rhyme scheme, with all the syntactical acrobatics that requires, or whether to try to capture in English the naturalness and lucidity of his style. Most of my predecessors, from the small selections by Strangford (1804), Hemans (1818), and Aubertin, down to Baer's *Selected Sonnets* (2005), have opted for the former. But with the question posed as I have done, there seems only one appropriate answer. A relatively relaxed rhyme scheme, mixing full and half rhymes with sometimes the merest echo of a vowel or consonant, allows for versions that read like modern English, while actually being closer to the way rhymes sound in Portuguese because they are so easy. I have also opted to transfer back to the nouns and verbs, what the poems are about and what they are doing, something of the richness of Camões's epithets. A simple noun followed by a line of four multisyllabic adjectives does not work well in English. In pursuing an English equivalent of Camões's manner, I have cut back on the descriptive words but increased the number of synonyms. In "Aquela cativa" (p. 253), for instance, Camões sticks throughout to the noun "cativa." It is the translation that has made her "slave," "captive," and "vassal." The reader must be the judge of how well this works.

The order in which, for the first time, the poems are presented here, loosely grouped in four sections, rests on two assumptions.[26] First, that poems referring to specific events were written more or less contemporaneously. Secondly, that Camões's poetic style matured detectably as he grew older. Both these assumptions may obviously be

---

[26] Portuguese scholars have been reluctant to speculate on where and when the majority of Camões's lyrics may have been written. The excesses of attribution, culminating in the 1880s, were matched by excesses of biographical speculation, with the poems (not all of them by Camões) raided for information about his life, the results being then applied to elucidate the poems. In sharp reaction, as I have described, twentieth-century Portuguese scholars worked tirelessly to establish what Camões actually wrote, eschewing biography for the more rigorous critical practices of formalism, mannerism, and (more recently) discourse theory. José Hermano Saraiva's bestselling but novelistic *Vida Ignorada de Camões* (Europa-America, 1978) seemed only to reconfirm the need to maintain this strict attendance to the actual texts.

Yet no one doubts Camões spent some two-thirds of his adult life in Africa and India, and it seems critically evasive not to recognize that his poetry shows the mark of these travels. A paper by Saraiva, presented to the Lisbon Academia das Ciências in 1982 (*Tome* xxii, 257–84), plausibly assigned forty-three of the major poems to four distinct periods. I have rejected only one of his suggestions, namely, that the eclogue "Que grande variedade vão fazendo" (p. 199) was written in 1570 after Camões's return to Portugal. Both the dedication and the letter from Goa make it clear that it belongs to the period shortly after his arrival in India. Saraiva, however, did not discuss the sonnets or songs. Subsequently, Maria de Lourdes Saraiva published a small edition of Camões's *Sonnets* (Europa-America, n.d.), dividing them into four periods more or less matching my own. Her three-volume edition of the *Lírica Completa* (Imprensa Nacional, 1986–2002) is organized by theme but makes suggestions by way of annotation about possible dates.

questioned. For a poet whose work circulated in manuscript for over thirty years, there is no knowing how stable these texts were.[27] The hymn "Junto de um seco, fero e estéril monte" (p. 192) may possibly have more of the 1570s than 1555 about it. But I suggest this hardly matters. Even if that poem were written late as Camões looked back on his travels, it would still reflect his thoughts about that period, and may be placed in that context. The hardest poems to place are the songs, many of which float free of any discernible background. But Camões did not spend his life as a learned doctor at the University of Coimbra, endlessly recycling existing tropes. His greatest work was produced in Africa and the East, and I have tried to underline that truth. Needless to say, the reader is not obliged to accept the arrangement proposed here in order to enjoy these superb poems. It remains astonishing that most English readers will be encountering them for the first time.

[27] The hymn "Manda-me Amor que cante docemente" (p. 135) exists in three versions, and there are differences between the versions of the ode "Aquele único exemplo" (p. 266) published in 1563, when Camões was alive, and in *Rimas*, 1595. Otherwise, we are largely in the dark.

PART ONE ▪ *Before Africa*

◈ Enquanto quis Fortuna que tivesse

When Fortune was disposed to give some
hope of eventual satisfaction,
the agreeable pleasures of invention
made me write of the likely outcome.

Love, however, fearing what I wrote
would be artless in its candor,
made of my talents a nightmare
to keep his stratagems inviolate.

You, then, whom Love compels to be subject
to various yearnings! When you read   10
in a brief book such varied cases,

that are plain truths, without defect . . .
once you experience love, I'm persuaded
you'll know what I'm on about in my verses.

◈ Eu cantarei do amor tão docemente

I'll sing of love in a manner so svelte,
with theme and style perfectly matched,
two thousand amorous parts of speech
will make hearts feel what they never felt.

I'll do it so love confers life,
painting its thousand delicate mysteries,
its blank rages, its heart-felt sighs,
it foolhardy courage, its remote grief.

But in writing of the highborn disdain
of your tender and fastidious eyes,   10
I'm content to play the lesser part.

For to sing of your face, a composition
in itself sublime and marvelous,
I lack knowledge, Lady, and wit and art.

Tanto de meu estado me acho incerto

So much of my life is equivocal,
I shiver with cold in the hot season;
I weep and laugh together without reason,
I embrace the world and clasp a bubble.

My impulses mutually contradict,
from my soul comes fire, from my eyes a fountain;
at times I hope, at times am uncertain,
at times I'm distracted, then reconnect.

Being earthbound, I soar to heaven,
an hour's a thousand years, and my genius   10
in a thousand years is to miss my hour.

If someone asks why I'm so driven,
I respond, I don't know. But I surmise
it was your face, my lady, I saw.

Amor é um fogo que arde sem se ver

Love is a fire that burns invisibly,
a wound that festers though inert,
a happiness more like a hurt,
a pain that rages painlessly.

It is not to want what's wanted most,
to walk alone in a multitude
dissatisfied with all that's good,
claiming the prize when all's lost.

It is to be prisoner by consent,
to be conquered and serve willingly,   10
with one's murderer to feel content.

So how could its blessings possibly
turn human hearts benevolent
when love itself is so contrary?

O fogo que na branda cera ardia

The flame on the soft candle burning
at the sight of that face I see in my heart,
kindled another in its sudden spurt
to attain the brightness that eclipses the sun.

Wherein two passions were inflamed
as presumption, blazing in its fury,
launched itself with splendid energy
to kiss that part of you whence it came.

Happy the flame that so dared
to quench its torments and its pains   10
in that face by which the world is shaken.

Your elements adore you, Lady,
and the white fire of that snow burns,
singeing hearts and the imagination.

Pede o desejo, Dama, que vos veja

Desire drives me, Lady, to possess you;
I don't follow why what it asks is wrong.
Is love so refined, so spiritual a thing
that who's driven forgets what he must do?

Nothing exists in nature's guise
without wishing that existence to endure;
desire then cannot want the desired
for it should not fail where it overflows.

But this pure passion in me is condemned,
as a stone is driven by the art of its gravity   10
to desire nature's very kernel,

so imagination (through the demands
I derive from my fallen humanity)
forces me, Lady, to ask this fundamental.

Quando da bela vista e doce riso

When my eyes are drawing sustenance
from the lovely face and sweet mirth,
I'm made to see paradise on earth,
so heightened becomes my fancy.

I am so removed from human good,
everything else I consider mere wind;
in such a sphere, as seems to my mind,
it takes very little to turn one mad.

In praising you, I offer no reasons,
for whoever senses your mystery,   10
senses clearly it can never be his.

So strange you appear to what's mundane,
it seems no strangeness, excellent lady,
whoever made you made the sky and stars.

Quem pode livre ser, gentile Senhora

Who, gentle lady, is not in thrall,
surveying you with a tranquil mind,
when the child god who was born blind
is at home there in your own pupils?

There he dictates, there reigns and woos,
there lives, venerated by all people;
your luminous, delicate face is an idol
that Love, adoring himself, adores.

Whoever sees blooming amid snow roses
encircled by twisted threads of gold,   10
if upon such light the eye should dwell,

it will see yet brighter rays, which to those
souls doubtful at heart are unrivalled,
as the sun's light outshines a crystal.

Tomou-me vossa vista soberana

The magnificent sight of you compelled
me to where I had weapons closer to hand,
proving whoever had hopes to defend
against those lovely eyes is self-beguiled.

To achieve a more resonant victory,
it armed me first with Reason;
I tried to protect myself, but in vain,
there's no human defense against Destiny.

But perhaps even if you had promised
your sense of yourself this victory,   10
your much ado about little is shrewd;

for however well I'm equipped and harnessed,
from conquering me you take no more glory
than I take in being conquered.

Vosso olhos, Senhora, que competem

Your eyes, Lady, that in their searing
voltage are more dazzling than the sun,
fill with such tenderness my own
that on meeting yours they melt in tears.

Overwhelmed, my senses submit,
blinded by such majesty;
and from their prison's sad obscurity,
full of fear, resort to flight.

You offer a fresh glance and, for sure,
the bitter contempt with which you view   10
me startles awake my languishing heart.

O strange disorder and gentle cure!
What will the favor you withhold do
when your very scorn reanimates?

Está o lascivo e doce passarinho

The sweet, irrepressible sparrow is tugging
its feathers in shape with its tiny beak;
free, spontaneous poetry, rocking
joyously on its rustic twig.

The ruthless hunter (who tracks
on tiptoe, dodging stealthily), glimpses it
and fires the arrow that dispatches it
to its eternal nest in the Stygian Lake.

Just in this manner, my carefree heart
(for all that this was long in store)   10
was wounded, where I was least apprised.

For the blind archer was waiting
in ambush, ready to take me unaware,
his hiding place your flawless eyes.

Quem vê, Senhora, claro e manifesto

Whoever, Lady, sees plainly on view
your beautiful eyes in their lustrous being
without being blinded in the act of seeing
is already not paying your face's due.

This seems to me an honest price,
but I, for the merit of deserving them,
gave both life and soul to serve them
apart from which I am without resource.

Enough that life and soul and hope
and as much as I have is all yours,   10
and the profit of this I alone know.

For such good fortune is beyond scope,
giving you all that is in my power
as the more I pay you, the more I owe.

Passo por meus trabalhos tão isento

I go about my business so exempt
from emotion, whether heartfelt or trivial,
it's only through my desire to feel
love delivers me further torment.

Yet Love pursues me with such spite,
tempering the antidote with a venom
that disturbs suffering's usual system,
since I don't consent to a broken heart.

Yet if Love fails to appreciate this subtlety,
and pays me my hurt with a feigned hurt,   10
it melts to pleasure, like the sun on snow.

But if he sees me content with my misery,
he rations the pain, struck with the thought
that the more he pays me, the more he'll owe.

Num jardim adornado de verdura

To a garden luxuriously verdant
and enameled with countless flowers,
there came one day the two goddesses
of Love, and of dense forests and Hunting.

Then Diana plucked a perfect rose
and Venus the best of the red lilies,
but exceeding by far all the other flowers
in beauty and grace were the violas.

They asked Cupid, who was standing near,
which of the blooms, in his opinion,   10
was sweetest, purest and most lovely?

The youngster answered with a grin:
all three are gorgeous, but I much prefer
viola-tion to mere rose and lily.

Lindo e sutil trançado, que ficaste

Prettily woven head-dress arrayed
in pledge of the remedy I am due,
alone at last, is it madness I see you
torn from the hair that you once tied?

Those golden ribbons, as she wove them,
more dazzling than the sun's rays;
is it to deny me what I pray
for, or to bind me she unraveled them?

You are in my hands, pretty riband,
and as my grief's palliative   10
I have to take you (no other availing).

And if my desire is not unburdened,
I warn you, in this game of love,
whoever takes part takes everything.

Presença bela, angelica figura

Lovely presence, modeled on angels,
in whom whatever heaven has she disposes;
happy appearance, suggesting roses,
from among which beauty personified smiles;

eyes that consist of such a blend
of white crystal inlaid with jet,
that in those of elegant green we catch sight
not of hope but of envy with no end.

Tenderness, judgment, and grace that dilate
your natural beauty through disdain   10
and through disdain takes the lovelier form:

these are the fetters of a captive heart
that sings of its anguish to the rattle of chains,
as mermaids sing in a storm.

Está-se a Primavera trasladando

Spring's very essence is depicted
in your frank and charming face, while in
your eyes, mouth, and brow's expression,
daisies, lilies, and roses are reflected.

In this way, nature, through the variety
of your face, manifests her power,
while mountain, meadow, forest, and river
all are enamored of you, Lady.

If now you are still reluctant the fruits
of these flowers should be plucked by lovers,   10
soon your eyes will no longer shine.

For, beautiful lady, Love accumulates
little in sowing you with paramours,
if it's in your nature to produce thorns.

Porque quereis, Senhora, que ofereça

Why intend, Lady, of one who serves you
for life I should suffer so much hurt?
If I by my birth have so little merit,
there's no one yet born who deserves you.

I knew intimately, whatever you ask,
I would come to merit what I wished of you;
Love won't accept so little is due
to such high ambition, at such risk.

So do the rewards match my discontent
with nothing in surplus; but you are in debt   10
being capable of so many disfavors,

and if the mettle of your attendants
must measure your own self-estimate,
you'll have only yourself by way of lovers.

Se pena por amar-vos se merece

If loving you deserves a heavy sentence,
who can escape it, or be exempt?
What heart, what understanding, what judgment
does not yield on seeing you, in obeisance?

What greater glory has life ever offered
than thinking of you at every moment?
At the sight of you, all the pain and torment
is not only unfelt, but unremembered.

But if whoever offends by loving you
truly deserves his sentence, you will kill   10
the world that's yours to the last man.

You can start with me, Lady, one who,
in my love for you, comprehends very well
just how much I should and how much I can.

O culto divino se celebrava

Divine worship was being consecrated
in the temple in which the whole of nature
praises the divine Maker, whose creatures
He redeemed through His sacred blood.

Love, despite the event being one where
passions were normally under control,
through the image of a human angel
ambushed me as she knelt in prayer.

I, trusting the place itself would defend
me, ignorant of his licentious play   10
and in no way bold enough to flee,

surrendered; but today I understand
he wanted me for you, my lady,
and I repent the time that I was free.

Amor, que o gesto humano n' alma escreve

Love, that stamps on the soul a human brow,
showed me bolts of lightning one day
where a crystal tear melted away
between roses in bloom and driven snow.

My eyes that in themselves lacked vision
to enquire the subject of their stare,
became their own fountain, that altered
pain to sweet and gentle passion.

Love swears that softness or weak intent
causes the first effect; and the imagination   10
goes mad if it worries about what is real.

Look how Love mutates in an instant
from its tears of honest devotion
to happy tears that are immortal.

Leda serenidade deleitosa

A happy, charming composure,
the image of an earthly paradise,
a sweet laugh between pearls and rubies,
the color of roses under gold and snow;

a prudent and gracious demeanor,
where shyness and subtlety impart
what can be done by wit and art
in being beautiful as of nature.

Speak of whom life and death perplex,
rare, delicate lady; all yours, in short;   10
I relax in discreet rapture.

These are the weapons with which Love attacks
and holds me captive, and yet cannot
divest me of the glory of surrender.

Se tanta pena tenho merecida

If I have merited such an ordeal
as my wage for bearing such adversity,
practice on me your cruelty, Lady,
having this heart at your disposal.

Experiment on it, if such is your fancy,
the whole gamut of your disfavor,
so I sustain in this life's warfare
even greater anguish and constancy.

But against your eyes, what could avail?
All that surrenders is by force,   10
but I shield myself with my heart,

for in such a hard and bitter struggle
it is good that, being defenseless,
my defense is to fling myself on the dart.

Diversos does reparte o Céu benino

The kindly heavens bestowed different
gifts, intending each to have just one;
so chastity adorned Diana the moon,
the jewel of the crystal firmament,

and grace, Cupid's beautiful mother,
at the sight of whom he lost his own,
and wisdom like yours to Pallas, and to Juno
courage, unique in ruling through worth.

But united now the same heavens bestow
their most lavish gifts, only less acclaimed   10
than those of the author of Genesis;

to their cost, lovely Lady, they awarded you,
Diana her chastity, Pallas her wisdom,
Juno her nobility, and Venus her grace.

Náiades, vós, que os rios habitais

Naiads, you who dwell in the rivers
that irrigate the pleasant meadows,
you will see pouring from my eyes
other streams, almost equal to yours.

Dryads, you who fire your darts,
shooting down the running deer,
you'll see other eyes triumphing here,
shooting down much worthier hearts.

Leave your marshes and clear fountains,
come, nymphs, if you wish to discover   10
how eyes exist that give birth to despair.

You'll see how days are passed in vain;
but you will not come in vain, to encounter
in yourself the darts, in me the water.

Pelos extremos raros que mostrou

For the rare excellencies they embodied,
for learning Pallas, Venus for beauty,
Juno for courage, Diana for chastity,
Africa, Europe, and Asia adored them.

That great wisdom which conjoined
spirit and body in generous alliance,
constructed from the four elements
this shining terrestrial machine.

But the greater miracle was from Nature,
endowing each one of you, ladies,   10
with that which the four of you share.

Sun and moon bequeathed you splendor
while light, grace, and purity were supplied
jointly by fire, earth, water, and air.

⊞ Senhora, se eu alcançasse

TO A LADY WHO ASKED HIM TO SEND
HER SOME OF HIS WORKS:

Lady, if I could contrive
for the instant you are disposed to look
that what's best about my book
should stand before you as if alive,
so you could see
my writings, as it were, in précis,
composed with such brio
that I go where they go,
you'd want to read them only for me;

for after witnessing a disclosure   10
so at ease with its anguish,
you would see in the flesh
what's only painted here:
as that perfect
love to which I'm subject,
harsh and cruel you'll regard here
as ink on paper
when blood in my heart is the fact.

Imagine a hypothesis
in which what Love ordains   20
is pain that a mere pen
lacks the means to declare itself;
what I suffer
in my heart on paper
demands to be translated,
and see how much better you read:
if it's truly myself I write of here?

Este tempo vão

TO THE OLD SONG:

*My heartbreak
the day I see you.*

This pointless age,
this empty life,
for others it passes
only not for me.
The days elapse
without bringing in view
the day I'll see you.

Consider my fate,
if so short a life
is well forfeit   10
to so long a hope!
If this is well-founded
all others will rue
the day I'll see you.

Heartfelt pain.
I comprehend you,
but I won't defend
what insults Love.
If you were stronger,
for the greater merit   20
I'd give you credit.

My heartbreak,
my dear mortgage,
to whom did I pledge
so great a truth?
Night and day
in my longing
you are forever mine.

Quando vos eu via

Life of my soul,
seeing you never,
this is no life
only to suffer.

It was to my advantage
when I had you in sight,
life seemed a delight;
I showed you homage
living like a page
boy, for the sake of seeing.
But now I don't
what's the point of being?

My life is without purpose
because in my grief   10
Love gives no relief,
the two being sworn foes.
It's perfidy that forces
me to live as I now do,
existing, Lady,
without seeing you.

I no longer dare,
my as-it-were-wife,
to call you my life
given my despair.   20
No one warned
this could come about;
you being my life's
what I can't live without.

Dous tormentos vejo

ANOTHER VERSE ON THE SAME SONG:

I know two torments
that drive me to the edge;
if I see you, I hedge,
if I don't see you, I want.
When I break cover,
my dilemma is clear,
whether I fear desire
or just desire the fear.

Nos seus olhos belos

TO THIS OLD SONG:

> Shepherdess of the hills
> of the Serra da Estrela,
> I am lost over her.

In her challenging
eyes, such beauty glows
as to scorch in the snows
whoever risks such a vision.
Don't, brilliant Dawn,
unfasten your hair:
I am lost over her.

These hills contain
for all their summits
no lovelier remit
than in her is penned.
Heaven blesses the land
that owns such a star:
I am lost over her.

With shepherds, she causes
a thousand broken hearts,
but you hear in these parts
only her praises.

Adoring, I lack phrases,
not knowing what to say of her,
but I know how to die for her.

Some who, revealing
their innermost hurt,
laugh, unaware that
in laughter's no healing.
I, sadly concealing
the torment I suffer,
am lost over her.

Desiring her own hand
to pluck them, flowers
in their envy wither
by the thousand.
None exist who don't find
all perfection in her:
I am lost over her.

If her eyes are bent
on running water,
their crystal light
will stop the current.
So he who, intent
on that water, appears there:
I am lost over her.

▦ Dotou em vós Natureza

TO THIS COMMON THEME:

> *You, Lady, have everything*
> *without your having green eyes.*

Endowed as you are by Nature
with the sum of perfection,
what in you is a blemish
is in others the fashion;
green's nothing to be ashamed of

so, given that they're yours,
how lovely are your green eyes.

Gold and blue are, by convention,
colors men give their lives for,
but the charm of this green 10
deprives color of all charm.
What remains is the flower
to be seen in eyes like yours
because they are yours—and green.

Ninguém vos pode tirar

TO THIS OLD SONG:

> *Your loveliness would take the prize*
> *if it weren't for those green eyes.*

None of us could allay
your sudden reluctance,
but, Lady, I have to say,
your eyes are not worth two pence.
You were given bad guidance
when you wanted them green;
I've pressed you, keep them hidden.

Like a garden is your forehead
where Cupid likes to play;
it resembles polished ivory 10
being white and well sculptured.
As for me, I long studied
the growth of all your beauties
so close to those green eyes.

The sun itself is dazzled
when you shake loose your tresses;
but there's some are unimpressed,
reckoning they look frizzy.
But in faith it seems crazy

you don't bother to disguise
possession of those green eyes.

Your lashes have demonstrated
their incendiary power,
if they weren't so elongated
and painted even more:
they long focused my desire,
without your being wise
to it, but for those green eyes.

Your pudding face in its sweetness
seems reluctant to provide sockets,
and being soft and luminous
it confiscates our hearts.
Even so, you'll find courtiers
ready to overlook its size,
but not with those green eyes.

Your laughter is composed
of so many new-born graces,
though there's those who accuse
it of dimpling your face;
for my part, I'm disposed
to yield my heart as a prize
in exchange for those green eyes.

Never was seen or recorded
such a graceful mouth,
redder than coral the outside
and whiter than snow the teeth;
it fires me, I take my oath.
I suffered from all you advertise;
but you don't need those green eyes.

To that throat of yours is due
words more eloquent than mine,
unless its beauty has in lieu
little shells of confection.
I'm aware of one who pines

to seize all you monopolize,
including those green eyes.

Those hands are like manacles,
they arrest at first sight;
they are white and mechanical,
punching above their weight,   60
while you claim as your right
in law to apprehend and seize
those who witness your green eyes.

Your style of flirtation
destroys those you talk to;
you have a scornful affectation
that I plan to copy from you.
Holy Mary, it's my chief woe;
I'm the one you have in thrall
with those cat's eyes, and all.   70

▨   **Tudo tendes singular**

      ANOTHER ON THE SAME THEME:

You have all that's unusual
with which to conquer hearts,
yet when you laugh dimples start
you struggle to conceal;
and then to heal
you've strength, backed by grace,
if it weren't for those green eyes.

Ah, Lady, you attain all
such beauty accomplishes,
except that you make promises   10
with those eyes you use to kill;
and if, by chance, you heal
them, they're the hearts you'd surprise,
if it weren't for those green eyes.

1 Entre estes penedos

Fresh are the gardens
with roses and jasmine;
youths water them
by whom Love is undone.

Among the boulders
encountered here,
fresh grasses appear,
and forested highlands.
From these rocks descend
streams to freshen
the flowers of others
by whom Love is undone.

With the water that flows
down from this jungle,   10
another stream mingles
that pours from the eyes:
to freshen white flowers,
both of them join
where other eyes wait
by which Love is undone.

Celestial gardens,
with stars for blossoms,
while Seraphim
stand guardian,   20
roses and jasmine
of various complexions;
and angels water them
by whom Love is undone.

Campo, que te estendes

TO THIS COMMON THEME:

> *Green are the meadows,*
> *lemon tinted,*
> *and so are the eyes*
> *of my heart.*

The meadow you tender
with its beautiful flowers,
along with the ewes
you offer pasture,
the grasses sustained there
bring the summer's heart,
and to me memories
of my heart.

Cattle you promenade
with serene relish,   10
you do not furnish
their provender;
what they feed on
are not grasses, but
the graces of those eyes
of my heart.

Eles verdes são

TO THIS COMMON THEME:

> *Girl with green eyes,*
> *why don't you see me?*

Your eyes are sea-green
and the usual trope
is that signifies hope
though the results are lean.
Your condition
is not eyes that see,
for you don't see me.

[47]

Unaffected by tears
they say what you have
are not eyes that observe,   10
nor sea-green eyes.
I am on my knees,
and you don't believe me
because you don't see me.

They must be real
because they're there;
eyes so rare
are not to conceal;
but they make me feel
they're not eyes that see   20
for you don't see me.

Those can't be green
eyes I have in view;
green is the hue
seen as good omen.
If your condition
were truly to see,
why not look at me?

A verdura amena

TO HIS OWN THEME:

> *If Helena abandons*
> *the meadow,*
> *thistles grow.*

You pleasant meadows,
the cattle you tend,
should know you depend
on Helena's eyes.
In the gentle breeze,
thistles flower
in the breath of her eyes.

They put blooms on the mountain,
they make crystal the rills;
if they do that on the hills   10
what will they do to humans?
They come in suspension
like dewy grass
in the light of her eyes.

Hearts are imprisoned
with inhuman panache,
from each eyelash
a soul is suspended.
Love surrenders,
and on his knees   20
wonders at your eyes.

Quem põe suas confianças

TO THIS THEME:

Whoever trusts
in the eyes of teenage girls
sees they're faithless . . .

Whoever puts his confidence
senselessly in teenage girls
subjects his mature will
to countless twists of chance.
You put hope in their countenance,
but then read in their pupils
they don't have faithful souls.

In opinions they contradict,
as in the case of wooing,
they are women in denying   10
but girls in desiring it.
If you give their eyes credit,
you'll see a thousand graces
to admire, and yet they're faithless.

They show you at one moment
favor even to tears,
then with a shift of those eyes
their thoughts are gone on the instant.
They lack any judgment,
in short, what's on show   20
is a beauty that's untrue.

☒ Aquele rosto que traz

TO DONA GUIOMAR DE BLASFÉ,
WHO BURNED HERSELF IN THE
FACE WITH A CANDLE:

> *Love, that offends all*
> *took, Lady, as its purpose*
> *your countenance should face*
> *what smolders in souls.*

The face that attracted
all the world to be scorched,
by a candle flame was touched
and so felt its own effect.
I know Love surrenders all;
perhaps its purpose
was your countenance should face
what smolders in souls.

☒ Vi-o moço e pequenino

TO THIS COMMON THEME:

> *When tiny I imbibed love,*
> *not understanding what was in me:*
> *now, what was my main belief*
> *kills with its acrimony.*

I saw Cupid when tiny
and at the same age learned
a girl could be inclined

to the good looks of a boy.
Love I heard it called,
and by that name I lived;
I was never so deceived
nor saw so much to appall.

Day by day this disquiet
advanced with my age,   10
for Love from its earliest stage
lives and grows in the heart.
This Love nursed itself in me,
lording it over my life.
Now, what was my main belief
kills with its acrimony.

The flowers produce thistles,
and her death deprived me
of the girl I used to carry
in the pupils of my eyes.   20
In this grief and this agony
I know myself at last;
I love, and I'm lost
for whom lost his love of me.

It seems a strange predicament
Love has arranged for me,
that barely out of infancy
I feel so grown-up a torment.
It's Love's consummation
I have to suffer so,   30
until there's pity from one who
pities this frustration.

Ua diz que me quer bem

TO THREE LADIES WHO SAID
THEY LOVED HIM:

I don't know if Helena's lying,
nor Maria, nor Joanna,
nor which one of them's the winner.

She wishes me well, one resolves,
the next swears she wishes me better;
but who will swear by a woman's patter
when they don't believe it themselves?
I can't not believe Helena,
Maria, or Joanna,
but in their wiles, who's the winner?

The first crosses her heart,
swearing my love is all she values;
I'm pining away, the second says,   10
while Joanna's distracted.
If I hint Helena's lying,
you'll soon see Joanna trying,
but none of them takes me in.

Quem tão mal vos empregou

TO A LADY UNHAPPILY MARRIED:

Young lady, I'm dumbfounded
seeing you used up so,
but sadder still at seeing you,
lovely and badly husbanded.

That man to whom you're now domestic
took no account of the cost,
having no idea how much I lost
when he took from me what he took.
But truth insists when loveliness
takes a form so splendid

that everyone says what's obvious:
lovely, and badly husbanded.

When it came to beauty, you took
as much as you esteemed,   10
and with it you condemned
me to live out my ill luck.
I died for you as a virgin,
I die since you gave your maidenhead;
my ways of dying are legion:
lovely, and badly husbanded!

Baixos e honestos andais

TO A LADY WHO AVERTED HER FACE:

Eyes, I don't deserve this
conditional bestowing;
to the floor, so easy-going,
to me, so furious.

Modest and maidenly behavior,
to go about refusing
those who covet only the blessing
you grant freely to the floor.
So little is my merit
you think more of the floor than me,
on which you confer the trophy
I'm forced to live without.

Os gostos, que tantas dores

TO THIS OLD SONG:

Little contentment
in searching for whom to make happy
when you don't even know me.

Your kindness so much torture
makes me value not at all;
I don't accept the little

when I never had the more.
It seems am empty favor
when it's only now you want
me, while remaining ignorant.

You tempt me with joy
when I'm already blind and deaf:
it's beneath me to trifle   10
when I deserve you every way.
Take some other highway,
for the good that's my due
won't be bettered by you.

Se me for, e vos deixar

TO THIS COMMON SONG:

If from this land I journey,
Love, I'll take you with me.

If I leave you and go away
(I say what might be true)
my heart which belongs to you
here with you has to stay.
So merely to convey
my heart, if I have to leave,
I'll be taking you, my love.

What harm can befall me
that with you would be bad?
What blessing so good   10
that without you I'd be happy?
The evil can't appall me,
the good can only improve
if I take you, my love.

Já agora certo conheço

TO THIS COMMON THEME:

Your good, Lady, I covet,
your bad I'm best without.

I know for sure at long last
it's worth every torment
if my being repentant
is bought at a just cost.
A good beginning engrossed
me, but the climax now tells
me what's bad's better expelled.

When a blessing's so dangerous
it comes with a warning sign,
the harm has an obligation   10
to be less perilous.
But, lady, so poisonous
was your good, as luck had it,
your bad I'm best without.

Reinando Amor em dous peitos

TO A LADY WHOM HE FAILED TO MEET:

Which of us deserves the blame
in this mishap I repent?
When you're around, I'm absent,
when I'm here, you don't come.

When Love reigns in two hearts
it weaves such blunders
that from compatible desires
it produces opposites.
It lives in us equipollent,
but being so unsound
it takes you off when I'm around,
when you appear I'm absent.

✶ Pues me distes tal herida

TO THIS THEME:

Eyes, that's enough,
your darts have dispatched me;
yet in my death you watch me,
bringing me back to life.

Since you inflict such grief
your aim being my death,
I am happy in my final breath
since in death you give me life.
Eyes, what's your brief,
given you've dispatched me,
when in my death you watch me
bringing me back to life?

Wounded mortally at your sight
though that's hardly what you want,   10
but if it's death you grant me
dying is sheer delight.
Eyes, accept this proof
given you've dispatched me,
when in my death you watch me
bringing me back to life.

✶ Desque uma vez mirè

TO THIS THEME:

What will I see to be content?

Since the first time, Lady,
I beheld your loveliness,
never has it been my choice
to turn my eyes away.
Since my life knows no joy
without you and this employ,
if you do not wish them seen,
what will I see to be content?

Tiempo perdido es aquel

TO THIS COMMON THEME:

Why inflict torments
that profit them so little?
I'm lost, but so imbecile
as to confess what I want.

Time's wasted that is given over
to causing me anxiety
since whatever you cause me
by so much less I suffer.
Why reveal what I endure?
Not for anything so small,
and who could be so imbecile
as to harbor this idea?

They should know Love decrees
about such a sweet dispute   10
nobody should yield part
in order to increase.
My torture is exquisite
even when it hurts me little;
and when much, I go imbecile
with raptures of delight.

ELEGY

Aquele mover dos olhos excelente

Those eyes, with their superb movement,
that ardent, living genius
her crystal face makes evident;

that unhurried look, completely at ease
which, individually written on the soul,
cannot be translated into verse;

[57]

that mien which is immeasurable,
testing to the limit human wit
so I offend in anything I scribble,

inflames with a sweet delusion my heart,   10
bewitching me, so my fantasy
is of no greater glory than being hurt.

That blessed day should be solemnized
when the sweet thought captured me,
distracting me from all else!

And how fortunate was the agony
that knew it was capable of heartache
given its ultimate cause was my sanity!

She who kills me intends the harm she makes;
she treats me with lies and disdain;   20
then she redeems me with what she dislikes.

And if, through such delectable scorn
some soul consumes his days in strife,
what delicious torment! what sweet pain!

And should implacable fate rebuff
death's sympathy for my distress,
what sweet death! what delicious life!

And if she shows me a gentle, human face,
who's to blame for the damage done?
what delicious lies! what sweet lip-service!   30

And if condemning this defect I rein
in my too-ambitious thoughts,
what sweet feigning! what delicious chicane!

So I now locate in a broken heart
the greater portion of my glory,
taking all the torment as the better part.

If I feel so good at the mere memory
of seeing you, my lady and fair conqueror,
what better than to be your victory?

If your mere sight makes me aware   40
how far am I from deserving you,
what better than have you as my paramour?

If what's good proceeds from knowing you,
and consists in winning and being won,
what more could I want than wanting you?

If I'm at all divided in my ambition,
at the sight alone of those serene eyes
what more than being lost could I gain?

If my low spirits, from my earliest days,
still do not deserve this punishment,   50
what more do I want than that more is not less?

The cause, in the end, reinforces the torment
since in spite of the suffering, which I defy,
in all my labors I am content;
for reason makes my pen joyful or melancholy.

❇ HYMN ❇

❇ Já a roxa manhã clara

Breaking open the doors of the east
clear red dawn approaches,
and the dark summits are touched
by her beams, jealous to be the first.
The sun that never rests
with his joyful, welcome face,
        following apace
his horses tired of their drudgery
as they scent on the grass the fresh dew,
while he spreads his happy, luminous rays.   10
The birds in their flight
from twig to twig, or alighting

with their soft, sweet melody,
are heralding the renewal of daylight.

As mild and lovely morning
unveils her face, the woodlands
are once again verdant,
so delightful, heavenly and serene.
      O delicious pain,
Love's doing, he being pre-eminent,   20
as he gives his consent
wherever I may happen to be
it's her seraphic face I constantly see,
so with my sad life I am content!
But you, pure Aurora,
have so many graces to offer
fortune, in forms so different
representing so much splendor.

The gentle, joyful light
reveals to my eyes her I die for,   30
the dawn's golden hair
cannot match what's before my sight:
      rays that translate
the black chaos of sentiment
into sweet discernment;
the dew drops on delicate flowers
become on my eyelids spent tears
shed through pleasure at my pain;
the tiny songbirds
are my vital spirits becoming heard   40
to make manifest that unique vision
in divine music the world applauds.

In the same way it occurs
that to someone on the point of death
even as their last breath
fails, some sacred vision appears;
      my heart being yours
as I die for you, my *senhora,*

my soul dwelling in your core
—while breaking free of its prison—   50
you appear before me as a vision
in the guise of lovely bright Aurora.
O joyful catastrophe!
O supreme, glorious epitaph!
—if desire does not impede—
for what I behold at the last restores life.

Yet, all that's natural
in sustaining life's purity
fails me just as swiftly
as the sun ceases to be spherical.   60
       If it seems feeble
to die in such a pathetic state,
it's Love they will castigate,
or you, where he has so little purchase
you provoked so long a divorce
that life fails, along with appetite.
If living is not an option
—I am only a man of flesh and bone—
Love gave me this life I'm forfeiting;
I'm not mine; if I die, the pain's your own.   70

The swan's song in his last extreme:
on the hard, cold memorial stone
I leave you in the company
of this lettering on my tomb,
that a shadow always obscures my dawn.

⊠ ODE ⊠

⊠ **Fermosa fera humana**

Dazzling, feral creature
in whose proud, untamed heart
restless Cupid's power

that conquers all is blunted,
as no matter how many he sharpens
all his darts are broken;

my Circe, my beloved
(not mine, but loved all the same)
to whom whatever good I had
by way of delicious freedom,   10
little by little I handed over,
and had I more, I'd still deliver:

since it's Nature's philosophy
to award you such opposite traits,
so perversely lovely,
you amuse yourself with the fires you set,
while remaining cold
longer than the moon illumines the world;

since you go about triumphing
in the spoils of your lost ones,   20
those you are depriving
of sense, direction, and all reason,
as though generous to all
with the very blessings that have them in thrall;

since it amuses you to observe
the nocturnal suitor
dressed to kill, shivering
in the rainstorms Jupiter
brings, outside the door that shuts off
fulfillment, worn out by his grief;   30

what makes you so confident
the goddess who reins in
overbearing pride won't
reward your tricks and disdain
with what you deserve,
firing in you the punishment of Love?

Take Flora, that courtesan,
rich with spoils of a thousand sighs,

weeping for her captain
conquered at Thessaly,   40
her mourning so sublime
altars were raised to her at Rome.

Or take from Lesbos
that famed poet Sappho,
writing of all that were lost
over her; she lost her own life
on that cliff that inspires threnody,
as the true lover's extreme remedy

—through the chosen Phaon,
more lissome than the three Graces,   50
whom Venus kept hidden
in a bed of detumescent lettuce;
he paid the cold penalty
for the harm he brought to so many.

And seeing herself forsaken
by the one for whom she had left
so many, she was driven
to hurl herself from the fatal cliff;
so the evil beloved of evil
finds for such a life, life must fail.   60

"Take me, unruly seas,
take me, for that other that flew!"
And so, borne on the breezes,
in her anger, she hurled herself.
Succour her! you suave
and omnipotent bird of Love!

Fold her in your wings,
kind Love, secure from danger;
anticipate the appalling
waves and extinguish the old fire.   70
Is it right so great a love
of life should be so destructive?

No: it's fitting there should be
for reckless whores who peddle love
a clear case where they may see
who captivates can become captive.
So Nemesis decrees her moral,
determined Love should conquer all.

⬚ ECLOGUE ⬚

⬚ As doces cantilenas que cantavam

> ENTITLED *To The Fawns*, ADDRESSED
> TO DOM ANTÓNIO DE NORONHA.

The sweet ballads, sung by the half-
goats that live in the mountains
and are the lovers of the wood nymphs,

I will inscribe as song; and hence
if Love maltreats those woodland deities,
we shepherds will not be impugned.

You, Lord Dom António, in whom are united
to perfection bright Apollo and Mars,
with your high intellect standing out,

if my own talent seems immature and vulgar,   10
it knows where to find indulgence as it strives
to match the result with you, its author.

In you my blemishes are absolved;
in you springs the fountain of Pegasus,
through which my song is conveyed to the world.

You see the exalted muses of Parnassus
are singing of you to the sweet lyre,
gathering in hand such an exalted cause.

You see golden Apollo, taking over
the praise of your lineage, to eclipse   20
what in your praise my own song endeavors;

either through envy of what I make public,
or to prevent my rough flute singing
what is reserved for the sonorous harp.

It will resound, my Lord, this silent tongue
—while Procne comforts Philomela
by sharing her weeping over her wrong,

and while Galateia to the halcyon
winds unbinds her golden hair:
while Tityrus takes his seat out of the sun;   30

while there survives in the field a single flower
(if you do not at this take offense)—
as to the Douro and Ganges it proclaims your honor.

And my own tongue already assents,
by granting my Eclogue should mark time
while Apollo recounts your achievements.

On hard Parnassus, on the very summit
amid a grove of self-seeded trees,
springs a clear and crystal stream,

out of which a gentle river flows   40
quietly over the white rocks, rippling
placidly and at ease.

The soft sound of its delicate babbling
stimulates the birds, whose song
makes the green mountain yet happier.

So clear are these waters in their journeying,
that in their depths the smooth pebbles
are one-to-one in their manner conferring.

In their world, they will never be stepped on
by wild beast or intruding shepherd,   50
being from that mountain forbidden.

No grass is seen there, on that sad,
pleasant, or baneful mountain, unless
at its center are equally featured

red lilies along with the white rose,
white violets, and the one whose hue
lovers connect with grief and heartsickness;

and on all sides myrtles grow
to hide the beauty of crystal Venus
from the fawn's impudent crew.   60

Mint and marjoram breathe their odors
while neither winter, nor summer's heat
destroy, nor drought withers.

From here, the unploughed, uninhabited
mountain parallels the river's course
with green trees along its route.

Here, a lovely nymph, divorced
by chance from her fellow mountain-goers,
to whom the highest ridges are foreclosed,

returned one day from the hunt, tiring   70
and wishing to relax in the forest shade
and take in her hands daybreaks of cold water.

And seeing the freshness of the glade
and how trees co-operated with the wind
to preserve the quiet of the midday;

and the playful antics of the birds that,
expert in changing key in their verses,
gave wing to delightful thoughts;

there had already lapsed, as she noted this,
the hour of high noon, when she determined   80
to search around for her loved sisters.

Afterwards, she freely informed them
she had never seen a spot nearby
that she loved to such extremes,

and she begged them that some other day
they should bathe in that crystal river
where such translucent water plays.

It was when Apollo, the great pastor,
had spun round the serene sun,
making the happy lover repine once more,   90

that the lovely nymphs, to settle the question,
went together to that mountain site
invading the cold, delightful dawn.

One had her golden hair dispersed
over her lovely bosom in disarray,
entangled in two thousand knots;

another, wearing her breasts bare
for greater effect, preferred braids,
finding irksome disordered hair.

Dinamene and Efire, whom Phoebus encountered   100
naked in a river, when they plunged
their delicate bodies in the clear water;

Syrinx and Nise, who fled the lunges
of lusty Pan, with Amanta and Elisa,
skilled with their bows, no matter the range;

and the lovely Daliana along with Belisa,
both coming from the Tagus, no one
so splendid as they, striding the grass:

each of these angelic maidens
made their way to the luxuriant heights,   110
where vivid stars lit up the heavens.

But two woodland Satyrs, caught
up in the same private fancy,
of what they had long wished to consummate,

so there soon was no mountain nor valley,
nor meadow nor single tree lacked knowledge
of where they had reached in their traveling.

How often as they made their passage
rivers stopped their course, at the pains
they complained of to the hard ridges.   120

how often love of such duration
would have conquered the absence of desire,
if only nymphs had hearts like humans!

But whoever is content with failure
commit themselves to endless patience,
so that love through happy grief endures.

Cyprian Cupid sought through this science
that, being resigned to these contraries,
they would have, he said, the experience.

Descending at last by precipitous ways   130
and shedding from their lovesick
eyes crystalline tributaries,

the satyrs encountered the familiar tracks
of those white, darling feet,
and their impatient strides quickened.

But finding the nymphs in the clear water
naked, and seemingly oblivious
to all they had seen and met,

they left them undisturbed, surveying
parts they had never gazed on, so they   140
could see without being caught observing.

But the thick undergrowth betrayed
their ambush, through the rustling
branches of a rough hazel tree,

showing one of the goddesses concealed,
and all raised to the heavens such a screech
as if the mountain itself had fallen;

at once in their nakedness they dashed
for the forest, but so fleetingly
as if a light breeze had freshened.   150

Like a flock of pigeons alerted by instinct
to the glorious eagle, whose stare
does not falter in the sun's brilliance,

and communicating to their wings the terror
of death, they cut
the air to find safety in the verdure,

so the nymphs, abandoning the booty
of the branches they had carried, flew
naked into the nearest wood.

But the lovers, now driven to fury   160
as they saw their cloven feet
were useless in attaining their desire,

pursued them with amorous shouts.
Only one, by not pausing for breath,
did they attain in their alacrity:
then afterwards, repleted, they held forth:

First Satire

Ah, runaway nymphs,
simply to deny your humanity
you ignore the dangers of the bush!
What makes you rebuff us?   170
We are not asking for your pity,
but why insult such glistening flesh?
Ah, nymphs, is it your wish
to die like Eurydice,
flying from her lover instead of from mortality?
Hespere, too, was bitten
by a viper never seen.
Observe how nymphs in the green meadow
lose their lives preserving their condition.

What tiger, what lion,   180
what monster so poisonous,
what pursues you with such enmity?
A gentle heart, imprisoned

by your unrelenting countenance,
that flies to you spontaneously, and you flee.
Observe how in a face so lovely
a heart so recalcitrant does not fit
unless you wish all to resign to their fate.
Even if you see your beauties in the river,
you do not trust its mirror   190
that brings its vengeance, disguised
as that hope that led you into error.

But ah, I do not allow
that any words of mine could offend,
even though sheer grief excuses me.
Nymphs, I admit I am a liar;
nothing that exists could pretend
not to be unmade by your beauty.
If devotion so steady,
deserves so much harm for so little good,   200
you take no account as my heart goes mad;
if they talk of impromptu frenzy
without sense of prophecy,
pray God you do not press my life beyond
measure through such growing obduracy,

Strange matters, larger than fable,
exist in the world and occur in nature,
leaving he who has never seen them astounded.
In the mountains of Libya,
are ferocious crocodiles, so bizarre   210
in shape, their very appearance confounds.
Hyenas give tongue
in a voice so like the human voice
whoever hears them is deceived.
And you, a savage race, whose sight
holds the world subordinate,
you have by nature, in one body,
the look and sound of humans, but are wild at heart.

Why fly to the forest,
nymphs, from those amorous laws   220
by which nature joins human hearts?
Why are you not embarrassed
there exist in you such obdurate flaws
when you possess more than nature's assets?
Given your beauty
is supernatural, you are not driven
to have hearts consumed with spleen;
but faced with Love, in whose hand
hearts are found,
for all your lovely elegance   230
you lack an amorous state of mind.

Love is a passionate friendship
placed by God in the world and nature
to propagate the things he made.
Love controls and shapes
whatever in this globe has jointure;
nothing without it is created;
through it is repeated
the loved world's prime cause
when lusty Adam took his last repose.   240
Love binds things, and harmonizes;
in this world it transforms
matter. Who lives that does not encounter it?
As for me, it ordains evil, which comes.

Among the various grasses of the meadow
are not male and female known
existing companionably one with another?
Are the elm trees not bowed
down with the clinging grapevines
as the trained bunches mature?   250
As the turtle dove suffers
the death of its one and only wife,
do you not witness its grief?
How many did Cupid on Mount Olympus
capture and abuse?

Better than my words, subtle Arachne
depicted it all on her canvas.

O great and grave indictment!
O hearts composed of diamond
and by entirely natural laws!   260
Are you indifferent
to Love so sweet that, ordained
by his power, even the gods are awed?
I warn you to be aware,
against Love there is no known shield:
vengeance in all is its method.
Soon, I shall watch you unwind
a thousand sighs to the wind,
tears, sad moans, and fresh complaint,
over one with some different love in mind.   270

He wished to say more,
that unhappy lover, who saw himself
unsupported in his grief and sadness;
but it fell to him to humor
the other companion, resentful
at treatment so harsh and capricious
—he whom coarseness
and a country education taught
to fancy, as a cry from the heart,
roused abruptly from a dream.   280
What more was there affirmed
you, mountains, will say, and you boulders,
and what is carved on your trees as emblem.

Second Satire

You nymphs weren't born of human stock,
nor were you nurtured by human mothers,
springing from some monstrous warlock
from Hircana there in the Caucasus;
it was there your bitter bile was sucked,
from there your hearts froze;

the sphinx reveals your natural race,   290
though what you show is a human face.

Even if your genesis was in the thick
forest, where no animal lives,
nor green vegetation nor hard rock
that knew anything whatsoever of Love,
or for whom that soft, tender shock
could not alter what they were made of,
why ignore that interminable memory
thrown up by your long and amorous history?

Take Arcadia, there in burning Sicily,   300
out of sheer love, the river Alpheus
plunged his clear water beneath the sea,
in pursuit of Arethusa, his darling nymph.
There, too, you can watch poor Acis
swimming whom the Cyclops Polyphemus,
jealous that Galateia should be his lover,
murdered so his blood became the river.

Look further, nymphs, to Venus's glades;
you'll observe Egeria transformed
into a spring of crystal water, distilled   310
on account of the death of Numa.
See the broken-hearted Byblis school
you in forfeiting all she had, to bloom
in tears of such green efficacy
they irrigated a fertile valley.

If the clear streams knew about passion,
it could equally happen to boulders.
Witness that pair of high-flown
lovers turned into rocks on Mount Ida;
Leteia on account of her brazen   320
folly, setting her beauty above the gods';
and Oleno because he courted the blame
rather than see his sweetheart condemned.

Or take examples from Cyprus: Iphis,
who for Anaxarete put his life on the block;
or that lovely nymph, whose pure voice
angry Juno imprisoned in the rock,
so that only the faintest sound echoes
if she attempts to bewail her luck.
And you too, Daphnis, the very first   330
to sing to the mountain sweet, pastoral verse.

Such love he bore to his tender friend
who became afterwards his bitter enemy
when another unknown nymph dragooned
him to gather up her magic remedies;
share the deep pain of her wound
as to satisfy her anger, his dear Chloe
changed him to stone. Adamant conclusion!
In the upshot, he repented. But in vain.

Study, nymphs, the spreading trees   340
as you gather your flowers in their shade,
how they were lovers in former days
and their trunks even now bear their load
of pain. You will see, if you have memories,
how Love turns the mulberries red,
for the blood of lovers marks Thisbe's
tomb in that vegetable testimony.

And look there, in fragrant Sabeya,
don't you see how, from her penitent tears
after joining her own father in pleasure,   350
Arabia is enriched, subsisting from myrrh?
Then take note, further, of the green bay,
a lovely nymph in a former era,
and that tree that was handsome Cyparesso,
both evergreen with the tears of Apollo.

This is Attis, the slender youth of Frigia,
transformed into a tall grove,
often torn by the wind in its rage
as just reward for his behavior;

to some lesser nymph he laid siege,   360
being at the time great Sibele's lover,
and the goddess to whom he had given his heart
wished he should forfeit his very wits.

In that sudden, wild eruption, it appeared
mountain and houses and trees were felled
as first the goddess seemed inspired
by her passion to see him gelded;
then down to that cursed mountain she careered
where even the wild animals wished him dead;
and so Atis forfeited in the forest gloom   370
after so much loss his human form.

Recall, nymphs, when the Greeks celebrated
in ancient times the rites of Bacchus,
when the loveliest nymphs were united
with the sacred dwellers of Mount Lycaeus,
and after the hillside was swathed in night,
were lost in the arms of Morpheus,
though the god of the Hellespont was not lethargic,
for a new love was keeping him awake;

but she, stretching her limbs *post coitus*,   380
found branches sprouting from her arms
while her feet were twisted into roots,
so of Lotus all that survived was her name.
Witness, wood nymphs, this calamitous
case, for your fate could easily be the same;
or be warned, also, by Syrinx who fled
from sacred Pan, and ended as a reed.

I must speak, too, of Phyllis, who, lost
in the sad yearning she daily felt,
came in the end to be so depressed   390
by the long pain of living desolate,
that to free her body came at last
to strangle herself with her own belt.
It was a leafless trunk on Mount Rodope
Demofonte embraced after his long delay.

In the very daisies, you can see Jacinto
whose fate Phoebus lamented in vain;
you can see in red blood Mount Idalio,
his mother's brother, his father's grandson.
Venus bewailed her deceased gigolo   400
cursing heaven and earth with good reason:
for failing to open on the instant, Earth,
and Heaven for collaborating in such a death.

And you, faithful Clicie, for whom true
constancy in all your lovers dies,
in the amorous laurel that forgets you
are also forgotten your yearning eyes;
no happy condition can continue
in a world that finds pleasure in lies;
but you, bright sunflower, for the Phoebus   410
you sigh for, constantly turn your face.

I recall all this to memory's page
because it makes your cruelty more bizarre,
given that breeding and long usage
have not changed or refined your nature.
I offer these my tears as a pledge
that throughout this globe in whatever quarter,
you don't and won't see, if you're observant,
anything from which Love is absent.

I said already that with Love it's the most   420
insensitive know the pain and glory;
observe how the most susceptible get lost
as birds while I tell the long story.
All the heartbreak true love costs
is borne on wings by way of memory,
and that light and ecstatic fluttering
hurts only in the mind's reiterating.

The sweet nightingale and the swallow,
how did they come to be changed, if not
through the love of the king who became a hoopoe,   430
Tereus of Thrace, who yet loves and calls out?

—calls out blamelessly to the melancholy
pheasant, named for the sands he inhabits
on the Phaesis; and calls out thither
to his cruel mother and his faithless father.

Witness whom Pallas despised for her chatter
—in lovers always the worst fault—
and she who succeeded her as suitor,
both birds, love's customary result:
the one for fleeing Neptune, the latter   440
for sharing her father's bed of guilt;
and Scylla, witness her father threatened
by making his greatest enemy her friend.

And Picus, who retained the royal colour
of purple in his woodpecker's plumage;
Esacus who, pursuing his amours,
caught death at an early age;
or witness the two most constant lovers
turned to fowl at the water's edge:
he was son-in-law to the winds, Aeolus,   450
but against fate no one is victorious.

In her worry, Alcyone was waiting,
straining her eyes for her absent husband,
but the angry winds in the waters'
tumult drove him to be drowned.
In dreams, he often appeared to her thoughts,
but hearts never lie in their foreboding:
only about good do our suspicions quibble:
about coming evil, the future's infallible.

Grief was instructing her eyes to shed   460
tears, as she scanned the horizon, pole to pole,
when she found on the beach the lifeless body,
the soul-less corpse that belonged to her soul.
Comfort her, you Aegean Nereids,
for to this sad duty you are called;
console her, emerge from your waters
if there can be any cure for despair.

But how stupid of me! To be rambling on
about tiny birds in their amorous nest!
Hasn't Love equal sway and dominion   470
over the mountain's most ferocious beasts?
Take the lion and lioness, how and when
did they attain such terrifying facets?
It was on account of Sibele's temple,
as was told to Adonis as example.

I would tell you who was the gentle cow,
but the Nile named her Io and reveres her;
in her North Pole dwelling, all know
the constellation of the Great Bear:
Actaeon's sad fate I should also   480
describe, metamorphosed into a deer;
better by far had he been struck blind
than find sepulcher in his deer hounds.

(here, two stanzas describing Diana's nakedness
were censored at publication)

Actaeon saw all this in the clear pool
where he glimpsed suddenly a stag in its mirror,
as Diana who had been entirely visible
gave assent to his becoming a deer.
But, like a sad lover who finds the profile
changed beyond knowledge, he disappeared.
His friends called out, unable to recognize   490
him they searched for was before their eyes.

He spoke to them with his eyes and a look,
for he no longer owned a human voice;
as each called out for him, his pack
of deer hounds rose up to give chase;
one man shouted, "Here, quick!"
on seeing the deer; "Actaeon, show your face,"
He called out again—"What inhibits him?"
The echoes responded, "It's him. It's him."

How much am I saying to no purpose,   500
O stubborn wood nymphs, and without discerning
those diamond hearts become less callous;
for whom alone my suffering yearns!
But the more you prove yourselves averse,
for however much of life remains,
no harm you cause me will be so grave
Love won't transform it into yet more love.

For your sake, nymphs, I have portrayed
a sweet garden of love, comprising
these waters, rocks, and these birds,   510
without becoming bird, beast, or daisy.
If I found onerous the pursuit of hearts
though it holds the key to hearts' ease,
and if, over time, some may be brought
to repent of causing so much hurt,

how much more leisurely would I relate
my whole tale, and you not be maddened?
And with how much water would I irrigate,
from happiness, the river of white sand?
Among the satisfactions for me, is that   520
this is no trouble but concentrates the mind;
while you, relishing the absurd situation,
will then regret your self-delusion.

But who am I complaining to, when I find
there is no sentiment in these boulders.
I scatter empty words to the wind,
and faster than the wind, she withdraws.
With life and my voice I am the less chagrined,
but time cannot control my ideas.
I continue, in short, in such endless grief   530
that only in death will I find relief.

Here the sad Satyr ended, his heart
wrenched by violent sobbing;
and the unfeeling hills reiterated
his last responses, as they trembled;

bus plunged himself in the waters
the light that animates the globe,
mid his shining flock reappeared
heavens the celestial shepherd.

❖ ELEGY ❖

❖ O Sulmonense Ovídio, desterrado

Ovid, born in Sulmo and banished
to remote, uncultured Tomis, imagined
he could see his scattered flesh,

his dear wife left abandoned,
his sweet children, his minions,
his eyes parted from his fatherland;

and unable to contain his passion,
he complained to the mountains and the rivers
of the sad, dark day he was born.

He reflected on the curse of the stars   10
and how, from where he stood, the sky,
air, and earth moved on in their order.

The fish swimming in the Black Sea
saw him, and ferocious beasts, following
their instinct, treated him with equanimity.

He witnessed from his own ducts flowing
homesick rivers of crystal sorrow,
the true mark of his inner-being.

Isolated, divided to the marrow,
he studied himself in a strange country,   20
the sad ache of which had no fellow.

With only his sweet muse for company,
he composed his nostalgic poems,
bathing the meadow in tearful elegy.

In like manner, I indulge my whims
contrasting this exiled life of pain
with the good I knew in another time.

Here I pass in contemplation
pleasures never to pass from the memory
of one who inscribed them on his brain.   30

Here I see how short-lived is glory,
disillusioning me, as simple change
exposes our lives as transitory.

With this reminder, I find it strange
I've done no wrong; it's sad to observe
how for no reason suffering impinges.

To suffer for some cause one believes
just punishment mitigates the pain, but
it hurts all the more when undeserved.

When dawn, unparalleled in beauty,   40
opens the door to the sun, and dew alights,
Philomela repeats her old complaint;

The anxiety that only slumber abates
reappears in dreams; what to other people
brings refreshment is for me an effort.

After waking blindly from sleep's
repose—or, more truly, being discomposed,
for it's poor wakening for the unhopeful—

I step out at a forlorn pace
to some small elevation, and sit giving   50
free rein to my accumulated woes;

then, exhausted by so much grieving,
extending homesick eyes to those parts
from which my imagination derives,

[81]

I see nothing of these rocky heights
nor the drought-stricken fields, but instead
see them as though flourishing, and full of delights.

I see the gentle Tagus in its winding bed
with those curved boats that, as they navigate
self-sufficient in their needs,   60

some scudding under their white
canvass, others driven by light oars,
gently parting the crystal waters.

But here I address waters that hear
nothing, my heart going out
in copious tears they patently ignore.

O fugitive breakers, wait!
not bearing me off in your company,
these tears of mine, at least, transport,

until there comes that joyful day   70
I go where you go, in contentment.
But who could endure such long delay?

There cannot come so good a moment,
for sooner life itself will end,
itself ending such bitter banishment.

Yet the sad death that must impend,
if it finds me so contrarious,
where will my impatient soul descend?

And if it arrives at the gates of Tartarus,
its memory replete with so much pain,   80
the River Lethe may not let me cross.

If Tantalus and Tycius should learn
of the torment that is approaching,
they will take their own penance as heaven.

I find this thought enlarging,
embracing a thousand sorrows, for
life's sustained by sad imagining.

Though all life passes, what I suffer
seems diminished, subsumed
in the glory of imagination's power,   90

until eternal darkness consumes
me, or I see that longed-for day
when fortune does as accustomed;
unless it has the wit to change my destiny.

✦ HYMN ✦

✦ A Instabilidade da Fortuna

The inconstancy of Fortune,
the pleasant strategies of blind Love
—pleasant had only they endured—
were my topics, to find some relief;
for as my suffering importunes
me, my song importunes the whole world.
And if past blessings and my present ordeal
toughen this voice in my sang-froid breast,
          my song's outburst
will give sure signal of my torment,   10
for an error, when all's error, is congruent.
Given it's in this truth I trust,
—if there's any truth in the pain I expound—
the world knows Love is inconsistent,
and that it only becomes reason's friend
lest wrongdoing be left unatoned.

Once Love made rules without reference to me;
once, in his blindness, he turned rational
only to accuse me without good cause,
though if I had erred in some detail   20
I was wise enough to avoid misery,
nor was he impeccable in his amours.
But to make use of his franchise

I invented my own destruction,
          casting myself down
in the eternal abyss of my torment,
nor was I presumptuous in my intent
assuming to place my aspirations
higher than he wished; and if he
ordained I should pay for being arrogant,   30
I knew it was this same Love condemned me
to fall into error, and further into agony.

That day those eyes I most cherish
became subject to a base maneuver
as I lodged them gently in my soul,
and like a miser always claiming more
I gave her my heart as a choice dish,
as though it were under my control.
Yet, set before her on the table,
this imagined end of my concupiscence,   40
          or other impudence,
that my tongue made free with as a game,
I die of thirst beside a stream
as the fruit of all my attendance.
If I try to pluck it, it's in vain,
and the water retreats if I want a dram.
So in hunger and thirst, here I remain:
not even Tantalus knew what I sustain.

Next, a base impudence tried to possess
her where my heart finds its home   50
and through this deceit attained her:
a cloud of sustained dreaming
imagined her in my arms, with success,
fancying what was my waking desire.
Because I boasted of my ardor
in gaining a good far surpassing
          my present distress,
I am tortured, being tied to a wheel,
rotating me in constant reversal
so if I rise to some good I descend apace,   60

and so all my hopes and despair hinge
on what's coming from behind, or turning tail;
and all this merely to take revenge,
like Ixion firmly fixed to change.

When that gentle, divine vision
was through my insolence violated
by my human lust, born of her loveliness,
without it knowing what it did,
blind Love firing his darts beyond reason
avenged the sin of such recklessness,   70
and beyond the pain that was my nemesis,
turned me still more of a scapegoat
            as giddy thought,
leaping as always between contrary poles,
has never its fill of these sad entrails,
concluding about appetite
the more it eats, the more it's hungry,
so in tormenting me it never fails.
I exist for nothing but this agony;
I'm another Tycius, and don't know why.   80

I was sustained by improper desires
that I treacherously preserved
in my deceitful, thieving heart.
In a manner, deceit itself was deceived,
for after I brought them within my power
I overwhelmed them with love, being without it.
At once, and with a punishment to fit,
avenging love forced me to feel,
            making me scale
that Everest of disdain I encountered   90
in you, with desire's heavy boulder
that from the summit of attainment must fall.
I turn to climb to the desired plateau;
it rolls away from my useless shoulder.
Don't be shocked, Sisyphus, at all this ado
as I ascend the mountain slopes of woe.

In this fashion, the highest good offered
to my baulked desire, is to feel
the loss of its loss the greater hurt.
As a miser to whom his dream reveals   100
buried treasure, with which to reward
and slake his insatiable thirst,
awakening in a desperate haste,
he goes excavating the spot he dreamed of,
        but all he can discover
on his ill-adventure is shale,
and his sheer greed is distilled
by the lack of all he coveted;
likewise, in love I was never judicious;
for those bounded by night's charcoal   110
never fully experience Hell's abyss
if they're ignorant of Paradise.

Song, no more—I don't know what I'm saying;
but to make my torment less intense,
proclaim the cause of this death sentence.

▩ ELEGY ▩

▩ Aquela que de amor descomedido

TO D. ANTÓNIO DE NORONHA,
THE AUTHOR BEING IN CEUTA

Echo who died of her helpless passion
for the toy boy Narcissus, who himself
pined away in self-contemplation,

was afterwards changed by Juno to a cave,
so that of her truly human figure
only the cadence of her voice survived.

In the same fashion, of my personal hurt,
already history, nothing remains
but this poem I scribble urgently,

and if its tenuous, threadbare existence   10
reflects love, it's because the thought
echoes its loss of the good that is present.

My lord, do not be at all startled
that overtaken by such ill fortune,
I steal this little space to inscribe it,

for whoever has the strength to go on
without killing himself by way of statement
has also the strength to write it down.

Nor is it I who write of my customary fate;
but within my heart, overwhelmed and broken,   20
the heartbreak writes, and I translate.

Pacing out my life of pain,
and declaring its unremitting sadness
to the burning sands of this African

beach, I study the sea's relentless
motion, as with its thunderous booming
it reverberates in the greater emptiness,

and with its furious white spume
it takes sorrowful hold
of the earth where it disperses foaming,   30

and earth in turn appears to yield
her beckoning womb helplessly
to the penetrating, salt-odorous tide.

In all such matters I feel such empathy
I scarcely know if I'm seeing what's out there
or whether it's determining me.

If I'm tempted by such misfortune to despair
I cannot, because love and the heart's
affections do not accommodate self-murder.

I meditate at times on the newness   40
and oddity of things, such as change,
if only I could direct its course,

and my mind, struck by this foreign
land, these new ways of being human,
a different people with customs I find strange,

I climb the mountain Heracles the Theban
divided from Gibraltar's Rock,
giving entrance to the Mediterranean,

and I try to imagine where he picked
the apple of the Hesperides,   50
killing the serpent that blocked

his march, while looking further, my fancies
are of the giant Antaeus, whose death-
blows doubled his strength as he swelled in size,

but who, held on high by Heracles, breathed
his last to the four winds, barred
from drawing strength from his mother Earth.

Yet not with what I'm now recording
nor by the endless fighting that is waged
can I shield myself from things remembered.   60

Everything I see around me changes
constantly, as fickle time ensures
only change can be unchanging.

I have seen how Spring, out of sheer joy,
was once again clothing river and meadow
and mountain in a thousand colors.

I have seen on high the harmony of birds
as they invited even the rocky mountains
to a gentle manner of gladness.

I have seen, in short, so much to content me,   70
yet for one evil, for all my fortitude,
a thousand delights cannot compensate.

So strong is my sense of change and remoteness,
if I visit the meadows, their very greenery
seems to my atrophy more like drought.

But this is again Fortune's customary
trick, that eyes discontent with what they discern
are discontented with the imaginary.

O, the insupportable twists and turns
of luck and of love, humbling   80
the innocent with such heavy penances!

Isn't it enough to test my good will
with fears and false hopes without
subjecting me also to the pains of exile?

You approach change, my lord, with a spirit
so tranquil you could never be assailed
by tears, sighs, and regrets,

and if you were brought face to face with trouble
you would not confront it resolutely
because you never cohabited with evil.   90

But I have lived quietly amid misery
and am not without that calmness of spirit
that controls the impulses of despondency.

Accepting I would never be a courtier,
I embraced Fortune's wheel, and she dealt me
further grief and fresh disaster.

I've said enough by now to imply
much more about which I'm keeping silent
to the one whose grave danger I have kept in view,

but if to brave hearts, a heart discontented   100
and grief-stricken disposes
whoever hears to offer encouragement,

I ask nothing more, my lord, than for news
freely given of my native land:
with that, at least, I can live at ease.

For if implacable Fortune commands
so long an absence from all good that my spirit
soars from the prison where it's chained,

to the roaring of the black waters
of Cocytus, on the verge of the gloomy groves,   110
I will sing what is written in my heart,

and deep within the dreadful cliffs
where Nature withholds all daylight,
amid fears and bitter suffering,

in a tremulous voice I will celebrate,
though tired and cold, the shining face
of Fancy, of whom I never lost sight.

And the musician of Thrace, sad Orpheus,
his Eurydice lost, will help me, stroking
his lyre, cutting the dark atmosphere.   120

The ghosts of lovers, re-echoing
old memories, will hear me and their tears
will make the very river overflow.

Proud Salmoneus's pinions will falter,
and Belo's murderous daughters will rival
him in weeping beyond the urns' measure.

Given that love is never forfeit in exile,
still less is it cancelled by dying obscurely,
for in the end the soul lives eternally
and love is the effect of soul, and endures.   130

❖ Transforma-se o amador na cousa amada

Lovers change themselves into the thing
beloved, by dint of endless imagining;
I've no room for further longing
since I possess what's most desired within.

If in her my soul is transfigured,
what higher need could the body attain?
Uniquely in her can it recline
for with her such a heart is anchored.

But this pure and lovely demi-goddess
that, as a verb-form with its subject,   10
so with my heart agrees terms,

is to thinking like a concept:
the living and pure love I'm composed
of like simple matter searches for form.

❖ Se as penas que Amor tão mal me trata

If the pangs that Love prescribes wish me
to spend such time accommodating them
that I witness fading that star's flame
whose glance lit up and extinguished me;

and if time that squanders all should ever
wither those roses that were never plucked,
and make the color of those dazzling locks
turn from subtle gold to fine silver;

then, too, you shall see altered, Lady,
those crabbed thoughts and uncivilized   10
ways no longer useful to your change;

you will long, then, for former days,
at a time when will be realized
through your repentance my revenge.

Vós que, d' olhos suaves e serenos

You whose eyes, so gentle and serene,
with just cause seize life a prisoner,
banishing every other care
as irrelevant, insignificant, and mean;

if you don't know what it is to be jealous,
never having loved, I hope to prove
that Love is paramount, once you know love,
as the reasons for it are seen to be less.

And no one considers any blemish
that's visible in the thing one loves   10
can undermine perfect devotion.

Before it increases, though causing anguish,
little by little the soft heart forgives:
so Love feeds on contradiction.

Aquela fera humana que enriquece

That cruel vixen who reinforces
her presumptuous tyranny
over my bewitchment, so love's agony
seems deficient even as it increases;

if heaven intended to show the earth
so much of itself as (it seems) in her,
why does my life so injure her?
How is she ennobled by my death?

But go ahead, exult in your triumph,
Lady, of capturing me to conquer: 10
I'll tell the world the whole story.

For the more I suffer from your mischief,
I go about basking in the splendor
of seeing you so enjoy killing me.

Oh! quão caro me custa o entender-te

Importunate Love, how much it costs
to understand you, when merely to engage
grief with grief you drag me to the stage
that my hatred and anger are reversed!

I reckoned to know you through and through,
drawing on all my experience and art;
now I see growing in my heart
the very cause of my losing you.

You lurked in my bosom so secretly
even I who housed you was unaware   10
you were lording it over me through your genius.

Now you've revealed yourself, in such a way
your self-exposure matches my flaw,
the one embarrassing, the other injurious.

Dai-me ua lei, Senhora, de querer-vos

Lay down some law, Lady, for wooing you
that I'll keep for fear of aggrieving you;
my good faith, that keeps me loving you,
will comply with it, obeying you.

I denied myself all but gazing at you
and in my heart of hearts admiring you;
and if this won't suffice to humor you,
at least it stops short of provoking you.

And if, Lady, this cruel and rare purview
that you lay down the law of my life   10
irks, a law for my death would suffice.

If you don't grant this, better you continue
not knowing how I live, in certain grief,
but resigned to my fate nonetheless.

O cisne, quando sente ser chegada

The swan, when he senses fast approaching
the hour that brings his dying moments,
pours forth song with a rising cadence
loud above his deserted beach.

He longs to have his life extended,
lamenting what is about to be lost,
and heartsick about the cost
bewails his calendar's sad end.

Precisely so, my lady, when I saw
the desperate outcome of my love,   10
dangling in its last extreme,

in sweeter, more harmonious airs
I put on record your disfavors:
La vuestra falso fé, y el amor mio.

Sempre a Razão vencida foi de Amor

Perennially, Love has conquered Reason;
but why, then, should the heart approve
Reason winning the battle over Love?
How fare the cases in comparison?

A new way of dying, a new ordeal,
a strangeness greatly to be wondered at,
that affection forfeits all its might
because suffering does not relax its rule.

For there never was a weakness in desire,
but before long there begins to gather   10
a contrary force, perpetually fighting;

while Reason, which finally wins the war,
is not, in my view, rational, but rather
my personal bias, and self-defeating.

Suspiros inflamados, que cantais

Ardent sighs, you rhyme the burden
I have lived with so contentedly,
but I leave you behind me as I die
lest in passing Lethe you'll be forgotten.

You'll remain forever, being written,
pointing your finger as a case
of damage done, though I confess
to others you may appear an omen.

To whoever, then, you see deluded
by Love and Fortune, though what they endure   10
some will take as their blessed fate,

I told them, having served you for decades:
while in Fortune, everything's unsure,
in Love there's nothing but deceit.

Fiou-se o coração, de muito isento

My heart had always set such store
on its independence, it was unprepared
for a love so unlawful, so beyond daring,
a torment I never felt before.

But the eyes dazzled in such fashion
as others I had seen in dreams,
while reason, afraid of what seemed,
fled, leaving the field to passion.

—O chaste Hippolytus, loved illegally
by Phaedra, your own stepmother,   10
who had no acquaintance with honor:

Love has avenged your virtue through me;
but so fully avenged is this other
crime, it now repents of what was done.

Um mover d' olhos, brando e piadoso

A shift of the eyes, gentle and piteous
without seeing; a gentle, honest smile,
as if forced; a sweet gesture, but bashful,
doubting any personal happiness;

an outcast, shy and barely audible,
a grave and demure serenity,
whose pure goodwill was the fitting
and gracious evidence of her soul;

a timorous daring; a gentleness;
a blameless fear; a tranquil mien: 10
a prolonged, unquestioning agony:

this was the unearthly loveliness
of my Circe, and the magic poison
that could metamorphose my fancy.

Fermosos olhos que na idade nossa

Beautiful eyes that for our present epoch
are the surest sign of paradise,
if you wish to see what power you possess
look at me who are your handiwork.

You will see how existing robs me
of that very laughter you brought to life;
you will see I want no more of love
for as time advances, so do my troubles.

And if you care to look inside this heart,
there you will see, as in a clear glass,   10
your own self, too, angelic and serene.

But I warn you, Lady, my image apart,
you won't like seeing your own likeness
taking such pleasure in all my pain.

Ondados fios d' ouro reluzente

Delicate weaves of gleaming gold
rearranged by a lovely hand,
even now over roses extended,
increasing your loveliness tenfold;

eyes, with so sweet a glance
lit up by a thousand rays,
if you inspire me from so far away,
how would it be but for my absence?

Discreet smile that emerges between
the greater elegance of coral and pearls,   10
whose heart does not feel the sweet echo?

If such beauty merely imagined, not seen,
makes the soul forget itself in new marvels,
what when she comes? Ah, who should know!

Bem sei, Amor, que é certo o que receio

I'm well aware, Love, what I fear is true;
but you, to make you appear more rare,
negate me from sheer whimsy, and you swear
on your golden bow, and I believe you.

I know what's going on in your mind,
and I'm not in the dark about my torture;
but then you take such trouble to assure,
I swear I'm lying, and am the more constrained.

I not only go along with this cozenage,
I even thank you, and privately refute   10
all I see and suffer of my distress.

O heavy pain to which I'm hostage!
In the just course of my self-deceit,
a blind youth keeps me in blindness!

Senhora, já dest' alma, perdoai

Pardon now, Lady, and from your heart all
these follies of one conquered by Cupid;
let your eyes fall with a kind regard
on this pure love that springs from the soul.

Observe only my extreme fidelity
and my other extremes will appear refined:
and if some penalty's in your mind,
take your revenge on me, Lady.

The pain that scorches my sad breast
should not make suffering its subject   10
where love so true implies servitude.

But beware, Lady, of some who attest
your being so proper in all your objects
could spring from some deep ingratitude.

Este amor que vos tenho, limpo e puro

This chaste, unsullied love I bear you,
untouched by any obscene imagining,
beginning when I was very young,
yearning only in my soul to procure you;

against mutability I am secure,
unperturbed by accident or fate,
nor any shift to high nor low estate
nor this present tense, nor any future.

The daisy and marigold fade quickly;
in the earth winter and summer reign;   10
for my love uniquely it is always May.

But watching you avoid me, Lady,
as ingratitude spurns me, this consigns
my love to the point of fainting away.

Já não sinto, Senhora, os desenganos

I no longer feel disillusioned, Lady,
over how you always treated my love,
nor at seeing the satisfaction I deserved
withheld after so many years' fidelity.

I lament only the anguish, only the distress
at seeing, Lady, for whom you exchanged me;
but such as he is, you have merely avenged me
for your ingratitude, your artifice.

Revenge achieves redoubled glory
in according guilt to the culpable   10
when the vindicated has a just suit.

But reviewing my all too easy victory
over your ill-treatment and denial,
I wish it were not so much to your hurt.

Num tão alto lugar, de tanto preço

On a place so exalted, of such credit,
I see my feelings focus their hopes
to the point that my appetite droops
at finding in myself so little merit.

When I recognize the peasant in me
I worry my love is a great presumption,
and to die for it beyond pretension
a blessing of which I'd never be worthy.

My natural birthright, all the more,
that causes such strong, painful growth   10
keeps it hardening hour by hour.

But I will not abandon my desire
for, even if this suffering caused my death,
un bel morir tutta la vita onora.

Olhos fermosos, em quem quis Natura

Beautiful eyes, by which Nature looks
to provide best proof of her vigor,
if you wish to understand your power
look at me, your finest handiwork.

Your countenance is copied in me,
in all I suffer, you are painted;
so if I endure redoubled torment,
so much more is the power of your beauty.

I want nothing more than this one desire,
to be yours: your ornament alone,   10
given that your pledge is sealed in me.

When you're in my sight, I don't remember
myself, or the world—this being no sin,
for in thinking of you I fulfill all duty.

Quando se vir com água o fogo arder

When flames are fuelled by cold water
and day blends with the dark night,
and the earth ascends to such a height
heaven becomes the inferior;

when Love's controlled by common sense,
and everyone's equal in their fortune,
at such somersaults I might abandon
my yearning after your elegance.

However, with no such change in view
in this world (as is clear, not yet),   10
don't count on my not admiring you;

it's enough to fix my hopes in you
my soul's reward in forfeiting it,
so as never to cease desiring you.

Diana prateada, esclarecia

Silver Diana, illuminated
by Phoebus's resplendent luster
reflected him as in a mirror
(being in her nature pellucid).

Infinite benevolence inspired
her, when there was revealed to me
your own face's glorious ray,
more gracious and loving than he that soared.

I, seeing myself so full of favor,
so close to being yours in every way,   10
praised the bright hour and the dark night,

for in these is my love's true color;
from which it follows, as the night the day,
I cannot be happy with you during sunlight.

Quando, Senhora, quis Amor que amasse

When, Lady, Love gave orders I should dote
on your great perfection and courtesy,
Love passed sentence that cruelty
should also grow to possess your heart.

I resolved nothing should estrange me,
neither cruel scorn nor harshness,
but my unique, dogged faithfulness
should exterminate your cold immunity.

And since you possess on offer here
the heart that's yours, as your sacrifice,   10
I have done my duty to your will.

You do not, Lady, make life more dear;
it will end, fulfilling its proper office
as your loyal defender and true vassal.

Que pode já fazer minha ventura

What today could make my fortune
turn for me to contentment?
What must I do to be confident
in what's wholly unfounded, or uncertain?

What severer or more taxing pain
could be greater than this nightmare?
Or how could my spirit fear
suffering, if its action is to refine?

Like that king whose cunning custom
was to take poison in small doses,   10
ensuring he would always be safe,

so, acclimatized to venom,
as I endure my daily reverses,
I fear nothing for my future life.

Quem presumir, Senhora, de louvar-vos

Whoever presumes to praise you, Lady,
based on human knowledge and not divine,
will always merit equal scorn
to the time he has spent on your study.

No one claims a beauty so rare
and marvelous can be enhanced,
and I imagine yours is a countenance
that God intends as an exemplar.

Happy the heart that had the power
and the will for an offering so superior   10
as the one, my lady, you gave me.

I'll guard it better than life itself, for,
given you granted me such a favor,
it will never be wiped from my memory.

Se de vosso fermoso e lindo gesto

If from the sheer beauty of your face
flowers that glisten in your eyes are born,
those in your breasts are hard thorns
pointed at me, very clear and obvious;

for though in your lovely, frank expression
a thousand fresh daisies spurt,
were there but blinders on my heart
it would not suffer its fatal pain.

An evil seen as good, a good despair,
inspiring me, raising in my thoughts   10
a thousand, competing fantasies,

constantly dreaming of which I wander,
while you care nothing for my hurt
that's the main source of your happiness.

Sempre, cruel Senhora, receei

Fearing your inability to trust
I always dreaded, cruel lady,
the cause lay in your frigidity
and that in loving you I should be lost.

In the end, all I hoped for is forfeit;
you already have hopes of another love.
As evident will be your false move
as my hiding forever all I have felt.

I gave you soul, life, and the sum of meaning;
all that is in me, Lady, is your doing.   10
The same love you promised, and revoked.

Now I am so bereft that, where I'm going
I scarcely know, but some future evening
this memory will cause you great heartache.

Sustenta meu viver ua esperança

One hope sustains my whole existence,
based on a blessing I've longed for
so long, the surer I become, the more
the slightest shift leaves me in suspense.

And when the prospect of this pleasure
elevates me so it feels all but gained,
I'm tormented to think it might be attained
by someone ignorant of who you are.

Sufficient that, caught in this snare,
I find fresh material for my pen,   10
articulating these antics;

in sighs the winds snatch and tear,
whistling around a stone,
I give voice to these sad topics.

Que modo tão sutil da natureza

How subtle of nature to inhibit
one of such tender years, avoiding
the world and its delusions by hiding
so much beauty in a nun's habit!

But to veil those grave, sovereign
eyes in their splendor is impossible.
Against their brilliance, among mere mortals,
I know of no denial, nor protection.

She who longs to be free of grief and pain,
experiencing both only in memory,   10
by the same logic is self-condemned;

for whoever deserved to see such glory
is forever her captive; so Love ordains
that in justice hers is the victory.

Pues lágrimas tratáis, mis ojos triste

So you deal in tears, my sad eyes,
and in weeping you pass the night and day;
gaze at this, one tear sent your way
by her for whom your own are copious.

Sense, my eyes, what you've just witnessed,
for what great fortune, if it's genuine!
The thousand tales you told for her alone
were for my benefit well expressed.

That thing that's above all else desired
cannot, however apparent, impose,   10
let alone this blessing I've gained.

But I declare, unless it's some fraud,
it's enough it should be a gift of tears
given through tears it was obtained.

SONGS

Dama d'estranho primor

TO A LADY:

Lady of strange perfection,
if my
persistence becomes tedious,
don't leave me comfortless
lest I change it to devotion.
If your conjecture's
to kill me with your air
of indifference,
I'll take my vengeance
by courting you all the more.   10

Perhaps it's your thought
that a cold heart
will gain its intention,
reckoning such affection
can only abate.
Don't set any store
on being by such means
invincible,
for faced with the impossible
Love delights in doing more.   20

But in the course selected
I contradict;
for all Love's power,
you accomplish more
by the pain you inflict.
But were it proved
between ourselves you've
the greater power, who
could outdo you
when you do more than Love?   30

On first seeing you, Lady,
I understood
Love himself had succumbed,
for the favors I asked him
he sought from you instead.
I don't doubt
in his passion he couldn't
withstand
for, instead of wounding,
Love was wounded by your sight.   40

Given a glimpse of you fills
me with woe,
what can I want of you,
knowing I can't prevail
where Love himself fails?
Pondering

well, I trust no one;
would to God
your intention should
prevail with my undoing.   50

Fix no hope in feeling sure
that my dear
devotion is superfluous,
for it's when my hope is less,
I feel greater desire.
My hope is scant,
but my creed is this taunt:
being your own,
I want you all I can,
and can't have as much as I want.   60

If only for being deluded
I feel owed
for my pains some redress;
though what I seek seems priceless
compared to how much I pursued.
This affair,
in the end, should inspire
no great to-do,
for whoever, Lady, desires you so
should of you so much more desire.   70

Suspeitas, que me queries?

ON HIS SUSPICIONS:

Suspicions, what do you want of me?
That I be willing to give space
to what, if true, would kill me?
That the one that gives rise
to you should be ready to confess?
That not finding her sorry,

the great accumulated pain
that makes my heart so weary
would, if she confessed her sin,
make me take it as forgiven?   10

Then observe what anomalies
barricade the heart, in that,
when it's most frustrated,
its own dearest enemies
rally to its ramparts.
Suspicions, I'm well aware,
with the utmost clarity,
that what I feared is for sure,
but nothing I conjectured
should ever emerge from me.   20

But I wanted this surety
from her who torments me,
because in such heavy straits
there's consolation in it,
and a respite from misery.
For if she were to swear
the simple, naked truth, bare
of prevarication and pretense,
I could not set at variance
my own desires from hers.   30

For the intimacies of an affair
are certain to be public,
and the pain of exposure
is a thousand times greater
than where merely suspected.
Yet enjoined to me alone
is a new mode of behavior
that from fear of the minor
I identify in the greater pain
the consolation for her.   40

At this, I'm embroiled in wrath,
in a fury of vengeance, that

madly overwhelms my thoughts;
and still madder, I take my oath
to wrench all loves from my heart.
Now, in my anger, I'm determined
to go away, shift my residence;
then, later, I am content
it was a good thing to be convinced
her lying was self-evident.   50

But afterwards, exhausted
by imagination's furies,
I break out at last
in sorrowful tears
and mourn sincerely.
And failing to conquer
the insidious creatures
of such plain disillusion,
I can do not other
than be reconciled to my pain,   60

entreating it to free me
from the vice of suspicion
that pierces through me,
and even confess its sin
of attempting to undo me.
Take care how you drive me,
Lady, to this extremity,
for given this state I am in,
for you to make confession
would be therapy for me.   70

But for all Love's prowess
in governing all paths,
there's poetry in such justice;
given it's your trespass
that's to end in my death.
Justice so badly witnessed
appears what color it's gilded;
it aims, when all's concluded,

that you should be confessed
and I'm the one that's dead.   80

So even now, make your confession,
while I maintain my dread
that on my very deathbed
I must grant Love absolution,
my lady, for all your sins.
And so it is I'm doomed,
for this is Love's embassy
put to the wrong uses,
for which I'm already condemned
to a hell of jealousy.   90

Se de dó vestida andais

TO A LADY DRESSED IN MOURNING:

I ask only this
in my bereavement and hurt,
you wear in your heart
what you show in your dress.

If you go dressed in mourning
for one who is no more alive,
why show no mercy for the lover
you have so often slain?
What bragging without words
in one, never caught without
cruelty in her heart,
and grief in her widow's weeds.

Se derivais da verdade

TO A LADY WHOSE DAUGHTER WAS
GIVEN A PIECE OF YELLOW SATIN,
WHICH MADE HER SUSPICIOUS:

If you derive correctly
this word *sitim* (meaning satin),

you'll discover literally
after the *si* (yes) comes the *tin-*
kle that's heard across the city.
I can see you understand me,
I'm not casting words to the wind;
I know throughout this land
in as much as you concede the "si"
the tinkle's close behind.   10

But whoever dodges rumor,
which threatens to reveal all,
must keep themselves well
away from satin, for by nature
silk will always rustle.
But a cloth, subtle and delicate,
such as calico or the like,
that warms and keeps quiet,
staying close, offers for your sake
more than satin, and never wears out.   20

But these silky types that deceive
their mistresses by the thousand
take more from you than they give;
they promise but only deliver
tales for the many-tongued.
If you refuse to give me credit
or prefer some other course,
note, for example, the curious
when the flames are well alight
in some close neighbor's house.   30

To feminine simplicity
faults come as a pair;
for some scion of nobility
she ignores two taller, innately
noble, and each more rare.
One Dom I know, grafted
in his name but not his nature . . .
I speak from long exposure,

but satin of this warp and weft
I've often cut to measure.   40

They tell me it was yellow,
and that such a gift signifies,
as God alone is my witness,
I'll love you (*amarei-lo*),
a thing I can't suppose.
For whoever knows how to live
by such cunning stratagems,
surely they can't thrive,
making gifts to lovely maidens
to turn them like themselves?   50

The one, my lady, who says this
long served in your wake,
but today's down on his luck,
though even now perhaps he bears
arrow-wounds for your sake.
And even if disdain
banishes him from serving,
he wishes you better fortune,
for of all your past lovers,
this love still remains.   60

▨ Nua casada fui pôr

TO THIS COMMON THEME:

> *Flirting with someone's wife*
> *I found could wreck my life.*

Upon someone else's wife
my eyes fell, of their own volition;
I though it was just flirtation
but they turned it into love.
This provoked the greater desire
where there could be no relief,
at the risk of making me suffer.

It didn't appear Love could
bring me to such an end
where, entering as a friend,   10
he promoted himself to lord.
He drags me from care to care
and from foreboding to foreboding,
each time suffering the more.

Não sei quem assela

TO THIS COMMON SONG:

I said, pretty girl,
where are you from
to make you so cruel
to whom wishes you well?

Whose seal of approval
stamped your loveliness
God knows, for the callous
can never be lovely.
You should be unmatched,
but reason swears
no one so tetchy
can ever be fair.

The display is lovely,
the actions are cruel,   10
so which of this double
will take the trophy?
Being virulent
does you no favor;
keeping radiant
wields the greater power.

Love, being beautiful,
depicts and approves;
if its love, she loves,
if she loves, she's merciful.   20
It's said that the gloss

explaining this by-word
is, she who is gorgeous
must want to be good.

Show mercy, my child,
to your beauty's foil;
in arid soil
the daisy's shriveled.
Pitiful thirst,
kept under wraps   30
as, being repressed,
you forfeit all hope.

▨ O coração envejoso

> TO HIS OWN THEME:

> *I put my heart in my eyes*
> *and my eyes on the floor*
> *so my heart should not be sore.*

My jealous heart
followed my eyes
with taunts and jeers—
it was not my favorite:
I turn back in pity
and, lest lord heart be sore,
cast my eyes on the floor.

▨ Peço-vos que me digais

> TO A LADY WHO WAS SAYING HER ROSARY:

I beg you to tell
me—these prayers you uttered,
are they for those you murdered,
or for yourself while you kill?
If they're for you, they're abortive,
for what kind of petition

could give satisfaction,
Lady, for so many lives?

If you observe how many run
merely to beg life of you,   10
why should God attend to you
when you attend to no one?
You cannot be acquitted
with hands ready to slay—
in one you carry a rosary,
in the other you bear a sword.

If you claim you intercede
on behalf of those you kill,
why pray for those departed souls
when it's by your prayers they're dead?   20
If in the grip of invocation
you raise you hands to heaven,
it's not to the divine,
but instead for execution.

And when, enraptured by your faith
you close those glorious eyes,
they shut out those who witness
you, so as not to see their death.
For that's how they're rewarded
who watch you at your prayer—   30
these observances you offer
are obsequies for the dead.

So, then, if you would worship
without causing such slaughter,
don't pray before spectators,
and look only to confer hope.
Or if you desire absolution,
having caused so much evil,
resurrect all those you killed
so none will need your orison.   40

▦ N'álma ua só ferida

TO THIS COMMON THEME:

If the soul could be seen
where imagination causes such hurt,
what must I do to have credit?

A soul that's merely wounded
shows a thousand signs of life:
the more it reveals its grief
the more it stays hidden.
If they're blind to my burden
because they don't wish to see it,
what must I do to have credit?

If only they could see
how I dissemble what I feel,
after such an ordeal   10
I suppose I should be happy.
But if those eyes that injure me
don't wish to see their remit,
what must I do to have credit?

▦ Esses alfinetes vão

LINES THAT HE SENT TO A LADY
WITH A PAPER OF PINS:

They venture, these little pins,
to prick you, nothing worse,
only so you get a sense
how sharp will be the ones
you prick me with in due course.
But the points of those stars
that come have tips so sharpened,
that whereas these others
leave no more than tiny scars,
your own cause real wounds.   10

Therefore, if you note well
when both are in combat,
they can never be equal;
if these here confer ill,
those there aggravate.
But if Love should agree
to weapons so disparate,
where you're the most doughty,
I'm content, my lady,
you take the greater delight.   20

They strike home, those pins
in your eyes, without
any special intent,
but what I send you are meant
to adjust your skirt.
And apart from all else
I wish this paper's contents
inserted, I say, and licensed,
myself being jealous
of every one of your garments.   30

For if they become your stay,
powerfully I envy them,
not only for being so employed
but because, Lady, they'll enjoy
where I can never come.
There they go and will continue
where alongside and underneath
perpetually they hold you,
and eventually impale you,
while here I pick my teeth.   40

🔲 Quando me quer enganar

TO A LADY WHO ALWAYS SWORE BY HER EYES:

When my perjured beauty
perceives the need for lies

in order to ratify
what she has to tell me,
she swears by her eyes.
Given that they both
entirely rule my well-being,
imagine the good faith
that addresses its appeal to them,
but cannot credit such an oath.   10

However, being in such affairs
sophisticated beyond saying,
in the absence of other auguries,
the more vigorously she swears
the surer I am she is lying.
But then, so as not to distress
eyes like those beyond compare,
I let myself be credulous,
in order not to constrain her,
to make them bear false witness.   20

Se trocar desejo

TO THIS COMMON THEME:

> *I exchanged this grief*
> *with myself, Lady,*
> *so you see the hazard*
> *of being without love.*

If I seek to convey
love between us,
it's so you may witness
the matter my way.
And being transposed
between us, this love,
you both have my reproof
and feel the blows.

Your sense of being loved
is to be unconfined,   10

and you warn it's mere wind
that I'm so deprived.
You would not be reproved
by your own worst foe,
that you court the woe
of being unloved.

But never took such form
this, my desire,
that she to whom I aspire
should come to harm. 20
I should be well served
if never my anger
shows you the danger
of being without love.

▓ Da lindeza vossa

THE DEVICE OF MIRAGUARDA:

To see and further to abstain
from seeing once again,
who could attain?

Your beauty,
Lady, once seen,
it's impossible anyone
can eschew.
Glimpsed only a day
to make such an impression,
who could abstain?

Better would be
in this concern
to see and obtain, 10
not try not to see.
To see and guard safely
would be best of all,
but who has such control?

Pois a tantas perdições

Since, ladies, this ruin
you hope to revivify,
happy the injury
that has such surgeons.
Since Fortune elevates
me to so dizzy a height
that you become my protectors,
happy the blight
that's set right,
ladies, through your overtures.   10

To act as my human quill
in my pain is what you undertake.
For myself, I have no wish to speak
that for myself speak very ill.
You are gorgeous,
you should be piteous,
for they share the same livery;
since Love makes of you roses
that seem miraculous,
make miracles of my love.   20

I beg of her you know
she should know what I suffer,
not because I value it myself
but because it's what you value.
What's seemly
and suits your sublimity
as you beg her on bended knees
will declare that in my agony
she can surely see
the omnipotence of those eyes.   30

Your immense beauty
along with such merit

makes me laugh at my hurt
when I realize who cures me.
Throughout my suffering
I beg you, in your sharing,
love-ladies so persuasive,
you never know the chagrin
of so desiring
where you're far from being loved. 40

Despois de sempre sofrer

TO THIS THEME BY FRANCISCO DE MORAIS:

A sad life is ordained
for loving one so far above me.
The evil you deal as pain
must serve as my reward.

Lady, after long enduring
all your disdain,
despite all my yearning
it's your pleasure to return
my courtship with this pain.
For those your eyes have sentenced
resistance is in vain,
and I'm ready for this recompense,
that for me, as penance,
a sad life is ordained. 10

Resignation to this truth
to such extremes brought me
I consented to my death,
given you, and even I, both
were conspiring against me.
But to suffer such affliction
wanting the greater trophy,
it's hardly beyond reason
pain should be my portion
for loving one so far above me. 20

The pain you deal as a blessing,
that, Lady, is lethal;
the pain you deal as an evil
injures much less,
being almost natural.
But, however, in this victory
that to me is a mere grain,
the greater grief's contained
in the hurt in which you glory
than the evil you deal as pain.   30

What greater good could befall
me than your service, I don't know.
But I'd like to learn without fail
if the more I'm at your disposal
the more service I will owe?
If your exalted station
is held in such high regard,
it's sufficient dispensation
my present desolation
must serve as my reward.   40

Minina mais que na idade

TO THIS THEME:

> *Child, lovely but ungracious,*
> *to me it's well known,*
> *he gives up being his own*
> *whom you wish yours.*

Child, more than in years,
if, purely for my benefit,
I don't see your desire
it's because someone else has it;
has it, and makes you ungracious.
But I
already took it as not mine,
given it was so little yours.

In your eyes and every part
I saw in you, when you glanced   10
such grace as entranced
willingly this heart.
But cruelly you refuse
to be mine:
if another had given his own,
you'd have had more of what's yours.

Child, take good care
of what you haven't encountered
(for you want not where you're wanted)
lest you want where there's no desire.   20
Look, don't be ungracious:
because I
long to be yours, not mine,
you my center, and not yours.

Para evitar dias maus

TO SOME LADIES WHO PLAYING NEAR A WINDOW LET
FALL THREE CARDS THAT STRUCK HIS HEAD:

To cancel out bad days
in this life of petty snubs,
they struck me with a lifeline,
so I now hold three clubs.

Despues que Amor me formó

TO THIS BALLAD BY BOSCÁN:

Well deserved was my perdition,
with my suffering I'm content;
I already feel rewarded,
then it's your great merit
to have satisfied my passion.

Once Cupid had fashioned me
all for love, as seems clear,

beyond the laws he prescribed me
he consented to watch over me
and guarded my desire.
But my soul that considered
such perfection a sin
allowed desire a door,
and since I broke so just a law,
well deserved was my perdition.   10

Love made himself manifest,
more benign than cruel,
worse than a tyrant, treacherous,
and in envy of my bitterness
demanded a joint deal.
I who hardly want
such sweet torment, though I sin,
resist and don't consent,
but if I accept the bargain,
with my suffering I'm content.   20

Observe, Lady, who governs
this unreal love of ours!
To satisfy another, he orders
that I for one glance of yours
am rewarded with this pain.
But you, so you may see
through such intended falsehood,
though you sense I am dead,
avoid looking, for if you do,
I already feel rewarded.   30

You will ask me, "What perquisite
so priceless do you hope for?"
Learn, if you don't know it,
you are yourself it, more than I suffer
though less than is your desert.
Who is there, so willing to hurt,
and so free in breaking hearts?
Desire? No, that's vanity.

Love? No, he's a tyrant.
Then? *It's your great merit.*   40

Love could not despoil me
of so priceless a prize,
though it was more to honor me,
it was you alone killed me
as you lent him those eyes.
You killed me between you,
but you with greater reason,
giving him the satisfaction,
to me for him and for you
to have satisfied my passion.   50

Se vos quereis embarcar

TO THIS THEME:

> *Whoever says the ship is listing,*
> *tell him he's lying, sister.*

If you wish to go on board
and that's why you're on the jetty,
embark at once! Why the delay?
Look, you have a full tide.
And if someone, with some other bid,
advises the ship is listing,
tell him he's lying, sister.

This is an ocean-going clipper,
rigging refitted throughout.
Povos has nothing like it—   10
sound in the helm, a sturdy ship.
But if, for being a pioneer,
someone warns it's listing,
tell him he's lying, sister.

Caterina é mais fermosa

TO THIS COMMON THEME:

> *Caterina's full of promises;*
> *but God-dammit, how she lies!*

To me, Caterina's lovelier
than the dawn's first light,
but she'd be the better beauty
if she weren't such a liar.
I see her today at prayer,
tomorrow what a surprise,
and I remind myself she lies.

Caterina gives me the lie
incessantly, and without wit,
but I'd overlook the lot   10
if she'd only once comply.
If only she'd converse with me
I'd be happy to give replies,
and stop saying she lies.

I said, "You cruel minx,
why are you so deceitful?"
You promise, and don't fulfill,
and without fulfillment, no thanks!
You need to stop and think:
the girl who vows then cheats   20
can't know how much she forfeits.

She swore, the dear strumpet,
on the salvation of her soul.
She deceived me. She controls
mine, but wouldn't care if she lost it.
I waste life in her pursuit;
I prosper if she promises,
and lose all when she lies.

I'd grant you your way
in however much you want   30

if only you'd consent
you'd be mine for a day.
All that would destroy
me, while you in your new guise
would laugh back at one who lies.

She swore yesterday she'd make it,
but she hasn't yet appeared;
I believe she gave her word
just in order to break it.
I laugh and weep as directed,   40
laugh when she makes her promises,
and weep when they're all lies.

Since you get your kicks from lying,
engaging to meet me now,
I'll let you make the vow
while I see to the complying.
You'll discover in the trying
who's most deeply satisfied:
the one who delivered, or who lied.

Cousa este corpo não tem

TO HIS OWN THEME:

> *Of my soul, and all I possess,*
> *I want you to divest me,*
> *so long as you reinstate me*
> *with, to gaze at you, my eyes.*

Something this corpse no longer has
where till now you've not triumphed,
after carrying off my life,
take my death throes likewise.
But I've still more to lose,
I want you to transport me,
so long as you reinstate me
with, to gaze at you, my eyes.

Foi a Esperança julgada

TO HIS OWN THEME:

> *I strangled my hope*
> *but Love was such a goose*
> *that it cut the noose.*

Hope was arraigned
on Fortune's testimony;
to the scaffold they bore me
so I should be suspended.
Came Love with his sword's end
and cut next to the noose . . .
Love, you were a goose!

Ua dama, de malvada

TO HIS OWN THEME:

> *I put my eyes in a sling*
> *and took my aim*
> *at her window pane.*

A lady, from sheer ill-will,
took her eyes in her hand
and flung them like pebbles,
aiming straight at my heart.
At once I seized my sling, and
put my own eyes in the socket:
Crack! I smashed her window.

E se a pena não me atiça

TO A LADY WHO ASKED THE AUTHOR WHO KILLED HIM:

> *They ask me who killed me:*
> *I don't wish to respond*
> *for I don't wish anyone blamed.*

If my pen does not incite me
to describe pain so atrocious,

I'm tempted to die
and then deliver you to justice.
But if you're secretly ambitious
to be the one held to blame,
"I'm indifferent" will be my claim.

Cum real de amor

TO THIS COMMON SONG:

He shakes my hand
when he owes me a guinea.

With a guinea of love
and two of belief
and three of faith
the traitor makes off.
False disfavor
is in hiding because he
owes me a guinea.

I requested a loan,
not wanting a covenant;
a malicious accountant   10
clapped me in irons.
Taken in chains,
to the Tronco he bears me
for a guinea he owes me.

Along the side road
exists a gap;
I make my escape
running at top speed.
On this and that side
the cheat makes his sally   20
that owes me a guinea.

I bought into love
without naming a price;
I should not be forced

to endure such disfavor.
I'll send in the bailiff
if it breaks my heart,
to recover my debt.

As I stand here moaning
he goes flying off—   30
he forever laughing,
I forever complaining.
Time and again
love makes his sortie
as if not in debt.

To tell the truth,
he already paid:
yet still he stayed,
owing me half.
My relief   40
is what he owes;
if only he dares.

🔲 Só porque é rapaz ruim

TO HIS OWN THEME:

> *Love conquered me, I don't deny it,*
> *with more force than I could deploy,*
> *for as he's both blind and a boy*
> *he dealt me the blow of the blind.*

Because the boy's so namby-pamby
I gave him a slap as a joke.
He said, "Wretch, do you think you can poke
me because you're bigger than I am?
So then, I'll replay you in kind . . ."
With these words, *bang, wallop,*
he paid me back. Boy, stop!
you're dealing me the blow of the blind.

Sem olhos vi o mal claro

TO A LADY WHO CALLED HIM
"FACE-WITHOUT-EYES":

Eyeless, I see all too clearly
what's consequent on having eyes,
for face-without-eyes was witness
to eyes that cost him dearly.
Speaking of eyes, I desist,
for you prefer eyes should fail;
seeing you, eyes prevail,
not seeing you, eyes don't exist.

Quem quer que viu, ou que leu

TO A LADY, NAMED FUÃ DOS ANJOS,
WHO CALLED HIM A DEVIL:

Lady, because you slander me
with a name that's not my due,
let the devil take you.

Check what you've seen or what's written;
you'll find it strangely original
that someone could inhabit hell
but have his thoughts in heaven.
But if you've any reason
to reckon such a name's my due,
then let the devil take you.

Damned more than anyone
I am, Lady, I confess;
but the devil's not desirous   10
angels should have good fortune.
However, it's not germane,
or if your nickname is my due,
it'll be because he takes you.

If like an angel (but not Lucifer)
you make the sign to exorcise,

he can hardly flee from the cross
whom you've already crucified.
But if I'm fated to suffer
a devil's name, give him his due   20
and take care he doesn't take you.

But now you're at your last call
with your hands raised to heaven,
I'm forever imploring the Divine
you give yourself to his devil.
Lady, I never fawn,
but since you make this name my due
I take it, so as to take you.

Não posso chegar ao cabo

TO A LADY WHO CALLED HIM A DEVIL:

Given you are the angel,
Lady, I can't make any sense
out of this misalliance
of your longing for the devil.
That I'm a constant creature
you have the clearest proof,
in that devils bring grief
to angels by their very nature.

Cinco galinhas e meia

TO D. ANTÓNIO, GENTLEMAN OF CASCAIS,
WHO PROMISED THE AUTHOR SIX STUFFED
CHICKENS FOR A COUPLET HE MADE,
AND SENT HIM A DOWN PAYMENT
OF HALF A CHICKEN:

Five and a half chickens
owes this Cascais *senhor*,
and the half that was delivered
makes me hungry for more.

Pois onde te hão-de falar

TO THIS PASTORAL VILANCETE:

"God save you, Vasco, dear,
but you ignore me, how so?"
"Sincerely, I'm not here."

"Where should one address you
if you're not where you appear?"
"If you know Madanela, there
in her you'll find the clue."
"And how should one pursue
you wherever they flee?"
"Well, I'm not in me."

"Having failed to find
you in you, why Madanela?"
"Because I lost myself in her   10
the same day I gained."
"A thing I don't understand
is you talk so eloquently."
"She is speaking within me."

"How come you're present here
if there's your life and soul?"
"Because in front of people
it's a lost soul that appears."
"If you're dead, it's only proper
everyone should flee."   20
"And I also flee from me."

▦ HYMN ▦

▦ Mande-me Amor que cante docemente

Love commanded me to sing
sweetly what was there printed on my heart

with the purpose of unburdening my soul,
and to make me content with my suffering
said I'd be captured by eyes so bright,
just the telling would make me cheerful.
I allowed Love to beguile
me in this fine manner for my benefit,
          in case he should regret it
and eclipse my genius with pain.   10
          But I was more venturesome
in virtue of the countenance that's my theme
and if what I sing is more than I imagine,
          I invoke her face's lovely vision,
more potent than Love in my fallen condition.

I lived once oblivious of Love
despising his bow and all his intrigues
though by them I was also sustained.
Deceitful Love, who's the origin of
desires a thousand times beleaguered,   20
made me laugh at all who yearned.
Then the sun was in Taurus and Procne returned,
Flora spread her cornucopia,
          as Love shook free his hair,
the golden locks flowing
          careless of the soft breezes,
as living fire flashed from his eyes
and roses were sown among the snows,
          with a smile so fashioned
as to conquer a heart of diamond.   30

Something, I don't know what, emanating
tenderly, caused such sharp surprise
it was felt by inanimate things,
and like the birds chattering
with unruly voices in their hedgerows,
so desire in me began burning.
The crystal streams ceased flowing
entranced by the pure, lovely sight;
          all greenery flourished

as if touched by the passing of some god;   40
       as the branches, envious
of the trampled grasses
—or because everything before it bowed—
       in short, nothing in life
failed to wonder at it, or I at myself.

When I saw it making percipient
things that had no minds, it behooved
me to take care what its effect might be.
I knew I had lost my judgment
and in this alone retained it; for Love   50
permitted that, letting me see.
Such revenge Love exacted on me
that human nature changed;
       the adamantine range
underwent a metamorphosis.
       O what a gentle shift
to transform a mountain bereft
of feeling to one with genius!
       Note the sweet deception,
as your customary profit from my pain!   60

So it was as feeling abandoned
all rational constraint, it irked me
to find thought subdued to a passion;
but in my inmost heart I found
thought's demise in a cause of such sublimity
made sense, as reason was undone.
So it happened when all was gone
its very damnation restored it;
       as each to its opposite
agreed to be subject.   70
       Such splendid harmony!
Who would not judge it heavenly
that a case could have such an effect
       that the heart's emotion
comes to be taken as reason?

Here I experienced Love's finesse,
how it was to feel with the insensible
and to lose in the feeling all identity.
In the end, I felt nature was in recess,
given I believed all was possible   80
for those lovely eyes, except desiring me.
I fell a victim to syncope
in place of the good sense I had lost,
          not knowing there was impressed
on my heart in the alphabet of memory
          the substance of this case,
jointly printed with that bright face
that's the origin of this long history.
          If well said, it's not
I who invent, I copied it from my heart.   90

Song, if whoever reads you
doubts those eyes of which you speak,
whether or not they lie,
it's but human instinct to reply;
what's divine transcends any critic.

⊞ ODE ⊞

⊞ **Pode um desejo imenso**

An immense yearning has the power
to glow in the heart so intensely
that for the gentle, living soul its fire
effaces from our mortal coil all stains
and purifies the spirit to such an extent
that it can read
with immortal eyes more than it sees written.

The flames that then take hold
spread such radiance
that a noble passion for good unfolds   10

bright as the day, larger than experience,
and sees beyond what it finds natural,
the grace and living color
of some greater other than the corporeal.

Given you are the clear template
of all living beauty
that timelessly I contemplate
in my soul that exalts and refines this quality,
don't imagine I don't see the image
that humankind never sees,   20
until over all others they are greatly privileged.

And should eyes be insufficient
to behold the measured
harmony, in its various excellent
colors of modesty and virtue;
of which Poetry, that until now sang
only of appearances,
makes mortal beauty equally becoming:

if such eyes don't see hair
as pure gold, as in the usual jargon,   30
if they don't see lovely eyes, so clear
they outshine the treasury of the sun,
if they don't see a face whose excellencies,
they will say, draw
metaphors from crystal, snow, and rose:

they observe in a flash that pure grace,
that heightened and austere light,
divine beauty's rays
to be imprinted on the soul and radiate
like a crystal broken from the sun   40
that shines beyond itself,
its borrowed flame a clarion.

And they observe gravity
along with living happiness,
combined in a mix of such quality

that one from the other never diverges;
and does not allow one to look askance
at gladness or pleasure,
nor the other at much revered stoicism.

And they see all that's noble   50
in an honest, well-considered opinion,
tempered with a sweet, happy smile,
at whose opening the meadow flowers open;
with discreet and gentle words
whose discourse
detains breezes and the high circling birds:

a shifting of your eyes
makes everything overflow,
whether by chance or artifice
the imagination cannot know;   60
from the ebb and flow of your presence,
your posture and movement,
beauty's very self could take lessons.

Something, I don't know what,
that emanates, I don't know how,
emerges invisibly, touching the sight,
though understanding it's not my purview;
something poetry of the Tuscan era,
most favored by Apollo,
never saw in Beatrice nor in Laura;   70

in you, Lady, in our own age
it can be on display
if genius, skill, and knowledge
are equal to your beauty;
as I found in my long separation,
and in my absence still see.
Desire gives such wings to imagination!

So if yearning can refine
the soul to such a pure point
that it takes you as an aspect of the divine,   80

I'll raise for you songs unprecedented,
known to the Betis, furbished by the Tiber,
though our clear Tagus
I see a little ruffled and perturbed.

Flowers have ceased to enamel
the meadow, thistles in their ugliness
swarm, and they surely fail
as metaphors for your eyes.
but let vile doggerel say what it likes:
the sun that is your very essence   90
will always be my unsullied light in darkness.

▨ EIGHTS ▨

▨ Quem pode ser no mundo tão quieto

Who could live so calmly on this planet
or know such freedom in his reflections,
whom long experience has made discreet,
in short, so far from conventional opinions
that, perhaps openly, perhaps in secret,
he is not shocked to the core of his emotions,
making sound judgment that much harder,
on seeing and writing of this world's disorder?

Who is there, knowing some clown who lived
by thefts, adulteries, and murders,   10
and in the people's judgment has deserved
eternal scourging, the most scurrilous satire,
if instead, Fortune guides him with favors,
though nothing finally could be weirder,
triumphantly to the pinnacle of fame,
who, however cynical, is not struck dumb?

Who is there, knowing some man whose conduct
Momus himself, the god of bickering,

in the court of the people judged perfect,
after scouring his heart for any minor sin,   20
when ill-fortune that targets the elect
sends all his virtuous entitlements packing,
who does not feel his heart turned to ice
no matter how often he's witnessed injustice?

Democritus of the gods pronounced
there were just two: punishment and reward.
But I can find no solid evidence
for what he dreamed up, or heard;
if both come through some route unnoticed
to those who don't deserve them, it's absurd   30
gods can be so unjust, so irrational—
as Democritus declared, but not St. Paul.

You caution me that, if ever again
this strange dissonance stuns our world,
I, the freest and most practiced of men,
have no cause for surprise, if I'm bewildered;
if Socrates of old could be quite certain
no grand event could ever have altered
his face, or those of his loyal and prudent
disciples, I, too, should hide my astonishment.   40

This sounds good advice, but I have to call
this habit of fortune so injurious
the more through use it seems traditional,
the more it's become warped and blasphemous;
for if heaven, friend to all,
is helpless to limit fortune's lease,
no one need be unduly shocked
that evil continues a hateful fact.

At this, another anomaly seems odder:
for despite the fact worldly fortune   50
lords it over all the world's disorder,
not one man anywhere is taken in.
There's no one ready to underscore
this theory of how we live as humans;

for where's the philosopher will reason
away his share of worldly ambition?

Diogenes trampled all over Plato's
rich mosaics with his dirty soles,
presuming in his arrogance to veto
those luxuries men adopt as idols.   60
"Diogenes, don't you see such a motto
proclaimed, as you do, to the utmost pole,
declares, for all the pleasure you despise,
fame and disciples are the fruits you prize?"

I ignore great kings, only schooled
in how to quench a ravenous appetite
for conquest and universal rule,
through propaganda and lavish rites.
I ignore all who presume to shield
careers vicious and lives dissolute   70
behind their line of noble ancestors,
hardly caring they appear impostors.

I ignore that courtier whose waking dream
is of being that favorite the king adores,
who sustains himself by what merely seems,
which many hearts take as fixed laws.
I ignore those cuckoos, hourly scheming
to fill their beaks with all kinds of treasure;
like men with dropsy, their complaint
is the more they swallow, the more they want.   80

I ignore the delusions of that clan
there's no man anywhere can refute,
not being subject to any doctrine
but what's established and obsolete.
But to mighty Caesar, I put my question,
and to divine Plato, that they relate
what led one to lands too far from home,
and what gained the other from conquering them?

Caesar declared: "I live in history:
conquering so many people of valor   90
I was the world's monarch, the memory
of my sublime deeds will remain forever."
True enough: but that power and glory,
how long did it last? Brutus, the conspirator,
and Cassius will say: "For all your commands,
your death was at your colleagues' hands."

Plato said: "It was to see Etna and the Nile
I went to Sicily, to Egypt, and to other parts,
to observe and describe in the grand style
of natural science, through my best arts."   100
But time is short. Are you happy to while
it away on books, Plato? You devote
hours to study, and end where you begun,
worshipping the false god of the sun.

For when from its dark, clammy fetters
the freed soul rises to be born anew,
it is preoccupied with greater matters
than any earthly fame can minister to.
If the corpse feels nothing on its litter,
someone will air the Cynic's view—   110
that the field where the dead find sepulcher
must have somehow banished dog and vulture.

He who stays earth-bound in his dreams,
untouched by great events, and merely thinks
of leading cattle to the cool streams,
milking them for all the milk he drinks,
how well predestined than man seems,
even if Fortune wheels him to the brink,
nothing could cause him greater grief
than weariness at so confined a life.   120

He'd see the sun's red face each dawn,
he'd watch the rippling of the clear spring,
without worrying where its waters were born
or who conceals the light every evening,

piping as his cattle saunter on:
types of mountain grass his only learning,
trusting in God would comprise his history
without the need for any grander mystery.

Of Thrasyllus is written, to be read
in the annals of profound antiquity,   130
that over many years he forfeited
all reason through some great infirmity
and when, being beside himself, he was mad,
he kept on asserting obstinately
that of the ships sailing the seven seas
those anchoring at Piraeus were all his.

He took himself to be a great lord
(over and above the happy days he passed)
for the ships he lost he simply ignored,
while in those that found harbor he rejoiced.   140
One day, this tale not being long delayed,
his wandering brother Crito regressed
from his travels, and finding him deprived
of reason was moved by brotherly love.

He dispatched him to doctors, warning
he must submit to the treatment he refused.
Sad irony that, his wits returning
destroyed that calm to which he was used.
Improbably, Apollo's ministering
restored him to the health he once prized.   150
Rational Thrasyllus could find no fault
with his brother's concern, only the result.

For knowing he was now under threat
of the responsibility good sense imposes,
rejoicing no more in his earlier state
of delusion in its various guises,
"O, enemy in a brother's mask," he broke out,
"why kidnap me from my bed of roses,
that quiet life of absolute freedom
only to be experienced in an asylum?"   160

"For what king was I ransomed? Or what duke?
For what lord, with so much to command?
Who had such power over nature to revoke
her order and make my world end?
It's only now my life feels the yoke;
I know how to work, and be disheartened.
Now I'm restored, this is my advice:
sound judgment's only found in madness."

You see, my Lord, very clearly in all this
how Fortune has power over everyone   170
except those who know little and fear less,
being incapable of high ambition.
He alone can mock human blindness,
for to him nothing could ever happen;
nor will he ever weigh in the balance
evil's terrors and hope's pretense.

But if sweet heaven should ever authorize
some quiet, humble, and sweet dwelling
where I might live alone with my muses
in place of this exile's nonbeing,   180
where no one exists to recognize
me, nor whom I acknowledge as princeling,
except for you, who's as content as I am
for I know already that's no problem;

and to the bank of some pure, limpid stream
that, springing in bubbles, would invite
some sweet bird to warble the theme
of her separation from her colorful mate;
then when snows cover our mountain home,
the biting cold will drive us to our hut,   190
rekindling our brains in sweet studies,
better food for the soul than all besides.

Petrarch will sing to us of that laurel
he burned for Daphne's tree, and his own Laura,
the same who with his rare, grand style
halted in full flow the crystalline river;

Sanazzaro would play his flute awhile,
on the mountain, in the village, or wherever,
and Castilian Garcilaso would serenade us,
repeating his praise of the proud Tagus;   200

and present, too, we would encounter her
whose memory and whose bright countenance
lives uniquely in my heart (for there
she exists, pure and manifest, in essence
through the high influence of my star),
relaxing her breast's virtuous resistance,
weaving roses in her braided hair,
outshining the sun, for those who stare;

and there, plucking flowers and fruit
or in winter settled by the fire,   210
I should tell how much my ambushed heart
has suffered by way of such desire;
I would not ask love should impart
mad Thrasyllus's insensate cure,
but rather double my intelligence,
being grounded in such good experience.

But where's my imagination veering?
Why do I deal in such happy tropes
when it's fortune's habit to be steering
an opposite course to all my hopes?   220
If with some new vision Love is inspiring
me, given this time and place where I mope
at my rejection, so lost in exile,
it can only be expressed as an ideal.

The conclusion is Love plotted with Fortune
and I their experiment in my agony;
Love drove me to a hopeless passion,
so Fortune had even more to deny me;
then time arranged my present condition,
expecting my life to end, Q.E.D.,   230
if it's for me to end it, which I don't reckon:
what I fear are the long years that beckon.

O Poeta Simónides, falando

Talking with captain Themistocles
one day, on matters of practical science,
the Greek poet Simonides

offered him some contrivance
just invented, to file
systematically all his experiences,

showing him such subtle rules
that nothing would fade from his memory
bank, however swiftly time rolls.

He surely merits fame and glory   10
who finds methods to stop oblivion
burying any remote history,

but the renowned captain whose opinion
was very different, given he had
thoughts that exacted their own pain,

"O illustrious Simonides," he said,
"do you really put such faith in your trick
of showing memory a fresh road?

If you could only show me the knack
of recalling nothing from my past,   20
you'd be doing me the better work!"

This excellent maxim, long ingested,
suits me, who found myself deported,
my cherished hopes all dashed.

O, how appropriately he shouted,
"Simonides, invent differently;
past and present aren't connected!"

If a man's forced to some other country,
in the search for some genuine resting place
that you, Fortune, dispose unjustly,   30

and if it's plain his labour's onerous
but, however hard, has to be done
with a lively spirit and cheerful face,

what does it serve that men burden
their minds with what's past, given all
passes, unless to regret and know pain?

If some other body could contain one's soul
—no, not in death, as Pythagoras hoped,
but in frail life under love's control—

and if this worldly love were of the type   40
that, in virtue of one, lovely object,
exists without soul, being strong and happy,

where this object fails becomes a fact
so life-denying, my own case
evokes the snake-haired fury Alecto;

why was I not bred by my stars
some barbarian, tough inhabitant
of Scythia in all its harshness?

Or the dread Caucasus, a feeble infant
suckled by some Hircanian tiger?   50
An outlaw, obdurate as diamond,

for such a barbarous, inhuman figure
would never bow to the hard yoke
of what confers life even when perjured;

or that payment in tears I took
for Lethe's waters, like the seas I traversed
to make me forget my ill-luck:

the good that vain hope might achieve,
or death prevent, or altered ways,
(at which evil some soul would grieve).   60

My Lord, you will accept how in evil days
good memories are a painful scourge
because they spring where hope dies.

And if you wish, in this homesick elegy,
to see them improved, don't waste pains
on reading more of this wretched page.

The god Aeolus had slackened the reins
of the serene and gentle Zephyrs,
and I already had freedom to yearn.

Neptune's trident was in place;   70
the prow divided the white billows,
the mariners took their ease.

The nymphs' chorus followed
the breezes, beloved Galateia
among them, lightly propelled.

In their tiny, silvery shells Panopeia
surfed the ocean, scattering spray,
along with Melanto, Dinamene, and Ligeia,

while I, blinkered by my memories,
conveyed my eyes on the restful waters,   80
and waters restlessly in my eyes.

My past good fortune, now so altered,
lay there before me, as plain
as if time was set at naught,

and with a face impassive and restrained,
and a deep sigh, barely audible,
so the mariners should not know my pain,

I spoke: "If you are susceptible,
bright nymphs, to love in its pure form,
and even now are not forgetful,   90

if, perhaps, you return some time
to the mouth of the Tagus, paying tribute
to Tethys, the lady you esteem,

and if you find the banks at low water
and collect the glittering specks of gold
the Tagus sands yield as their fruit,

write there in verse, elegant and bold,
using your shells, that you glimpsed me;
it may perhaps make some heart tender,

recounting what you saw of me,   100
so the Tagus shepherds I sang to there
will hear from you sighs you heard from me."

The nymphs showed me by gestures
and by waves in their gentle movement,
they were ready to grant my prayer.

But these memories, always present
in calm seas and fair weather,
persisted when all was turbulent,

for reaching that Cape, known further
as Good Hope, my sense of raw   110
change brought unhappiness still nearer,

being governed by a new star,
sure evidence of the second pole
as it glistened in a new hemisphere;

then black clouds advanced at nightfall
as the brief dusk was nitrous
and the ocean turned foul.

In such a storm, the world's apparatus
seemed about to implode;
the waves became vertiginous.   120

Fierce Boreas and Notus conjured
howling gales, tearing
the concave sails from the masthead;

the rigging whistled in the uproar;
the blaspheming of the shocked
mariners curdled the atmosphere.

Austere, terrible Jupiter shook
the bolts forged by Vulcan's hammers,
leaving earth's poles thunderstruck!

Yet Love showed himself in this extreme   130
all-powerful, not disposed to flee,
—the greater the challenge, the more firm—

as I spoke out, with death before me:
"Lady, should you just once grieve, all
I suffered will vanish from my memory."

In this crisis, nothing could forestall
constant Love's true nature
in any heart it had entered for real.

Some cause, my Lord, ordained for sure
that love is never truly courtly   140
while in the presence of its cure.

In this manner, it was my destiny
to reach the distant and longed-for
Goa, the grave of honest poverty.

I saw in our own people such hauteur
and in the land's owners so little, against whom
it was at once necessary to make war.

Some island the King of Porcá claimed
had been taken by the King of Pimenta;
we were sent to retake it, and did the same.   150

With a huge armada, fitted out
by Goa's Vice-Roy, we pressed on
with every armed man located,

and with very little effort we won
against a people skilled only with bows,
punishing them with death and arson.

It was an island of many waterways
like an exotic, transplanted Venice,
so we moved around in canoes

during the two days we were fixed   160
there, though there were others who remained
to cross the cold waters of the Styx

—beyond all doubt the best medicine
for those harnessed for life
to others ambitious to be gentlemen.

O, happy those who work the land, if
only they knew their own good!
To live among fields, utterly safe!

The honest soil yields them food,
the clear spring gives them pure water,   170
they milk their ewes by the hundred;

they don't study the angry ocean by night,
voyaging for India's rubies;
they don't know the fearful summons to fight;

that man lives happily with his trees,
and no hankering after gold coins
breaks in on the rural peace.

For all he may lack of perfumed gowns
or of lovely Assyrian purple,
or of gold-embroidered turbans;   180

if they exist without Paros marble,
or Corinthian sun-dried delights,
or garnets, hyacinth stones, or emeralds,

and if their houses are not gold-plated,
the fields are painted with a thousand flowers
where their kid-goats frolic and eat.

There the meadow displays its colors,
the branches bend with pleasant fruits,
and shepherds' fields are a place of culture;

Titirus and Silenus practiced letters;   190
sacred justice, after all, fled
to the serene heavens from just those parts.

Happy that man who has succeeded
passing his days in the sweet company
of the gentle lambs he bred!

That way he'd easily come to know
of all things their natural causes:
how originates rain and the cold snow;

the sun's labors, which never pause,
and why the moon gives us borrowed light   200
and dares to obstruct Phoebus's rays;

and how rapidly the heavens rotate,
drawn by the *primum mobile*,
and whether Venus is kind or obdurate.

But how could he grasp what I have to say
about having to pursue dreadful Mars,
my eyes always on my jeopardy?

Yet it must be, my Lord, by whatever muse,
that even if fate has such authority
to divide me so far from all I prize,   210

it can't divide me from the prime duty
of my muscular verse, while death postpones
my passage to Rhadamanthus's court,
if sad people can enjoy such fortune!

❖ Quando vejo que meu destino ordena

When I see my destiny applied
as a trial to set me apart from you,
turning my back on so much I value,
so the blame and penalty coincide;

the harsh treatment to which I'm condemned,
as I revolve it in my memory,
hardens my feelings to such a degree
that the anguish of absence is lessened.

How can it be, when this reversal
of all I want most is so extreme,   10
I don't also give up on life?

I will not be so bitterly equivocal;
for, Lady, the pain of parting would seem
much worse were I nonchalant in my grief.

❖ Se algu' hora em vós a piedade

If just once compassion for my chronic
torment had found room in your heart,
Love would not have agreed to my being parted
from those eyes, for which I am homesick.

I left your side; but my desire for you,
by its nature bearing you in my soul,
makes me believe this absence is unreal
though still evil, being all too true.

I will embark, Lady, and with this departure
sad tears will take their own reprisal   10
in those eyes you gave sustenance.

And so I'll give life to my torture;
in short, I shall cherish you in my exile,
entombed in your negligence.

Em flor vos arrancou, de então crecida

In your earliest bloom, cruel fortune
(ah, Don António, sir) tore you away
from where your mighty feats in arms that day
left the fame of the ancients in oblivion.

The one thing equitable in such grief,
providing, as I know, some grain of solace,
is that given your earthly end was glorious
you could not have lived a greater life.

If my humble verse had such energy
that my art could equal my desires,   10
you should furnish me with rare material.

And celebrated in a lengthy elegy,
dying at the hands of insatiable Mars,
you should live in the memory of all people.

Se tomar minha pena em penitencia

If I accept my sentence penitently
for the error into which my thoughts fell,
this in no way eases, but doubles my hell,
so I'm forced to bear all patiently.

And if death's pallor in my appearance
and my vain sighs scattered to the wind
are not enough to change your mind,
my suffering rests in your conscience.

And if through whatever bitter change
Love punishes all unbridled longings   10
(I see good in the pain that's my sentence),

and if Love fails to take his revenge,
he will be forced (for so Love dragoons)
that I alone suffer for your offense.

Quem quiser ver d'Amor ua excelência

Whoever wants to witness Love at his best,
his refinements burnished to perfection,
observe where I was dispatched by Fortune,
putting fidelity to the ultimate test.

Where memories are killed by long absence
on the fearful ocean or in dire war,
there my longing is most secure,
the dangers strengthening my endurance.

Wherever I'm placed by relentless fate
in sorrow, death, injury, or perdition,   10
or in sublime and prosperous anchorage;

in short, whether in high or low estate,
until implacable death tracks me down,
on my tongue your name, in my heart your image.

Por cima destas agues, forte e firme

Resolute and strong, buoyed by these breakers
I went wherever my luck ordained,
since, buoyed by the tears that rained
for me from those bright eyes, I could embark.

I had reached the end of my setting
out, with every obstacle foreclosed,
when rivers of love interposed
to obstruct the finality of my parting.

I set out in that most desperate state
in which death, glorious and inevitable,   10
makes those already lost tenacious.

In what shape or unfamiliar light
could furious death ever appall
one delivered to him, bound and helpless?

Doces aguas e claras do Mondego

Sweet pure waters of the Mondego,
sweet memory's calm center,
where long-held and treacherous desire
blinded me so many years ago;

I'm far removed, but I still revere
those old memories I keep in view
that refuse to admit any change in you,
but the further I travel, the more I draw near.

Well might Fortune, that heart's engine,
bear me to new and strange countries,   10
a prey to distant seas and winds;

but my heart your constant companion,
borne by light imagination, flies
to your waters and bathes on your strand.

Senhora minha, se a Fortuna imiga

My lady, if it is Fortune's will
to plot my death with the highest powers,
conveying my eyes where they cannot see yours,
consigning me to the greatest peril,

I carry with me a heart sworn,
in the greater dispatch of sea, fire, and anger,
always to be constant, one that longs
with you alone to have eternal union.

In that heart, where Fortune's impotent,
I'll bear you ardently where not cold or famine   10
nor frivolous dangers can drive you out.

In the front line, in an echoing, strident
voice, boasting your name alone,
I'll put hurricanes and the enemy to flight.

No mundo poucos anos, e cansados

I passed on earth a few weary years
replete with unhappiness and hardships;
so soon was the light of my day eclipsed
I did not see five times five birthdays.

I traveled lands and ploughed oceans
searching for some remedy for living;
but he whom Fortune denies favors
will never attain his ambitions.

Portugal raised me, in Alenquer,
my dear and fertile home. But the detested   10
climate where my dust finds burial

made me food for fishes in the rough breakers
that beat on Abyssinia's desert coast,
so remote from my happy native soil.

Como quando do mar tempestuoso

As when an adroit, exhausted mariner,
swimming from some dreadful shipwreck
in mountainous seas, has saved his neck
yet only to speak of it makes him shudder;

and he swears even if he sees the ocean
no longer heaving but placid and secure
he will venture out on it no more
unless profiting hugely for his pains;

so, Lady, suffering your face's torment,
in similar manner I withdrew,   10
vowing never again to be lost;

but my heart, where you were never absent,
for the simple dividend of seeing you,
steers me back to that dangerous coast.

Senhor João Lopes, o meu baixo estado

My Lord João Lopes, my low degree
I saw yesterday set at so high a level
that you, who are envied by all people,
would have longed to change places with me.

I saw the soft and delicate gesture
that already made you happy and hapless
launch to the winds a voice so melodious
it calmed the entire atmosphere.

I saw her in a few words convey such
as could be said in many; in my solitude   10
I was in despair at such gentle speech.

But cursed be Fortune and blind Cupid:
the one because hearts constrain so much,
the other because of unequal blood.

De vós me aparto, ó vida! Em tal mudança

Life, I abandon you! In such a demise
I am already alive with death's sentiment.
I do not know the point of contentment
if he who comes closest has the most to lose.

But I give you this steadfast assurance
that once my torments have killed me,
in the erasing waters of River Lethe
will assuredly die all remembrance.

Formerly, in your absence, my eyes were sad
that at anything else would show spirit;   10
before you forget them, they are forgetting you.

Formerly, in this memory, they felt troubled
that with oblivion, they would not merit
glory for suffering the pain they went through.

▦ Todo o animal da calma repousava

All animals were resting from the noon's heat;
Liso alone did not feel its flame,
for relief for what burned within him
lay in the nymph for whom he sought.

The very mountains seemed to shake
at the sad sounds of the grief he uttered;
but nothing could move that hard heart
whose desires on another were focused.

Wearying as through the woods he traipsed
he carved on the trunk of a layered beech   10
these words in sad reflection:

"No one should ever fix their hopes
on a woman's heart, for it's their nature
to be constant only in alteration."

▦ Seguia aquele fogo, que o guiava

Leander followed the fire that steered
him into the currents and the gale;
when his strength and breath began to fail,
love refashioned him, and restored.

Even as he felt his heart giving way
he did not lose courage, but in thought
(since he lacked words) entreated
the waves, sure they would comply:

"O waves" (said the youth in soliloquy),
"I don't ask for life; I only demand   10
you take care of Hero; she must not see me.

"Receive and bear my dead body
to that lighthouse; be in this my friend,
for my greater blessing, you merely envy."

Por sua ninfa, Céfalo deixava

On account of his nymph, Cephalus broke up
with Aurora, who became distraught
despite her heralding the bright
day with the purple flowers she copied.

He who adored the lovely Procris,
and for her sake forsook all others,
wished to prove he would find in her
the same faith *mutatis mutandis*.

Weaving the plot, he came in disguise,
and dissembling further, he offered cash: 10
she broke her weak word, and consented.

How subtly guile brings its own distress!
Observe how blindly a lover will rush
to ensure he will always be discontent!

Sentindo-se tomada a bela esposa

Perceiving she was taken, the lovely Procris,
wife of Cephalus, consented to the rape;
she fled from her husband to the mountaintop
but I don't know whether from design or disgrace.

Because he, as it happened, being horn mad
out of blind love and violent lust,
followed in her footsteps like one lost,
having already pardoned the guilty jade.

Oppressed by such studied deception,
he flung himself at the cruel nymph's   10
feet, begging forgiveness, begging for life.

O the power of misplaced passion,
that though he was the one who was cheated,
he asked pardon from a faithless wife!

Os vestidos Elisa revolvia

Dido rummaged among the garments
Aeneas had left by way of memory,
sweet spoils of former glory,
sweet so long as Fortune consented.

Among them she found the superb sword,
a weapon with its own sad history,
and like one laying claim to victory,
speaking only to herself, she said:

"Untarnished sword, if you've survived
to execute his design who wished   10
to leave you embedded in my life,

know that with me it's you that's deceived:
to separate me from such anguish
the pain of parting was enough."

Ferido sem ter cura perecia

Wounded, and with no apparent remedy,
by Achilles, who had been dipped in water
so nothing iron could inflict a cut,
the strong and brave Telephus trembled.

He sought prescription, to be cured,
from Apollo's oracle at Delphi.
"Be wounded again," came the reply,
"by the same Achilles," and so was restored.

Obviously, Lady, my fate's diagnosis
is that, pierced by your loveliness, the pill's   10
to see you and adore you as at first.

But such is your beauty, my prognosis
is that of a patient swollen with dropsy:
the more I drink in, the greater my thirst.

O raio cristalino s' estendia

Mottled dawn was spreading her crystal
beams over the world when Nise,
the tender, courteous shepherdess,
was parting from where she left her soul.

Even as her eyes eclipsed the sun,
raising her face bathed in tears,
tired of herself, of fate and the years,
she spoke, fixing her eyes on heaven:

"Be born, bright sun, with your serene glow,
be resplendent, purple Aurora,   10
and gladden all hearts in distress;

as for me, from today on, know
nevermore will you see me content, nor
so heartsick another shepherdess."

Apartava-se Nise de Montano

Nise was parted from Montano,
though in his broken heart she stayed,
and in memory the shepherd portrayed
her, keeping alive his old delusion.

By the beaches of the Indian Ocean
on his curved pastoral crook he leant,
while his eyes were fixed on the distant
waters that showed scant feeling for his pain.

Then, in his grief and yearning, he stated:
"I worship her who preferred to leave me,   10
my witnesses are heaven and its stars.

But if you waves know any pity,
take these selfsame tears I shed,
for it was you removed their cause!"

Tomava Daliana por vingança

Daliana's revenge against the scorn
of the shepherd she so bitterly loved
was to marry cowman Gil, to reprove
such crass error and faithless disdain.

Her dependable trust, her self-possession,
her fresh face modeled on roses,
withered as her unhappiness
wrought its cruel alteration.

It was hybrid flower in barren soil,
sweet fruit plucked by a coarse hand,   10
her memory of vows that were broken,

turning green meadow to arid hills,
as selfish lies and passion feigned
left planet-struck the loveliest woman.

Quantas vezes do fuso s' esquecia

As often as Daliana at the spinning wheel
forgot herself, tears bathing her breast,
so often from his bitter fear and distrust
her husband, Laurenio, turned pale.

She desired Silvio rather than him
but to visit him was beyond her resource.
How could she cure Laurenio's distress,
lacking the remedy for her own harm?

He who understood this clearly said,
sobbing under the extreme pressure   10
of a sorrow that stirred him to pity,

"How can it be that nature's discord
creates such polarities of desire
in those subject to the same destiny?"

Em fermosa Leteia se confia

Leteia put her faith in beauty
and as little by little her pride advanced,
turning to outright arrogance,
she challenged the heavenly deities.

But this presumption was short-lived
(for delay gives birth to many errors)
as the gods gave effect to the measures
that such foolishness deserved.

Oleno, who had plainly lost his head,
not accepting that Cupid could approve   10
for his wife's beauty such retribution,

sought to be punished in her stead;
but so death should not divide them, Love
turned each to obdurate stone.

Num bosque que das Ninfas se habitava

To a wood where the nymphs had tenure
the lovely nymph Silvia came one day;
and underneath a shady tree
gathered the yellow flowers.

Cupid, whose custom was to keep
his siesta in the cool shade,
hung the arrows and the bow he carried
on a branch before he fell asleep.

The nymph with apt timing devises
a plan of action and does not stall,   10
but steals the arms from the scornful boy.

The arrows she brings in her eyes and lets fly
—O shepherds, run from her who kills all
but for me, who lives by being destroyed.

Enquanto Febo os montes acendia

While Phoebus was lighting up the mountains
of Heaven with his radiant clarity,
to relieve the boredom of her chastity
Diana was killing time in hunting.

Then Venus, who was descending secretly
to fetter the desire of Anchises,
seeing Diana so undisguised
addressed her half-jokingly:

"You come with your nets to the thick wood
to ensnare the fast-running deer,   10
but my own nets capture the mind."

"Better," the chaste goddess replied,
"to take the nimble deer in my snare
than be caught in one by your husband."

Na metade do Céu subido ardia

The sun, that gentle shepherd, had climbed
to his bright zenith when the goats
abandoned their pasture to scent out
the soothing freshness of cold streams.

From the burning rays, the small birds
had sheltered in the depths of trees,
and instead of their tuneful phrases
only strident cicadas could he heard,

when the shepherd Liso, in a green meadow,
went in search of Natercia, cruel nymph,   10
with a thousand moans bewailing his lot:

"Why reject me, whose whole life's
yours, for one who loves you not?" he sighed,
and Echo responded, "loves you not."

Já a saudosa Aurora destoucava

Ardent Aurora had shaken free
her slender tresses of gold,
and the flowers of the enameled
fields were sprinkled with crystal dew,

when Silvio and Laurente drove
their handsome cattle to pasture,
both cowmen, both knowing rupture
they felt a similar love.

Laurente, shedding a heartfelt tear,
said: "Gentle nymph, I don't understand   10
how one doesn't die from living alone,

for without you what has life to offer?"
"Love denies that," Silvio responds,
"for it sins against hopes of return."

O filho de Latona esclarecido

Apollo, Latona's enlightened son,
who gladdens human hearts each daybreak,
killed the python, the dreadful snake
that so terrified Thessaly's population.

He shot with his bow, and was wounded in turn
by the arrow tipped with glistening gold;
so, on the beaches of Thessaly, spellbound
by the nymph Peneia, he was overcome.

Nothing availed him, for all his misery,
neither knowledge, persistence, nor respect   10
for the fact of his being exalted and sovereign.

If such a one, even through treachery,
could not win her love, what should I expect
from her who is herself more than human?

Aquela triste e leda madrugada

That fretful and lovely dawn,
replete with every kind of ache,
so long as the world recalls heartbreak
I wish that hour forever known.

Dawn alone, when, finely variegated,
she rose, bringing clarity to the world,
saw separated from each other's hold
who never again will be separated.

She alone observed the tears
flowing from each other's eyes   10
and swelling to a veritable river.

She witnessed the grief-stricken vows
that could turn hell's fires to ice
and bring respite to souls damned for ever.

Amor, co a esperança já perdida

With all hope already forfeit, Love,
I visited your holy shrine
and to mark my shipwreck, as a sign,
instead of clothes I laid down my life.

What more do you want of me, having undone
all the glory I ever achieved?
Don't presume to force me, who am baffled
about how to return to what I never abandoned.

You see before you soul, life, and hope,
sweet spoils of my former happy days   10
when I pursued her whom I still revere.

On these trophies exercise your phobia;
then if you continue eaten up with malice,
be satisfied that I shed such tears.

Cara minha inimiga, em cuja mão

My dearest enemy, in whose hand
my happiness was ever at venture,
you lack an earthly sepulcher
and I a tombstone to attend.

Eternally, the pirate waves
will enjoy your pilgrim loveliness;
but while my own life endures
in this heart you will remain alive.

And if my rough verse can prolong,
by its excellence, the history   10
of pure, true love on your behalf,

you will be famous in my song,
for so long as the world knows memory
my writing will be your epitaph.

Quando de minhas mágoas a comprida

When prolonged reflection on my grief
dulls my eyes in sleep, I discern
in vivid dreams that dear person
who was for so long the dream of my life.

There in the empty landscape, straining
my pupils at the shimmering vistas,
I pursue her. And she then appears
remoter than ever, and more driven.

"Don't avoid me, gentle shade," I cry out.
She (her eyes brimming with tender shame,   10
like one who speaks what cannot be)

turns to flee me. "Dina-," I shout,
and before I have added "-mene," I fathom
even that brief illusion's denied me.

Ah! minha Dinamene! Assi deixaste

Ah, my Dinamene, so you abandoned
him who never stopped yearning for you!
Ah, nymph, I cannot discern you,
given life was what so soon you scorned.

How have you now forever parted
from one so unprepared to lose you?
Could these waves have refused you
had you not seen what troubled your heart?

Not to tell you how hard death quit
me, when you consented its black veil   10
so early on should cover your eyes!

O sea, o heaven, oh my dark fate!
What future pain will I feel, and so value,
that have so little to live for in sadness?

O céu, a terra, o vento sossegado

The heavens, the earth, the tranquil breeze . . .
the waves dispersing on the beach . . .
the fish slumbering in the reach . . .
the night peaceful and at ease . . .

Fisherman Aónio, as he wandered
where the light winds ruffled the spume,
wept as he pronounced the beloved name
that could no more than be conjured.

"Waves," he said, "before I die of love,
give me back my nymph whom, so untimely,   10
you made liege-woman of death."

No one answered. The sea beat far off.
The casuarinas stirred gently.
The wind returned his voice in the same breath.

[173]

Indo o triste pastor todo embedido

The sad shepherd wandered, caught
in the shadow of his sweet fancies,
his complaints mirroring the breeze
in the tender sighs pouring from his heart.

"To whom shall I complain, blind and ill-starred,
since in the rocks I find no sentiment?
With whom speak? Or express my torment
since the more I shout, the less I am heard?

"O lovely nymph, why do you not respond?
Does spying on me so endear me?   10
Is it your cue I should always accuse?

"The more I see you, the more you are hidden!
The more harm you see, the more you torture me!
So with suffering increases its cause."

Ah! imiga cruel, que apartamento

Ah, my cruel enemy, what scission
is this you make with your native strand?
Who exiles you from your fatherland,
glory of eyes, and fancy's paragon?

Do you venture to try Fortune's lists,
the cruel winds and obdurate war,
mountainous seas in a turmoil of water
as one wave and its opposite crest?

But as you depart, without willing departure,
may the heavens offer you better odds,   10
than any fallible hopes you take.

And find comfort in this formula:
there remains at your parting more that is good
than your illusions when you disembark.

Posto me tem Fortuna em tal estado

Fortune has brought me to such a shift
as to leave me prostrate at her feet;
I've lost so much I've nothing to forfeit,
and changed so much, change loses its drift.

Everything good for me is at an end—
from hereon I take my life as lived,
and, where the harm's so well perceived,
reasons for living should be better defined.

Were asking to suffice, I long for death,
for no other longing fits the case,   10
as I'll treat one evil with another.

That things can improve I've little faith,
so given this evil has only one redress,
don't blame me for seeking such a cure.

SONGS

Se de saudade

TO THIS COMMON THEME:

> *If I'm borne on waters*
> *I take them in my eyes.*

Whether I die
of heartache or not,
my eyes will relate
the truth about me.
It's for them I enroll,
daring the oceans
that match the emotions
I bear in my soul.

The waters that vainly
force me to cry,   10
if they are of the sea,
they are also of loving.
Doubly through them
I discharge my cares;
if the power of the waters
bears me, I bear them.

All of them sadden,
all are of salt;
and yet this melting
feels Elysian.   20
Run, sweet waters,
in you I delight,
the pain beneath notice
I bear in my heart.

Polo meu apartamento

TO THIS THEME:

> *I saw tears in bright eyes*
> *that time I came away:*
> *oh what grief, oh what joy!*

At my departure
all swam in tears.
Who supposed in such sorrows
I should find pleasure?
Let good sense measure
which the stronger torment,
whether pain or enjoyment.

When further bereft
I acknowledged to my heart,
in the midst of great hurt,   10
the greater joy left.

And so if my heart lifts,
it was because it sustained
that joy in me, amidst this pain.

The blessing Love declined
at the time I wanted it,
when I was parting from it
she confessed she was mine.
What now, if Fortune
baffles, shall I do,   20
defrauded of this joy?

But was Love cheated
in trying to defend
me from her rage at being abandoned
through the pain of being parted?
Now I'm doubly tormented,
rediscovering at each day's
end the origin of bliss.

Nunca o prazer se conhece

TO THIS COMMON THEME:

> *love's service will be rewarded.*
> *if for you alone it travails,*
> *sad times will fade away*
> *if only some hour you recall.*

No pleasure in living memory
came without pain to punish it;
blessings are so temporary
—if contentment flourishes,
duty soon crushes it.
Good things always defraud
and nothing obstructs like evil,
but it's everywhere recorded
where contentment knows travail,
love's service will be rewarded.   10

Whatever has been my labor
in bringing you happiness,
nothing, Lady, has been onerous,
if only at some hour
I see in you some awareness.
Howsoever evil deals me evil
I will take it all as beneficial,
and though the flesh wearies
the soul will be at ease
if for you alone it travails.   20

Whoever has already suffered
takes your cruelty as normal;
he will find it familiar,
and far better to travail
in your service further.
Sorrows will be effaced,
even those felt profoundly;
the years will not remind me,
for, like all else that's past,
sad times will fade away.   30

Were it to be repaid,
this service so onerous,
I should not feel so harrowed;
but if it was so yesterday,
why not tomorrow?
From fatigue I'd not recoil
even should you advise it.
Hard labor, death—I'll face it,
all, in short, I'd connive at
if only some hour you recall.   40

⊞ Se só no ver puramente

TO THIS COMMON THEME:

I see her painted on my soul,
when my desire longs for her,
it's her real self that's invisible.

If only seeing her inherent
self changed me to what I see,
from a vision so excellent
it will pain me to be absent,
though it was not of me.
Because the heart in thrall
transports her image so well,
and memory so takes wing,
if I don't see her in person
I see her painted on my soul.   10

Desire that takes advantage
of the least that's conceded,
in your case seeks and pleads
like a patient who badgers
for what's most prohibited.
Eyeless because absent,
I feel chagrined, and deplore
finding myself so poor
I have nothing left to grant
when my desire longs for her.   20

Like one who's been blinded
(it's a matter well attested
that nature has ordained
to be doubled in the mind's
eye what's veiled from one's sight),
so am I, who am not insensible
to visions of what's desirable;
in both memory and constancy
nature agrees with me
it's her real self that's invisible.   30

Amor, cuja providência

> *without you and with my sorrow,*
> *look with whom, and without whom.*

Love, whose providence
was always to be accurate,
for he who bore you in his heart
in respect of the pain of absence,
wished the exchange of souls absolute.
And given my constant harrowing,
I and my pain as companions,
I opted to bite the arrow
so as not to live alone,
without you and with my sorrow.   10

But this soul I brought with me
because it is your domain
left me eyeless and without strategy;
I'd have known better company
in staying where you remain.
For my advantage, I roam
where my ill star leads, without
the soul you gave heart-room,
and in the evil of living apart
look with whom, and without whom.   20

Querendo Amor esconder-vos

ANOTHER TO THE SAME THEME:

Love, wishing to secret you
where I would not discover you
in the excitement of loving you,
blinded me at the sight of you
taking my eyes without my perceiving.
Being eyeless but alert,
when I saw I didn't see you,

as Love still possessed my heart,
I continued as you now can view,
without you, and with my hurt.   10

⬚ Vêm-se rosas e boninas

TO A LADY CALLED GRAÇA DE MORAIS:

Eyes where flowers by the thousand
look out in such gracious style—
it appears that the passions
are dwelling where you dwell.

On seeing you, what's visible
are roses and daisies
and a thousand hearts blazing
in the fire of those pupils.
I will tell of my afflictions,
of my sighing and bewailing,
and I'll say more, that the passions
are dwelling where you dwell.

⬚ È muito para notar

TO A LADY WHO WAS ILL:

In the fever in which you burn
I will be your medicine
if you will be mine.

It's a matter for history,
of a remedy so sure
that you will only be cured
if you're cured along with me.
Should you wish to swap, Lady,
we both have the medicine;
I yours, and you my own.

Note that Love has no desire
(given we continue as equals)
that my ardor should be cooled   10

by relieving your fever.
I feel your pain here,
and, if you feel my own,
let's give and take the medicine.

Olhai que dura sentença

TO ANOTHER LADY WHO WAS ILL:

Observe what a harsh judgment
Love delivers without review—
because I lost myself in you,
he looks in me for your ailment.
It's surely obvious
only in you may I be traced;
that if Love looks for myself in me
he will encounter only
the form I already possessed.

And Lady, should Love infect   10
you, it will follow inevitably
that the illness he locates in me
makes your own self-inflicted.
It's no mere metaphor—
Love is planning my murder
by a means never imagined,
in that you're forced to be obliged
to regret in order to recover.

But you continue ungrateful
and my suffering's of the type   20
that in denying all hope
you threaten my survival.
For if justice,
as we see in this case,
proclaims it is even-handed,
you will enjoy Love's pardon
having already this party's forgiveness.

But what I fear, finally,
is that in this private war
your illness has no cure   30
if you are not restored to me.
It's a verity
concerning your humanity
about which no one cavils;
that Love for human souls,
too, is a maker of infirmity.

Não sabendo Amor curar

TO YET ANOTHER LADY WHO WAS ILL:

Love pronounced the sentence:
Lady, you should be ill,
to make apparent to people
how sweet and lovely is sickness.

Love, not knowing any cure,
chose to make of your illness
something beautiful to witness
and delightful to endure.
Then, seeing the alteration
in you, fashionable people
demanded also to be ill
for the glory of infection.

And I swear to you, truly,
that health itself is envious   10
at seeing such loveliness
evinced by your infirmity.
But, lady, don't relinquish
your ill health too quick
because people can fall sick
from nothing more than a wish.

Lovely lady, being afflicted
by the selfsame fever,
I confess it's my hot desire

to lie down with you in bed. 20
In relieving this ailment,
there would be, if you complied,
no healthy man more satisfied
than I with my complaint.

⊠ Todo o trabalhado bem

TO THIS COMMON THEME:

Without fortune is more than enough . . .

All cultivated virtue
promises delicious fruit,
but the tasks that fall due
to those fortune eschews
offer little while the cost is great.
The hard stone breaks all,
though labor, if they tough
it out, makes men immortal;
but to make a fortune your goal
without fortune is more than enough. 10

⊠ Pois o ver-vos tenho em mais

TO THIS COMMON THEME:

My soul, remember her.

So on seeing you I choose
the thousand lives you could give me
as well as what you offer me,
my fulfillment that you refuse,
my eyes that you don't deny.
And if I come to such a state,
guided by my star,
when you feel regret,
my life, put an end to it,
my soul, remember her. 10

Tem tal jurdição Amor

TO THIS COMMON THEME:

>   *All for some infatuation . . .*

You wield such authority, Love,
in the hearts where you reside
that, obeying your prerogative,
from all human solicitude
their exemption is approved.
And for just such a reason,
most like a sovereign liege,
Love will not permit damage;
but allowing me an opinion,
I wept in bitter knowledge,   10
all for some infatuation.

Campos cheios de prazer

TO THIS COMMON THEME:

>   *Blissful meadows,*
>   *make yourselves melancholy*
>   *for the days when you saw me—*
>   *happiness is of a time that was.*

Meadows full of pleasure,
you are sprouting anew
and I rejoice to see you;
but already I fear
that seeing me saddens you.
Since you gladden the scrutiny
of despairing eyes,
it's my wish you don't see me,
so hence you will always be
blissful meadows.   10

However, if contingently
you sympathize with my torment,
you'll know it's Love's way

that all discontents me
except discontent.
You woodlands that presently
in my eyes can witness
more joy than despondency,
if your aim is my happiness,
make yourself melancholy.   20

You once saw me joyful,
but after deceitful Love
made my life so melancholy,
I rejoice to see you cheerful,
for it doubles my grief.
And if you still sustain
this relish for what I suffer,
judge how much more I yearn
for hours of not seeing you than
for the days when you saw me.   30

The effects of drought and rain
on you are unequal,
since for you it's only natural
ill changes to good fortune
while for me it's to greater ill.
If you enquire, green meadows,
in respect of the different
seasons my love disposes,
suffering's what's always present,
happiness is of a time that was.   40

Os privilégios que os Reis

TO HIS OWN THEME:

> *Shoeless, she ventures in the snow,*
> *as those in the cause of Love go.*

There's no monarch who bestows
the privileges Love can offer
that make any lover

free from all human laws.
Deaths and cruel wars,
iron, cold, fire, and ice,
are all normal in Love's service.

The lovely girl cares not a straw
for the cold and all the pain.
See in this how more sovereign   10
Love is, beyond nature,
while neither shame nor nurture
prevents her tackling ice,
doing all this in Love's service.

The more tasks Love imposes,
the more she hazards;
she passes through blizzards
whiter than actual snows:
whatever the cold, she ventures . . .
Observe in what furnace   20
burns the grief of Love's service.

Leva na cabeça o pote

TO THIS THEME:

> Leanor walks barefoot through
> springtime to the well:
> she is lovely, and vulnerable.

On her head she bears her water pot,
in her hand the silver lid;
scarlet silk is the girdle
of her camel-hair waistcoat;
the weave of her bodice
is whiter than a fresh snowfall;
she is lovely, and vulnerable.

Her neck scarf reveals her throat,
her braided hair is golden
and red the restraining ribbon,   10

so enchanting the world halts.
Such grace is in her beauty,
beauty beyond parallel:
she is lovely, and vulnerable.

Posto o pensamento nele

TO THIS COMMON SONG:

> *At the fountain is Leanor*
> *rinsing her water pot and weeping,*
> *asking of her companions,*
> *"Have you seen my love there?"*

Her thoughts fixed on him
because Love is all-compelling,
she sang; but her song
was merely sighs for him.
In this Leanor
was dissembling her passion,
asking of her companions,
"Have you seen my love there?"

Her face resting on her palm,
her eyes on the ground, praying   10
that, now tired of weeping,
it should offer her some calm.
In this manner, Leanor
suspends from time to time
her pain; and when it resumes
the pain weighs heavier.

No tears tumble from her eyes,
not that her pain assuaged
Love, for in the greatest anguish
the grief dries up the tears.   20
But after hearing of her man
news she found disturbing,

I saw her on the instant sobbing—
study the extremes of pain!

Não vos guardei, quando vinha

TO THIS THEME:

> *Iron, fire, cold, heat—in all*
> *these the world will cease,*
> *but never will they displace*
> *you, my soul, from within my soul.*

I did not guard you, as you came near,
in some tower, by force or trickery;
I held you the more securely
in yourself, my soul's proprietor.
Neither cold nor heat control
there, nor wield authority;
in life, indeed, but no way
in you, whom I have as my soul.

De maneira me sucede

TO THIS THEME:

> *The heart that's given*
> *to all for nothing else is fit—*
> *so passes life's benefit,*
> *so passes death's pain.*

In some way it comes about
with what I fear and what desire
that I always meet with what I fear,
and never with what I covet.
Life and soul I committed myself
to Fortune in good faith;
it will deliver me a death
much as it promises in life.

▨ Por cousa tão pouca

TO THIS OLD SONG:

A turban captivates dumb John.

Over something so trite
you're completely enamored?
You love the headgear,
not she who tied it?
I'm blind and distracted
over you, dumb John,
and you over a turban!

You're in love with some fabric?
You might as well be a slave.
Don't you know true love   10
displays herself naked?
But you're distracted
over a thing like a turban,
and I over you, dumb John.

What would anyone say
about how you're behaving?
How could you deceive me
over something so ordinary?
He'd have to be merry
you're in love with a turban   20
not with me, dumb John.

Whoever loves as I do
deserves to be loved,
not wander aggrieved
through loving you.
Love what's true
and forget your turban—
that's good advice, dumb John.

Everyone's flabbergasted
by your stupidity;   30
on account of your idiocy

Gonçalo's aghast
and goes singing this skit:
look how a turban's
captivated dumb John.

Did you ever notice
my own hairdo,
adorable, too,
if that's your bias?
Don't be lugubrious: 40
love me, dumb John,
and not some turban.

(Dumb John blubbered.
Maria wailed,
and so revealed
the pain that throbbed.
Her eyes stabbed,
but not the turban
that did for dumb John.)

Why, I don't know,   50
you love a wardrobe
when the selfsame Cupid
wears not even a bow.
Do you know why you so
fancy a turban?
It's because you're dumb, John.

Juravas-me que outros cabras

TO THIS THEME:

> *I demand of you, Domingas,*
> *since you give me so much pain,*
> *that you say you want vengeance—*
> *I'll be a lot less concerned.*

You swore that leading other goats
to pasture was your pleasure,

but I, not to feel heart-sore,
assumed they were just words.
Now, you want your vengeance
for some petty fault of mine,
and by what you've done, Domingas,
I can't be taken in.

All things seek their destiny:
the stream descends to the Tagus,   10
and your whole being's focus
is to avenge yourself on me.
Domingas, you seem to forget
how well I tend my herd.
Please God, if you retaliate
against a lady so wretched!

In my fancy, I draw your face;
I call you, the mountain answers;
I search the spring, I search the rivers;
I go half-mad, and don't notice.   20
I shout "Domingas" to the valley,
the echo comes back "do minhas."
Have you not gained your vengeance
in seeing me turned so silly?

✳ HYMN ✳

✳ Junto um seco, fero e estéril monte

Under a parched and barren mountain,
treeless, unfarmed, utterly bare,
the most tedious place in all nature,
where no birds drift, no animals make their lair,
without one flowing river or simple fountain,
nor a palm frond's sweet whispering,
and named in the current vernacular

Arabia Felix, or by inversion, unhappy;
     somewhere nature
       has located in a gulf   10
where an arm of the sea shoals off
Abbasiya from Arabia the Bitter,
where Berenice was founded by Ptolemy,
     and a place the sun blazes
on so ferociously it vanishes;

here looms the cape, where Africa's
coastline, continuing from the south,
stops. It is named Aromata, though
under the turning heavens of the world's youth,
Aromata was named in the lingua franca   20
of the inhabitants Guardafui.
Here, where the ocean tries to force through
its tumultuous fury to this gulf,
     I took myself and there met
      my fortune in the wild,
and here in this corner of the world,
so hostile and unbearably remote,
I asked brief life for a brief
     respite, since the token
of remaining would be a life broken.   30

Here I whiled away wretched days,
sad, unwilling, utterly solitary,
toilsome, full of grief and resentment,
and suffering as my adversaries
not only a life of hot suns and cold seas,
with burning winds, harsh and pestilent,
but my fancies, the apt instrument
to seduce me from my true nature,
     and I saw, too, reviving
      to my chagrin, the memory   40
of the brief and superseded glory
I knew among mankind when I was alive,

re-doubling the effect of my torture
        by recalling my untold
hours of happiness in the world.

Here was I, consuming time and life,
and raised on the wings of such fancies
to so great a height, I plunged down
(and think how light a descent that was!)
from daydreams and illusory relief   50
to despair of one day being reborn.
Here my imagination was suborned
by fits of sudden weeping, and sighs
        that outdid the winds.
        Here, my afflicted soul
was again imprisoned in corporeal
form, ambushed by pain, chagrined,
and rudderless, exposed to the arrows
        of imperious Fortune—
proud, implacable, and importuning.   60

I had no place to lay myself down,
nor any remaining hope where my head
might lean a little by way of repose.
All was pain to me, a thing to be endured,
not just that it seemed so, but was ordained
in destiny's never gentle decrees.
O that I could tame these thundering seas!
These winds, with their truculent voice,
        that seem a law unto themselves!
        But severe heaven and the stars,   70
along with endlessly ferocious fate, amuse
themselves with my perpetual fevers,
exercising their malignant noise
        against this flesh and bone,
this vile earthworm, and so puny.

If only I could banish by such labors
the certain knowledge that sooner or later
I'd recall those eyes I once had sight of;

and if this sad voice, bursting out,
should reach to those angelic ears   80
of her for whose smile I once lived;
and now, as the memory revives,
turning over in my feverish brain
        times now extinct
        of my sweet trespasses,
of the gentle pain and madness
endured and longed for on her account,
she who (long afterwards) had shown
        some touch of pity
for all her former asperity.   90

If I could know this, it would lend
comfort to the time I am still allowed;
to know this would allay my suffering.
O Lady, Lady, you are so endowed
that even here, on this remote strand,
you sustain me, in my sweet feigning.
With you, simply by imagining,
I soar above the toil and pain
        and as thoughts of you revive,
        I can summon up courage   100
in the face of death's grim visage,
and my conjoined hopes are kept alive,
making my countenance more serene
        as the torments metamorphose
to sweet and happy memories.

So it is I remain here, questioning
the amorous winds that sigh for you
from whatever place you are, Lady,
and the migrating birds, if they saw you—
what your habits are, what you are doing,   110
where, when, with whom, what time of day?
Here, my wearisome days make way
for a new spirit, ready to conquer
        fortune and toil,
        if only to observe you,

if only to find and serve you
as time promises me all will be whole;
Yet ardent desire, which never suffers
        delay, against good sense
opens the wounds of fresh disturbance.   120

So I live; and if someone should ask you,
        song, how I exist,
you can reply it is because I exist.

⊠ ODE ⊠

⊠ Aquele moço fero

That indomitable youth Achilles
raised in a cave on Mount Petreton
by the strict centaur Chiron,
and whose immense valor
was suckled by tigresses;

in the waters of the Styx his mother
bathed her infant, to ordain
that no sharpened iron
should ever penetrate his rib cage
as he became his own armor.   10

The flesh turned hard enough
to resist all known weapons.
Such blindness! For it can happen
the heart can be smitten
in ways more hurtful than losing life.

For where the furious might
of the Trojans pierced armor and shield,
he was seen impaled
on the sharpened iron
of Cupid, all powerful in every heart.   20

There he was possessed
by a gentle slave he loved and served;
he was seen to survive
living in a furnace since
she of her master was visibly mistress.

In the hand that had brandished Pelias,
he took the soft lyre;
he was all songs and sighs,
not as the old centaur taught him
but as the youth, the eyeless.   30

So who, then, should be impugned
if from earliest infancy
one were given to misery,
in one's cradle being designated
unable to avoid Cupid's wound?

Who, then, being oppressed
by a child with greater power
was, from his first hour,
made over to that blind lover
as tears bathed his tender breast?   40

And if now he was struck
by the invading arrow with its herbs,
and if love is served
by service to a lovely slave,
why was I preserved to know such luck?

The well-sculptured guise,
the graceful gait and stance,
the delicate countenance
that at first sight seems
to teach beauty its own business;   50

how could anyone with a brain
avoid being enslaved?
For whoever perceived
that sweet, obliging look
cares no longer to be a free man.

There were other hearts, enriched
by fate with the highest knowledge
but nevertheless in bondage
to blind, frivolous Cupid,
transported by a divine rapture.   60

The most famous Jewish king,
the great sage and lover,
nevertheless to other
pagan gods made his sacrifice:
knowing much, he was the more wrong.

Wise Aristotle on his promenades
taught the secrets of philosophy,
but for Hermiaz, though she
was a eunuch's concubine,
raised up altars instead to the gods.   70

Altars to his whore he raised,
the famous philosopher-lover.
The never-ending rumor
hurts, and he weeps with guilt
as of sacrilege he stands accused.

He quits at once his native soil,
atoning for his guilt in exile.
But oh, that special hell
exposes the huge fallacy
that the wisest hearts are impregnable.   80

It's on the superior mind,
with a wit unrivalled
and blood most subtle,
the most receptive subject,
that the sweet, gentle passion gets imprinted.

❋ ECLOGUE ❋

❋ Que grande variedade vão fazendo

ON THE DEATH OF D. ANTÓNIO DE NORONHA,
WHO DIED IN AFRICA, AND ON THE DEATH
OF DOM JOÃO, PRINCE OF PORTUGAL,
FATHER OF KING SEBASTIAN.

Umbrano

What changes the headlong hours
bring about, Frondélio, my friend!
How things move on and metamorphose
into other things, various and splendid.
One day passes to the next without pause,
its identical hours preordained;
but however alike their quantity,
there's no comparing their quality.

I saw the various flowers of the meadow
stirring envy among the stars in heaven;   10
I saw shepherds going about, arrayed
from all those parts of the world in fashion;
and I saw at war with nature's colors
garments so superb and so finely woven
that were the materials not so rare,
the handiwork, richer still, would be spare.

And I saw roses no longer white
and the bright day all but obscured
in the face of the two dangerous transits
when Venus was more than ever adored;   20
then, I saw in shepherdesses such beauty
that Love was afraid of the very word,
though Reason trembled more, being free
of any proper sense of mystery.

Now all is changed utterly
and our hearts feel the immense wrong;
and it seems all-powerful Jupiter
is annoyed the world endures so long.
The Tagus flows muddy and dispirited,
the birds abandon their sweet singing,   30
and cattle, aware of the wasting grass,
by more than not grazing, diminish us.

Frondélio

Umbrano, brother, it is nature's statute,
fixed, without exception, and permanent,
that all good is followed by adversity
and that no pleasure can be constant:
to the bright day succeeds the dark night,
to sweet summer relentless winter,
and if there's one thing you may be sure
of, this is nature's unchanging law.   40

All joy, however splendid and elaborate
at the threshold, comes to a sad end;
if any hour is a sheer delight,
I watch out for the harm impending.
Don't you know the venomous snake inhabits
the flowers of the fresh, green lowlands?
Contentment, you deceive no one,
being even more capricious than Reason.

It's God's pleasure that harsh Fate
is delighted by the worst troubles;   50
that unforeseen misery has the habit
of dashing the hopes of unwary people:
I see this oak tree, blasted
by the lightning bolt to charcoal;
it takes no genius to understand
it's a brutal ploughman farms my land.

Umbrano

So long as we Portuguese shepherds cut
our crooks from the dependable olive tree,
along with the ancient valor that exalted
our name and distinguished us globally,   60
don't be anxious, Frondélio, my compatriot,
that we'll cease, in any age, to be free,
or that this indomitable neck
will submit to any presumptuous yoke.

And if the foe in his effrontery,
to left and right of us, should rise up,
do not believe our impregnable country,
whose stout heart no challenge has stopped
since our capture of Ceuta's Mount Atlante
till now, when we drink from India's Hidaspe,   70
can lie helpless before alien might
while sun, earth, and the heavens rotate.

Frondélio

Umbrano, reckoning you're secure
without the backing of might or reason
is false and vain; being cocksure
is not always favored by Fortune.
There, alongside Hope's altar,
dour, just Nemesis restrains,
imposing this dread law as her bridle:
do not transgress what is possible.   80

And if you attend to the vast dangers
that every day become more obvious,
you will control these mental errors
that appear to you in daring's guise.
Do you not see the wolves of Tangiers,
apart from all their cowardice,
kill the dogs guarding the herds,
and not just the dogs but the shepherds?

And Ceuta's well-fortified fold
at Mount Atlas, have you not heard   90
how in a most savage and bloody
massacre it has been left uninhabited?
O disastrous event! O cruel world,
that humans are powerless to resist.
And there, too, my Tiónio, while still
in the very flower of life, was killed.

Umbrano

I bathe my whole bosom with tears
at this dreadful matter you relate,
when I see how accomplished, how wise,
and how deserving of a greater part   100
was your shepherd who, for no good cause,
yielded his fleeting life to the Fates,
but there's no grass can satiate cattle,
nor young blood the furious god of battle.

But if it were not too much of a burden
—the sad death you have already conveyed—
to sing about this dreadful event
those tender verses you sang yesterday
when bringing home the cattle, when
you were apart from us other shepherds . . .   110
I, for instance, was rounding up my ewes,
and could not listen as I would choose.

Frondélio

What should you wish to recall to mind
such pain, so much misfortune?
To broadcast empty sighs to the wind
on account of grief is no medicine.
But since you are mourning for your friend,
on the sad and somber death of Tiónio,
I will put your desire into sweet practice
if a grieving heart does not choke my voice.   120

Umbrano

Sing now, shepherd, while the cattle stroll
in safety in the moist pasture;
and where it springs on the tall hill
the sacred Tagus, in human posture,
eyes on the ground, hand shielding
his face, is ready to hear you,
while there wait in sad silence the Naiads,
their eyes brimming with the purest fluids.

The meadow unobtrusively displays
its white and vermilion blossoms;   130
the sweet, industrious honeybees
are airborne with their soft humming;
the gentle and passive ewes,
unmindful of grazing, are inclining
their heads to the divine melody
of the crystal Tagus as it passes by.

Through the trees the breeze purls
its accompaniment to the clear river;
in the shade, the talkative dove murmurs
to the cooling air all it suffers.   140
Play, Frondélio, strike the sweet lyre,
as from the shady green poplar,
the gentle nightingale in her longing
summons you to heartfelt song.

Frondélio [singing]

That day the tender ewes took no pleasure
in the waters, and the lambs filled
the meadow with their amorous bleating.
The she-goats avoided the willows
in their misery, but they refused
grazing for themselves and milk to the kid-goats.   150
Prodigious sights
were manifest that day,
when Fate opened the way

to a sad and ferocious event.
And crow, you also made acknowledgment
while flying with your ominous caw—
on the right hand, you harped on
tyrannical death's grim law.

My Tiónio, the crystal-clear Tagus
and the riparian trees you have now abandoned   160
bewail a loss that is eternal.
I don't know why you left so soon
but Destiny must take the onus
by which land and sea are ruled.
And the endless, cruel
darkness, bitter and sad,
so early visited—
did your youth not suffer
you to outwit spring's verdure?
We are not accustomed to an ordeal,   170
such that neither beast in the high moors
nor shepherd here in the fields is consoled.

The fawns, sure guard of pastors,
no longer chase the nymphs in the thicket,
nor do the nymphs give tasks to the deer.
Everything, as you see, is full of disquiet;
the honeybees deny the flowers,
and to flowers dawn denies the dew.
And I with my song strew
sadness the day long,   180
the flute that sang,
touching the very trees when touched,
slips out of tune through heartache;
everything I see grieves on this mountain
and you, too, issue
turbulent and sad, you once-clear fountain.

The nymphs of the Tagus and the Oreads
of the rough mountains know too well
what drove you to hard, cruel war,

as the general opinion will tell,   190
there cannot be in this world any sadness
in whose causes Love has no share.
In such manner
in your yearning eyes,
your listless paces,
in the face that love and frantic thought
turned to wan violet,
these offered to all the surest sign
of the bonfire lit
by love which can not be hidden.   200

Then before the eyes there jerk
phantoms and fantastic pictures,
and exercises in false reasoning,
and there by the solitary thickets
among the lonely boulders that never talk,
he spoke out and disclosed his agony.
In a long oblivion,
he loitered self-absorbed
and so lost to the world
that when some shepherd enquired   210
the cause of his sadness, he appeared
as one who lived only for melancholy,
smiling as wearily he answered,
"If I didn't live like this, I would die."

But how he was marked by this passion,
and how much was evident in his face,
was understood by his resourceful father,
who dragged him from apathy by the device
of dispatching him far from its origin,
for absence finally is the cure.   220
But harsh, deceitful war—
of young lives so covetous!
So soon as his generous
heart was reanimated by the memory
of all his forefathers' glory,
you struck him down in the cruel strife

of a fortuitous victory,
the cruel epitome of a sad life.

I see you, Tiónio, in a vision
as you stain the greedy spear   230
in that infidel Mauritanian blood
on your Spanish jennet, trained for war,
as eager as you with the ambition
to see the people of Tangiers destroyed.
O conscious fraud!
O life cut short,
that merit, frustrated
by the overwhelming might of the enemy,
could not help itself in jeopardy
because Destiny acquiesced,   240
and so bore away
of the Tagus shepherds by far the gentlest.

It was so with Euryalus, Aeneas's comrade,
among the army of the Rutulians, assuaging
the fury of hard, proud battle,
his face's crystal color changing
as down his white shoulders blood
streamed, dyeing the hillside purple.
As when a flower to which the soil
denies nourishment   250
—because the season is inclement
and withholds life-giving moisture—
bows its neck and begins to tire:
so do I depict you, Tiónio, yielding your spirit
back to its creator,
who alone is eternal and infinite.

From the stiffening mouth, his life's breath,
together with the name of the splendid
enemy, Marfia, now transpired.
And you, gentle lady, are you not bound   260
to everlasting mourning over the hard death
of one who lived his life through yours?

For you, he gave to the echoes
countless groans.
For your sake, he determined on
a life of pure belligerency.
But your ingratitude will now place
your love elsewhere, like one
incapable of a fixed purpose
in your exercise of women's reason.   270

Shepherds of the this pleasant, chilly heath
who wish Tiónio's calamitous history
proclaimed as far as the highest hill,
I will raise on the banks of this estuary
a memorial adorned with wreaths
that will give pause to the toughest sailor
while the weariest foot-traveler,
witnessing such grief,
will shed tears of relief,
as he reads carved on the hard granite: 280
I am memory, replete
to bear witness everywhere
to the most gentle spirit
ever driven from the world by love or war.

Umbrano

As quiet repose to one exhausted
in the shade of some spreading trees,
or as to the thirsty and overheated
a cold spring or the rising breeze,
so to me was your elegant ode,
your rhymed, harmonious numbers;   290
and even now, the soft, sweet theme
tranquillizes and leaves me dreaming.

So long as cold-blooded fish find succor
in the riverbed's sandy houses,
and these rolling waters declare
the ancient lordship of the broad seas,

and while these grasses give pasture
to the querulous goats, I am witness:
by your song's virtue, the shepherd you adore
will live in these your verses evermore.   300

Now little by little the sun is failing
and the mountains extend their shadows:
the sky is adorned with a thousand flowers
that appear so cheerful to our gaze;
as we guide on foot down from these hills
our herds, that are now assuaged
with all they have eaten: so Frondélio, friend,
come, I'll go with you to the cattle mound.

Frondélio

First, Umbrano, my friend, if it's your opinion,
let us conduct the ewes by this river course,   310
for if by chance I am not deceived,
it resounds from here what echoes in my ears;
such sweet modulation seems barely human,
and if you support me in this cause,
I wish to see what its source could be;
the tone astounds, and the voice I envy.

Umbrano

I'll go with you, since the more I draw nigh
the more the voice you heard at first
seems rare and excellent, and I don't deny
it saddens the soul in my breast.   320
You see how the winds are dying?
No rumble from the mountain persists,
And no bird is flying—as if overwhelmed
by song, they have all succumbed.

All the same, brother, it seems better to me
we should not go where we are intruders,
but hidden in the foliage of this tree
we can keep watch on the whole glade:

as for our shepherd's bags and crooks, we
can hang them here, though the branch is slender;   330
but climbing's for those who weigh least,
so permit me, Frondélio, to go up first.

Frondélio

Wait, I'll help you up if you wish—
you will climb noiselessly and without effort,
and when you're securely in position,
you can give me your hand in support.
But first, share with me your vision;
whence springs that song of such art?
Who is uttering that rare, sweet sound?
Speak, for I can see you are astounded.   340

Umbrano

Matters not normal in the thick woods,
and never witnessed, Frondélio, I now discern.
I see in the greenery beautiful Naiads,
whose divine appearance courts heaven.
One, uncommonly lovely, who, compared
to the others, seems a lady of distinction,
weeps on a sad grave without check,
as pearls are distilled on her radiant cheek.

Of all these other demigoddesses
surrounding the body that is interred,   350
one, who is watering the moist sand, has
decorated the tomb with flowers;
others burning Arabian incense
fill the air with a sublime odor;
while yet others further on are gently
swaddling in rich cloth the new *infante*.

One, set apart from the rest by weeping
that saddens even the mountain, declares
that after cruel death had chopped
the flower that lives among the stars,   360

there remains this dearest princely copy
of him whose power was averred
from the Douro, Montego, Tagus, and Guardiana
to the distant seas of Taprobana.

She states more, that if this little one
in dawning meets unseasonable night,
the crystal Tagus will mirror the frown
of Allecto, in all her furious spite.
But if he is preserved by destiny,
the stars promise to be his by right   370
the spreading pasture of Ampelusa
where Atlas was petrified by Medusa.

So the nymph in her beauty prophesied,
reciting with abundant tears;
but just as the clear moon is eclipsed
in its station in the first heavenly sphere,
so I see a noble heart draped
in black, overcome by great despair;
behold, Frondélio, take my hand and climb,
all the more so since grief leaves me dumb.   380

Frondélio

O sad death, accursed and irregular,
that leaves so many beauties derelict!
To that goddess so refined and fair,
you should at least show more respect.
She is for sure Aónia, beloved daughter
of that great shepherd we know as fact
curbed the Danube and ruled Iberia,
and shocked the wild Turks of nearest Asia.

He died, sweet Aónio, well-descended
and mighty (to this, human life   390
is subject) and Aónia's dear husband.
Such is overbearing Fate's brief!
But as to that strange and pitiful sound

with which the nymph outwits her grief—
pause, Umbrano, take note and see
how eloquent Castilian verse can be.

Aónia

Soul and first love of my own soul,
happy spirit, in whose being
my own existed while such was God's will!

Gentle shade, from your prison fleeing   400
this world to return to the true home
of your engendering and proceeding!

Acknowledge there the sad alms
to which the eyes that saw you now give vent,
if such memories survive the tomb;

given the high heavens do not warrant
my accompanying you on such a journey,
desiring you alone as their ornament,

they will never allow your memory
to want for me as your companion,   410
who am adorned by your clay,

nor will you cease, while time remains,
to dwell in me with sempiternal weeping
until my life and very soul are gone.

But you, gentle spirit, all along
are treading other fields and flowers,
and hearing other panpipes and a different song:

now with astonishment you admire
there among the supernal that Essence
the world faces and follows with your power;   420

now Venus owns you, Citerian Venus
in her third home, because you
loved becoming her newest fondness;

now the sun admires you, if you can view
it ablaze as it climbs through the constellations,
lighting up the lands you flew.

If, seeing these marvels, you have not resigned
all memory of me, because your hand omitted
to pass through the waters of oblivion,

turn your eyes briefly down to this plot,   430
and you will witness one inconsolable
on this deaf marble, and vainly crying out.

But if there may enter those golden
constellations tears and loving sighs
such as move the supreme choir of angels,

the light of your most beautiful eyes
I shall see very soon, and be seen;
for, whatever insufferable Fate decrees,
even for the saddest, death will happen.

⊞ ODE ⊞

⊞ Naquele tempo brando

In that peaceful instant
when pure, lovely Thetis,
with the world's beauty quietly evident,
was resting from her efforts,
youthful Peleus was troubled
with intense desire by the boy Cupid.

In violent reaction
the lovely nymph had already fled
when, in the stormy season,
Notus stirs the ocean fluid,   10
raising up in the sea such Alps
the land appears beyond all help.

With his heart's agony burning his soul,
young Peleus waited for
one of those days Apollo
scorches the earth with relentless fire,
unloosing those golden tresses
where Clicie had treasured loving caresses.

It was the month when Phoebus
loiters with the heavenly twins;   20
the winds are curbed by Aeolus,
so the pleasant diversion
should be calm and tranquil:
so Love drives all and conquers all.

The resplendent day
rouses amorous flesh
in blind idolatry
that pleases and distresses
as the eyeless boy persuades all
such feelings must be eternal.   30

When the lovely nymph,
revered by all who came,
in the pure, translucent stream
was bathing her crystal limbs,
observing which the intelligent
waters rejoiced in being transparent—

the diamond breasts
at whose nipples love is born,
her expression that exists
to turn night to rare morning,   40
her generous lips
where love feeds hope with hopes;

her rubies, hidden
like her pearls among roses,
her delightful garden,
where Heaven plants lovely faces,

a bust to envy
as Apollo did shimmering Daphne—

a sudden movement
of those eyes that blinded Cupid,   50
who henceforth in his torment
was from them never separated,
as from that time the perpetual
boy finds a home in her pupils:

Cupid's net once cast,
as men desire above all else,
Love draws the trussed-
up hearts he has entangled
with fervid emotion,
by which he assumes his dominion.   60

Peleus, the amorous youth,
who had Neptune as mentor,
witnessing heaven on earth
expressed in such a lovely figure,
was momentarily tongue-tied,
as Love took away every word.

As he sought clear sight
of her who struck from so far off,
his vision was forfeited,
for Love sets no store on pure love,   70
all being blind and dumb
within his absolute realm.

Now the youth steels
himself for battle, now assaults,
now takes counsel,
now advances, now falters,
but too late; Cupid's
fresh arrow has his heart impounded.

Straightaway he rushed at
the source of his untreated wound;   80
irresistibly in heat,
the closer he came, the blinder
to himself, as with a groan
he fired his charge into the lovely maiden.

From Peleus's satisfaction
was born of this amorous union
(to Phrygian Troy's destruction)
Achilles, the strong Larissan,
who, to make him impregnable,
was dipped in the Stygian ripple.   90

▥ SONNETS ▥

▥ Busque Amor novas artes, novo engenho

Invent fresh arts and cunning, Love,
to destroy me, and new frustrations;
but you can't remove my expectations,
by taking away what I don't have.

Look where my hopes are grounded!
Observe what perilous guarantees
that I don't fear even on the wildest seas,
contrast or change, the ship having foundered.

But insofar as I'm not unhappy
when hope fails, Love maintains within   10
an evil that destroys, and in secret;

some days there pitches camp in me
I know not what, nor where it is born,
nor whence it comes, nor why it hurts.

Alegres campos, verdes arvoredos

Cheerful meadows, leafy groves,
cold and crystal-clear waters,
reflecting you in their perfect mirrors
as they plunge from the rocks above;

rough boulders, forested hills,
laid out in irregular agreement,
I knew without my suffering's consent
I could not make my eyes cheerful.

Since you do not see me as formerly,
enchanting leaves convey no pleasure   10
nor waters tumbling in full flood.

I will plant in you sad memories,
watering them with heartfelt tears
that will spring in yearning for my good.

Lembranças saudosas, se cuidas

Heartfelt memories, if it's your pleasure
to end my life in its present station,
I don't live so beguiled by affliction
as not to expect a great deal more.

For a long time you have seasoned me
to exist despairing of any good;
while with Fortune I have as long agreed
to endure whatever tasks you send me.

Chained to the oar, I have patience
with what life brings, with its vexations,   10
and let fancy suppose whatever it wishes,

for since there's no other hindrance
to such a collapse of inspiration,
I'll be harbor for those in anguish.

Quando o sol encoberto vai mostrando

When the sun, half-hidden, displays
to the world quiet and fitful beams,
pacing the long beach of my dreams
I begin imagining my enemy.

Here I see her with her hair coiled,
there supporting her cheek, so lovely,
here talking happily, there pensive,
one moment silent, the next mercurial.

Here she was seated, there she glanced
at me, raising those eyes so unengaged,   10
here anxious a little, there assured;

here she was saddened, there she rejoiced;
and so, with such tired imagining,
goes on this empty life that endures.

Tempo é já que minha confiança

It's high time my confidence
backed away from false opinion,
but Love is not governed by Reason;
therefore I cannot forfeit assurance.

Life, yes; but harsh displacement
won't let so much as a heart breathe,
and am I to find salvation in death?
Yes, but desire is not attainment.

So I live and hope like a galley-slave;
O hard law of Love, which won't suffer   10
peace for a heart in enthrallment.

I repeat: like a vassal is how I live,
for I seek the fugitive luster
of a vain hope that's my torment.

Oh! Como se me alonga, de ano em ano

O, how it drags me along year by year,
my weary peregrination!
How it constricts, hurrying to its conclusion
my short and pointless mortal career!

It eats up time and increases the pain;
it denies me a remedy I once had;
if based on experience one can look ahead,
any great hope is a great illusion.

I pursue this blessing that's unattainable;
on the open highway, it will disappear;   10
countless times, I stumble and give up.

When it flees, I tarry; and in the interval,
raising my eyes to see it it's still there,
I lose sight of the vision, and of hope.

Grão tempo há já que soube da Ventura

For a long time I've known a fatal star
has predetermined my existence,
as my protracted, lived experience
was a secure guide to the future.

Ferocious Love and implacable Fortune—
you've made an excellent trial of your power.
Lay waste, destroy, let nothing endure!
Conquer this life that still drags on!

Love knew of Fortune what I lacked
and, so I should feel my deprivation,   10
kept supplying visions of the impossible.

But, given my planet denied me luck,
you have lived, Lady, in this heart of mine,
where destiny has never had control.

Sete anos de pastor Jacob servia

Seven years Jacob served as a shepherd
for Laban, lovely Rachel's father,
laboring not for the father but
anxious only for her as his reward.

The days of waiting passed as a mere
day in the happiness of seeing her,
but supremely cautious the father
in Rachel's stead beguiled him with Leah.

Hurt by how wrongly, after his labors,
the pastor had been cheated   10
of his shepherdess wife,

he embarked on a second seven years,
saying, "I would work on, were it not
for so long a loving so short a life."

Pensamentos, que agora novamente

Old thoughts, which now, newly minted,
resurrect in me old yearnings,
I ask you: are you still burning
to make me yet more discontented?

What fantasies are those you beam
every hour before my eyes,
assaulting with dreams and shadows
one who cannot be content with dreams?

I see, thoughts, you are much confused,
yet why do you disdain to unravel   10
what you bring to so disturb me?

You don't refuse me, if you care to refuse,
but if I'm the one with whom you struggle,
I'll join to help you murder me.

Ditoso seja aquele que somente

Happy that man whose one complaint
is of amorous rebuffs,
because time will always yield him enough
hope he can one day be content.

Happy is he who, being exiled,
feels no more than the pain of memory,
because, dreading mutability,
he fears pain less when really felt.

In short, happy is he, whatever his state,
though deceit, exile, and public scorn   10
torment his very heart-strings;

but sad that man who feels contrite
about errors that are beyond pardon,
unaware in his heart of any sinning.

No mundo quis um tempo que se achasse

Time's project in life was to study
whether good came through accident or luck,
and so its conclusions could be checked,
resolved Fortune should be tested on me.

But because my fate made clear to me
that to live without hope was my best option,
never in this protracted life of mine
has it let me glimpse what I could envy.

I changed my habits, my country and station
to see if my fortune, too, would alter,   10
entrusting my life to a frail vessel.

But (following what the heavens had shown)
I already knew, as I pursued my adventure,
I'd encountered what was not mine to call.

Se, depois d' esperança tão perdida

After so many hopes foundered, if
Love peradventure could agree
on some brief hour of joy for me
after so much sorrow in so long a life;

in a heart by now feeble and careworn,
were my fortune suddenly to ascend,
I'd lack that with which to respond
to happiness so grudgingly given.

I'm not unique in not being shown
one hour of living joyfully, but Love   10
after a lifetime of harsh restraint,

still dispenses so much pain
that, beyond joy, he's deprived me of
the relish for an hour of being content.

Apolo e os nove Musas, discantando

Apollo and the nine Muses, singing
to the golden lyre, inspired me
by joining their sweet harmony
when I took up my pen, beginning:

"Happy the day and the hour when
such tender eyes wounded me!
Happy the feelings felt to be
transcendent in their yearning!"

So was I singing when Love turned
Fortune's wheel to hope, shiftiing   10
so gently it was barely perceptible.

Then it changed to night my clear dawn,
and if for me any hope is left
it will be worse, if such is possible.

[221]

A Morte, que da vida o nó desata

Death that unravels the knot of life
had tried to sever the knots Love braids
through Absence, that cruel sword,
and Time, that brings all to grief.

Two adversaries, mutually ruinous,
Death enlists against Love, and so they fight:
Reason, first, versus cruel Fate,
and thankless Fate opposing Reason.

But while Death masquerades as imperial
in separating soul from body, Love   10
unites them and consummates;

and so Love carries the triumphal
palm eternally over Death, in spite of
Absence and Time, Reason and Fate.

Alma minha gentil, que te partiste

Dear gentle soul, you that departed
this life so soon and reluctantly,
rest in heaven eternally
while I remain here, broken-hearted.

If there in the ethereal skies
memories are still allowed to move,
do not forget that ardent love
you once saw shining in my eyes.

And if you judge there might be merit,
however small, in this pain that stays,   10
grieving with nothing to repair it,

petition God, who cut short your days,
to take me to you, in that reckless spirit
he used to summon you from my gaze.

Doces lembranças da passada glória

Sweet memories of former glory
that Fortune elected to commandeer,
leave me to rest in peace for an hour,
for yours is a paltry victory.

On my heart is stamped the long history
of past blessings that never were
(or should not have been) but now, and here,
for myself they're a mere memory.

I live in the past, I die oblivious
of some that should always be rehearsed,   10
if memory were a happy pageant.

But who would wish to be born twice!
I've known how to manage my good past,
if only I could fathom this dubious present!

Males, que contra mim vos conjurastes

Misfortunes, seeing that you plot against
me, how long must your malice last?
If it's done to make me know your worst,
what you've done already should be sufficient.

But if you insist, because you presume
to undermine my being so bold,
the likelier cause, to which I hold,
is you think she herself is to blame.

And so your purpose, through my death,
is to end the misfortune of this love,   10
terminating so long a contest,

for the outcome would please us both:
you, because your victory's proved,
I, since that concludes your conquest.

Em prisões baixas fui um tempo atado

In vile prisons I was once fettered
as shameful punishment for my sins;
even now I drag along the irons
that death, to my chagrin, has since shattered.

I sacrificed my life as my warning
that Love demands more than lambs or heifers;
I saw wretchedness, I saw exile and grief.
It strikes me now all this was ordained.

I was content with little, maintaining
before me the ambiguous sport   10
of what a thing it would be to know bliss.

But by my star, as I now know, combining
blind death and dubious fate
gave me little relish for happiness.

Foi já num tempo doce cousa amar

Being in love was once a tender
thing, while hope sustained illusion;
the heart, utterly taken in,
undid itself in ardor.

O decrepit hope, vain and threadbare,
how change opens ones eyes!
The more happiness appears wise,
the less one believes it can endure.

Whoever faces such an ordeal
after a happy and prosperous life   10
has cause to lament his living well.

But whoever really knows the world
will not be surprised by any grief,
suffering being business as usual.

Que poderei do mundo já querer

What now in this world could I long for,
having placed in it so much love,
to meet only with vexation and disfavor
with death ahead, then nothing more?

For life seems not worth the living,
and I know great torment does not kill—
if something exists to bring greater evil
I'll deal with it, as I do everything.

Death, reluctantly, was my guarantee
against whatever harm came; I already lost   10
what fear had taught me to abandon.

Life for me was one long veto,
while in death, what seemed the worst
was that for this alone was I born.

Pois meus olhos não cansam de chorar

Since my eyes never tire of bewailing
sorrows that never tire of wearying
me; since there rages unassuaged the fire
over one my fervor could never fail;

nor does blind Love tire of being my pilot
into parts from which there is no return,
nor prevent the whole world from listening
while my feeble voice still permits.

And if in rivers, valleys, and mountains,
pity exists, or if love dwells   10
in beasts, birds, waters, plants, and stones,

they hear the tale of my misfortunes,
and cure their ordeals with my hell,
for great pain has the power to assuage pain.

✸ Mudam-se os tempos, mudam-se as vontades

The times change, along with fashions,
ways of being and of trust change;
all the world's made up of change,
consistent only in alteration.

Everything we see seems novel
and altered from all we ever dreamed;
evil endures as grief remembered,
good, if one finds it, as fond recall.

Time covers the earth with a green blanket
that before was mantled with snow,   10
and it turns my own sweet song to lament;

but besides this daily vicissitude,
one further change is the greater woe
that it changes no longer as was its wont.

✸ Conversação doméstica afeiçoa

Domestic talk captivates,
whether in kind and bantering fashion
or with some amorous intention
without regard to someone's status.

If later, perhaps, some disloyalty
grieves you, as it turns disdainful,
gentle Love pardons all
by turning truth to fantasy.

Nor is what I say mere conjecture,
with appearances taken on oath   10
to fashion polite literature.

I have examined all my behavior
and speak nothing but pure truths,
living experience my teacher.

Despois que quis Amor que eu só passasse

After Love sought that I alone should be
victim of what so many suffer,
he gave me to Fortune, having on offer
no further torment to exhibit through me.

She, because Love had already overstepped
every punishment Heaven allowed,
did what for no one else was permitted,
ordering fresh torments be dreamed up.

So here I am—with my varied curses
and copious examples for all those   10
subject to these same tyrants' control—

in deranged, harmonious verses.
Pitiful, those whose only recourse
is to be content with so very little.

Com grandes esperanças já cantei

With vast ambition I once sang, and kept
the gods on Olympus captive, listening;
later, I wept on account of my singing
and today I sing because I wept.

If recalling old roads, I pass them
again, memory alone is more than enough,
for the pain of revisiting past grief
is worse than the time I first paced them.

If then it's clear that one torment
gives rise to another within the heart,   10
then never can I know felicity.

But what if this theory is a figment?
O, indolent and blind conceit!
Am I still dreaming I could be happy?

No tempo que de Amor viver soía

In those days when Love was a fine game
I wasn't always a galley slave;
one day free, another in love,
my fire had an indiscriminate flame.

Heaven did not will that I should burn
in one hearth only, for she wished to try
whether a spell of constancy
would make any change in my fortune.

And if, at intervals, I was free,
it was like one resting from a heavy weight   10
only to resume with greater force.

Love should be praised for my misery,
since he adopted as a mere sport
this, my drawn-out wretchedness.

Quem fosse acompanhando juntamente

Whoever had by way of companion
in lush green meadows that tiny bird
which, lacking the blessing it once enjoyed,
knows not how to be happy again;

and whoever was shut away from people,
she, as a comrade and a neighbor,
should help me sigh away this nightmare,
I with her in the sorrow both feel.

Happy bird, at least, if nature
to her first gift does not add a second,   10
so only through grieving is she consoled.

But sad he, long Fortune's creature,
who even to breathe is deprived of wind,
and ultimately deprived of the world.

Cantando estava um dia bem seguro

I was singing, happy as the day was long,
when Silvio who was passing remarked
(Silvio, an old shepherd with the knack
of predicting the future from bird-song):

"Meris, when you want to know your fortune,
there will come to attack you the same day
two wolves; on the instant, that melody
will abandon you with its pure, sweet tone."

So it proved; for the first slaughtered
so many cattle I owned and pastured,   10
looking forward to immense returns,

and the second, to my horror, butchered
the gentle lamb I so much adored,
to my heart's perpetual mourning.

Julga-me a gente toda por perdido

Everyone considers me a lost cause,
seeing me so addicted to grief,
cutting myself off from life,
overlooked in humanity's affairs.

But I who have criss-crossed the globe
being, as it were, doubly cognizant,
remain at bottom a deluded peasant,
whom my sufferings have not ennobled.

Land, sea, and the winds revolve;
other men seek riches and honor,   10
conquering iron, fire, cold, and calm.

I alone in my beggary contrive
to be happy to bear, engraved forever
on my heart's core, your beautiful form.

Que me quereis, perpétua saudades

What do you want of me, endless regret?
What hopes do you even now cozen
me with, for seasons past will not return,
or if they return, time still is forfeit.

The cause is in years, not just that you fly,
but are so light-headed in your haste.
Not everyone is equal to your taste
or always happy with your authority.

What we want changes so, it becomes
as if something different, for the days   10
have already tarnished our first aim,

while hopes of future happiness
are hostage to Fortune and hollow Time,
which eavesdrop on contentment, like spies.

Erros meus, má fortuna, amor ardente

My errors, ill fortune, and ardent love
all connived together in my loss:
but errors and fortune were superfluous
in that love alone for me did quite enough.

I survived all. But I have still present
the great torment of things in the past,
and those desperate passions impressed
me I should never hope to be content.

In all my life's discourse, I was wrong.
I gave Fortune good cause to castigate   10
hopes that in the end had little purchase.

Love had always a deceitful tongue.
O, who could ever do enough to satiate
this, my iron-willed, avenging genius!

Eu cantei já, e agora vou chorando

I once sang, and now hear me lamenting
those days I sang with so much trust;
it seems that in that song so long past
my tears were doing the inventing.

I sang: but if someone asks me when
I don't know, being, however, much mistaken,
for so wretched is my present condition
I was judging the past to be free of pain.

What drove me to sing so cunningly?
Fulfillment? No! It was the future's map   10
I sang, but even then to the clanking of chains.

Of whom shall I complain, when all lie?
What blame should I place on false hopes
when error counts for less than Fortune?

Na desesperação já repousava

Out of desperation I laid to rest
a heart to suffering long inured,
and with everlasting pain assured,
I feared nothing and for nothing lusted;

but a thought, utterly insubstantial,
promised some good could be dispensed
in a vision so lively that its semblance
stayed haunting my bewitched soul.

What credit the heart grants
so readily to what it most desires,   10
forgetting destiny's heart of stone!

Leave me to dream, for I'm content;
even should it lead to greater misery,
there remains the glory of imagination.

✳ Eu vivia de lágrimas isento

I lived once untaxed by tears
in a delusion of such sweet rapture
that, even given some happier suitor,
a pang was worth more than countless honors.

Seeing such a paradigm possessed me,
of no riches was it jealous;
it lived well, utterly unsuspicious,
as sweet love's sentiments obsessed me.

It was envious Fortune robbed me
of my happy and contented state   10
as though that blessing had never existed,

in exchange for which it fobbed me
off with scenes that destroy me each minute,
being memories of a happier past.

✳ Lembranças que lembrais meu bem passado

Memories, you recall my happy times,
so I feel, all the more, my present evil;
let me live contentedly, if you will—
don't leave me to die on such terms.

If, however, it is all ordained
I must live, as is obvious, in discontent,
good comes, if it comes, by accident,
while dearth brings my sorrows to an end.

How much better to lose one's being,
canceling images from the memory   10
for the damage they do to one's reason.

Just as he who is lost loses nothing,
hope drags in its wake its own glory,
given life must always be lived in pain.

Ah! Fortuna cruel! Ah! duros Fados!

Ah, implacable Fates! Ah cruel stars,
how nimbly you switch to hurting me!
Time was you used to comfort me;
now you comfort yourself with my cares.

You allowed me memories of my former life
in prescribing agony upon agony;
in a single hour you took both from me,
leaving in their wake redoubled mischief.

Ah, pleasure, how much I'd benefit
from not having known you, now so far off   10
whether I ever saw you seems dubious;

without you, I've nothing left to forfeit,
unless it were this, my weary life,
which, to my greater loss, I don't lose.

Quando cuido no tempo que, contente

When I reflect on how I was content
seeing pearls and snow, roses and gold,
as one who dreams of treasure untold,
I seem to have it all here in the present.

But as soon as this visitation fails
and I realize how far from you is my home,
what I imagine appears an omen,
that imagination can no longer avail.

Once there were days in which by chance
I would see you, Lady, if I may say so,   10
with a confident heart and fearlessly;

now, surrounded by evil, I place no assurance
in my own dreams, or in your sorrow:
I cannot unravel this mystery.

Quem vos levou de mim, saudoso estado

Who robbed me of my state of trust
as you abused me utterly beyond reason?
Who was it? With whom did you cozen
me, suddenly oblivious of our happy past?

You changed my peace to sullen grief,
hard, cruel, and determined by you;
constancy being your gift, you withdrew
just at the point I had pledged my life.

I endured that calamity as a stoic:
Fortune that has everything at its feet,   10
Love that rewarded me with disgust.

I know in such matters, nothing's intrinsic;
for one who's born in tears, it's right
he's repaid in tears for what he's lost.

Cá nesta Babilonia, donde mana

Here in this Babylon, source of the pus
that gathers round the world's disease,
here where pure love is never prized
but she who rules and profanes is Venus;

where evil's refined, and what harms is good,
and more effective than honor is tyranny;
and where a blind, false monarchy
takes its name in vain to outwit God;

here in this labyrinth, where the noble
with vigor and knowledge go begging   10
at the doors of envy and corruption;

here, in this dark sea of troubles,
I comply with nature's level-pegging.
See if I forget you, Zion!

Na ribeira do Eufrates assentado

Seated on the bank of the Euphrates,
my flowing thoughts hit on the memory
of that all-too-short time of glory
I spent, sweet Zion, within your gates.

I was asked about the source of the pain
afflicting me: "Why not sing of the good
times past, and of those cards
you played to trump ill fortune?

"Don't you know who sings forgets
his pain, however deep and rigorous?   10
Sing then, and don't sigh away your breath."

With sighs I answered: "When regrets
steal upon me, the only pious
response is not to sing, unless of death."

Doce contentamento já passado

Sweet ease of mind, already gone,
in which all my blessing then was,
who stopped you being my dear spouse,
abandoning me to live alone?

Who cautioned me when I was in thrall
to those brief hours of contentment,
when my fortune gave assent
I should live to be illusion's fool?

My destiny was cruel and hard,
in that what brought about my shipwreck   10
was such as no one could monitor.

No human being is deluded,
nor could there be any certain check
to what's ordained in his star.

Doce sonho, suave e soberano

Sweet sleep, gentle and paramount,
if only you weren't so ruled by the clock!
Ah, from such sleep whoever awoke
without having to face disenchantment?

Delightful blessing! Sweet falsehood,
if you could only deceive me further,
if then my wretched life could expire
and in sheer pleasure I'd die proud!

Happy when not myself, I had
sleeping what waking I wished to have.   10
Observe the cards my Fortune deals me!

In short, in my dreams I was overjoyed.
It made better sense to be deceived,
for in the real world I was always unhappy.

Fortuna em mim guardando seu direito

Fortune, exacting from me its tribute
in my green youth, destroyed my joy.
O, how much ended on that day,
whose sad memory still burns in my heart!

On looking back, I freely suspect
that so much blessing could only end,
so no one would say the world could pretend
in its deceit to a thing so perfect.

But if Fortune arranged this to offer
me some relief by way of discount   10
on a feeling whose memory brings despair,

what accusation could make me suffer,
if the reason for my torment
is the means to endure the nightmare?

Memória do meu bem, cortado em flores

Memorial to the good times, carved in flowers,
by order of my sad and malicious Fates,
leave me in peace with all my regrets
in this anxious inquest into my amours.

Enough for me, the present and my worries
about consequences I expect to be worse
without past pleasures, newly rehearsed
to disturb my peace with their sorrows.

I lost so much in an hour, but in a style
so measured and easygoing I profited: 10
away, then, thoughts of that glory.

End this life of barren exile;
so along with my pain I'll terminate
a thousand lives, not just one hard memory.

O dia em que eu nasci, moura e pereça

That black, terminal day I was born,
let it be expunged from the almanac;
may it never return or, if venturing back,
let it suffer the same eclipse as the sun.

Let the sky darken, and the sun run wild,
let signs herald the world's end,
let the air rain blood, monsters portend,
the mother be stranger to her own child.

Let astonished people, their hearts aghast
in their ignorance, their faces dazed,   10
reckon the world already lost.

O timid creatures, don't be amazed
this day brought forth the most accursed
wretch on whom mankind ever gazed!

O tempo acaba o ano, o mês e a hora

Time ends year, month, and hour,
vigor, art, strength, and stealth;
time puts an end to fame and wealth,
time laments its own departure.

Time hunts down and ends all current
ingratitude and whatever rudeness;
but it cannot end my sadness
while you, Lady, withhold your consent.

Time turns the brightest day to night,
the happiest joy to desolate weeping: 10
time calms the wildest tempest.

But most fixed of all is that diamond heart
where, unassuaged by time, my hope's
mingled pain and pleasure coexist.

Quando a suprema dor muito me aperta

When my suffering's so great it causes
me to say I long for oblivion,
the force behind this reflection
contradicts my actual purpose.

And so the light of a well-ordered brain
awakes me from a grave fallacy,
showing that only self-deceit or fancy
could accommodate such consolation.

For this same image that, mentally,
represents the joy I'm bereft of   10
brings you strangely to my presence.

So I bear happiness painfully,
for within me its cause is suffered
as a good I assent to, even in your absence.

▦ Querendo escrever um dia

Wishing to write out one day
the suffering I hoarded,
considering what I should display,
I met Love, who paused to say,
"Let me dictate the record."
And since to read myself aright
it was no small journal
he desired I create,
from his wings I plucked the quill
with which he made me write.   10

No sooner had I plucked it
than he said, "You have my favor,
so brush up your faculties—
that feather you're equipped
with will make your writings soar."
And being made to suffer
all he wished I should set out,
I could at last make answer;
he gave the pen with which to write
of the pain I endure.   20

I who saw through these puns
asked, "What should I review?"
He answered me at once,
"Your own sublime impressions
and of her to whom I gave you;
and since it's my dearest theme
to balance antitheses,
write because you so esteem
the miracles of a lovely face
and the sadness of all dreamers."   30

[239]

Lady, through whom grows purer
the ideal of my fancy,
listen, and be well aware,
it's through your being so fair
that Love redoubles my agony.
Though you're too far away
to attend to my words
or offer any remedy,
I listen, because Love declares
miraculous the record.   40

The Record

According to some authors,
close by the clear source
of the Ganges, mountain dwellers
there among the glaciers
subsist on the scent of flowers.
If emotions yield calories
sufficient, and in residue,
it should cause no surprise
that if they subsist on odors,
I'm sustained by seeing you.   50

There was once a tree renowned
because, amid the general joy,
it alone was saddened,
for it blossomed when benighted
and lost its leaves by day.
For me, who knows what penalty
the sight of your face exacts—
the act of seeing weighs heavily—
for I haven't learned the trick
of being famed for melancholy.   60

The great king Mithridates
was nurtured on poison
so that, being used to it,
he could not be affected

when afterwards it was given.
I from my infancy
was suckled on frustration
and so it became my destiny,
I cannot be harmed by pain
until the day I'm made to die.   70

Whoever has the royal disease
and for a long time feels drained,
by one of nature's miracles
is restored by the vision
of some mammal that flies.
For all the harm Love plants in me,
when I see that Phoenix soar
I am altogether healthy,
though, like a man with dropsy,
the more I drink, the more I want.   80

Of the puff adder it's a maxim
(if he's looking for a date,
and hoping they'll conjugate)
he puts away his venom,
for it gets in the way of mating.
Just so, when I expose myself
to your unrelenting face,
the poison of my suffering
I set aside, so as not to lose
the joy of such relief.   90

Love, wishing to expand his empire,
made the heart-free Pygmalion
fall in love with a carved icon,
which, to confirm his power,
he changed to a living woman.
In what court will I be able
to present myself as the victim
if I pursue some doll
who, instead of taking human form,
converts herself to marble?   100

Of some river source it was known,
and the proof was in what happened,
that if a man made it his bond,
and if his vows were foresworn,
he was immediately struck blind.
You, my Lady, despot
of my autonomy,
unjustly you dictate
when I speak to you truly
I am banished from your sight.   110

It's written and sung of the palm
that it's so sturdy no burden
can do its profile any harm,
but that out of sheer presumption,
it stands erect and firm.
That heavy pain you use to ensure
the constancy of which I sing
not only makes me doubly heartsore
but multiplies my longing,
so I desire you the more.   120

If someone wishes with his eyes
a swallow should crash-land,
on the instant its mother flies
to that green marshland
so it'll be reborn and rise.
I who have my eyes fixed
steadfastly on yours, that are stars,
am blinded in my antics,
but reason is reborn as my tears
frolic with the painful facts.   130

It was we who found, navigating
there at the rising of the sun,
an unknown river of wonders,
in that branches cast into it
are metamorphosed to stone.
It's a thing makes the people stare;

more reason to be astonished
that a heart so potent,
watered with burning tears,
should transform itself to diamond.   140

The silent eel can administer
to a line cast in calm seas
a current of such vigor
as to utterly paralyze
the wrist of any angler.
If once my eyes are transfixed
by that wonderful scourge,
they are held with no knowledge
of how to switch off the electric
something that compels the urge.   150

These are the visible ciphers
of many you inscribe on me,
nor could you want for more:
if to see yourself is your desire,
in me read yourself clearly.
If you want to see for what purpose
you placed in me so much good,
it is because Love so chooses:
and to see you in you, you should
see me in myself likewise.   160

Of the pain I suffered at your hand,
which even now I dismiss,
learn, if you will attend,
I no longer know what to propound,
nor how you could know less.
But given I'm still ignorant
who could withstand such a fate,
Lady, I remain content
you should have my torment
as the object of your sight.   170

What a mixture of contraries
love forces us to tolerate,

as that inexpressible sight
that lights up all my days
should leave me so disconsolate.
But I offer this support
of the pain that so offends,
with the candle as exhibit;
though the wind blows it out,
it flares up in the same wind.   180

It was proved on a certain day
of that bird they give my name
if, where it lived, it saw the lady
of that house commit adultery,
it died of pure shame.
The grief is beyond measure
and no remedy avails,
but, oh fortunate creature,
that life itself should fail
on witnessing such an evil!   190

The enchantments of desire
would today be delightful
were they not assailed
by memories of my fear
of being displaced by a rival.
Such chilling jealousies
in which nightmares reason
are like Harpies
who foul delicacies,
transforming them to poison.   200

I feel this infinite pain
leaves me no more to relate
lest I should adulterate
the happiness of which I've written
with what more I have to write.
I have no vocation to expound
scandal, only to provide a gloss,
so of all that is heard in this,

nothing more should resound
than the glory of your service.   210

▨ Tenho-me persuadido

TO HIS OWN THEME:

> *What's the point of fleeing,*
> *death, danger, and grief,*
> *when I bear them in myself?*

I, for the best of reasons,
have accepted as evident
that I can never be content
given the fact that I was born.
I bear within one person
my torment as my better half,
myself a danger to myself.

But were I liberated
it would be no release,
for being no more myself, I'd lose   10
that from which I derive this good,
forfeiting this fortitude,
so that either I live in anguish,
or exist without danger. Or relish.

▨ Costumadas artes são

TO THIS OLD SONG:

> *False, ungrateful man,*
> *what you say is not true:*
> *you claim to be dying for me*
> *when it's me who dies for you.*

It's the fashionable art
to deceive the innocent,
with touching performances
from a carefree heart.
I love, and you're indifferent,

[245]

hurting me anew
as you claim to die on my account
when it's me who dies for you.

Observe which of us two
is closer to being finished;   10
I'm the one who's punished,
though the verdict names you.
When I deal in greater candor
you push me to
hatred and even murder,
when it's me who dies for you.

Para quem vos soube olhar

TO HIS OWN THEME:

> *If I'm reconciled to my pain*
> *it's because I recognize*
> *desire for you throughout the world*
> *but worthiness in no one.*

Those you momentarily admired
were faced with this quandary,
of knowing themselves unworthy
while unable not to desire.
Now, for all my thought,
there seems no remedy,
unless desire can furnish steady
wings for the merit.

Trataram-me com cautela

TO THIS OLD SONG:

> *My eyes were separated*
> *from me, far removed . . .*
> *False loves,*
> *false, evil hypocrites!*

They treated me with foresight
the more simply to beguile;
I gave them power over my soul—
they fled off with it.
There's no seeing them, nor seeing it,
from me far removed . . .
False loves,
false, evil hypocrites!

I gave them their liberty
and, in the end, a better life;   10
they went, and of this plain rebuff
they made necessity.
Who was it had her will,
from me far removed?
False loves,
and cruel as they killed.

No one put seas or land
between us, that being vain;
it was rather her condition
it was sweet to transcend.   20
She alone wished to be separate,
from me far removed!
False loves,
and would to God, hypocrites.

Se desejos fui já ter

TO THIS COMMON THEME:

> *Observe how I spent my days*
> *overwhelmed by despair;*
> *no wonder that I fear desire*
> *and badly lack joys.*

If I were still to have desires
that serve only to torment me;
if blessings could only bring me joy
before despondency overpowers . . .
I spent years, I spent whole days
overwhelmed by my despair
that simply not to feel desire,
I'd forfeit a thousand joys,

De ver-vos a não vos ver

TO HIS OWN THEME:

> *Since it harms me to see you,*
> *I don't wish, so as not to lose you,*
> *anyone should see me see you.*

To see you, and not to see,
are both mortal extremes;
and in me they take such form
that in either case I die.
But first I wish to satisfy
my heart—so as not to lose you,
it could live without seeing you.

Amid such danger
what remedy can I have,
when it's by seeing you I live?   10
If I don't see you, it's danger,
so I choose to be a stranger
to myself, so no one sees me see you,
Lady, so as not to lose you.

Quem viver sempre num ser

TO THIS COMMON THEME:

> *There's one good that comes and goes;*
> *it's called being just as well*
> *as you need to understand evil.*

He who lived his life in the same tenor
though it was spent in poverty,
not knowing the rewards of property
nor the pain of being made poor:
he did not win only to surrender,
but gained, life being uniform,
not to know good nor suffer harm.

Nunca em prazeres passados

TO THIS THEME:

> *Hope was drifting away;*
> *understanding my delusions—*
> *of evil stayed the pains,*
> *and of the good only the memory.*

Never in past enjoyments
did I feel any security,
promising such enchantments
as were yet to be apparent
when Fortune took them from me.
And like one mistrustful
my luck could ever vary,
surrounded by this quarrel,
however I could dissemble,
hope was drifting away.   10

It was not a case of folly
turning aside all hope;
I lay the blame on a destiny
that no one, even trustworthy
Love, could possibly shore up.

I put myself in his power,
not afraid of his pains
as I gave my heart entire,
yet only when it was mine no more,
understanding my delusions.   20

I stayed with harm to spare,
at which its origin advised
I should relate all I saw:
Love admits desire,
but lies in what he promised.
For myself, if he favored me
with the highest satisfaction,
it was only to deceive me;
of the good he deprived me,
and of evil stayed the pains.   30

And if pain's what I must endure,
so mismatched as if I'm damned,
I aspire afresh to suffer more—
the reason, given its nature,
I'm resolved not to offend.
Redouble pain, curtail life,
strengthen faith, cut security
for giving me so little relief:
what's printed on the heart is grief,
and of the good only the memory.   40

◼ Eu, para levar a palma

TO THIS THEME:

> *With good cause I can complain*
> *of you, as you yourself deplored,*
> *because, Lady, when you're bled*
> *the body should be your own.*

I, to gain the laurel
of deserving to be yours,

rejoice that my body suffers
for you, given you're its soul.
You complain of being invalid,
and I, too, can complain
in that your body being mine,
it's from my heart you're bled.

Without seeking to quarrel
over what you're possessed of,   10
by being so little moved
you cause sickness to my soul.
Since it's two you threaten,
oh! let this not turn bad:
may this body of yours bleed,
it being my heart you quicken.

Yet, if you're still curious,
you take the wrong medicine
in that for bleeding to be done,
some heart must stay bloodless.   20
Since through me you cure
disorder, which you give my heart,
if you are bled again, let
it be this body that's yours.

Perdigão, que o pensamento

TO THIS OLD SONG:

> *Partridge lost his quill,*
> *there's no harm won't befall him.*

Partridge, whose winged fancy
aspired to a high estate,
lost a feather in his flight
and won the pen of despondency.
He finds in the breeze no buoyancy
for his pennants to haul him:
there's no harm won't befall him.

He wished to soar to a high tower
but found his plumage clipped,
and, observing himself plucked,   10
pines away in despair.
If he cries out for succor,
stoke the fire to forestall him:
there's no harm won't befall him.

⊠ Se n' alma e no pensamento

TO A LADY WHO CAUSED HIM SOME PAIN:

If my heart and mind take
you as their proud device,
this doesn't in any way oppress,
for not to suffer heartache
would be an insult to your face.
And because whatever Love ordains
matches this heart's desire,
to death's row I'm condemned;
there's nothing else I aspire
to but pain, pain, pain.   10

⊠ De Amor e seus danos

TO THIS THEME:

> *Who knows*
> *where Love is born*
> *is he who sows.*

To Love and his losses
I made myself artisan;
I sowed passion
and gathered lies.
My years were not witness
to a man who harvested
what he sowed.

I saw fields flowering
in thistles with their dyes,
lovely to the eyes   10
but a bleak living.
The cattle wandering
such doomed pasture
were born in a bad hour.

Over so much atrophy
I labored in vain.
I planted grain
and harvested grief.
I never saw love
long endure   20
and not end in despair.

Aquela cativa

TO A CAPTIVE WHO BECAME HIS LOVER
IN INDIA, CALLED BARBARA:

That slave I own
who holds me captive,
living for her alone
who scorns I should live,
no hybrid rose
drenched in dew
had ever to these eyes
half such beauty.

The flowers in the field,
and the stars above   10
in their radiance, yield
to my love.
Distinct in feature,
eyes dark and at rest,
tired creature,
but not of conquest.

Here dwells the sweetness
by which I live,
she being mistress
of whom she is captive.   20
Her hair is raven,
and the fashion responds,
forgetting its given
preference for blonde.

Love being Negro
at so sweet a figure,
the blanketing snow
vows to change color.
Gladly obedient
and naturally clever;   30
this may be expedient,
but barbarous, never!

Quiet presence
that silences storms;
all my disturbance
finds peace in her arms.
This is the vassal
who makes me her slave,
being the muscle
that keeps me alive.   40

Quererdes profano amor

TO A WOMAN WHO WAS WHIPPED BY
A MAN THEY CALLED CORESMA, IN INDIA:

You should not show displeasure
if the same fate were yours,
for when a woman turns to vice,
someone called Coresma
should be the one to chastise.

You seek out illicit love
during Lent, it's penitence;

by whips and penances
you are much improved.
Don't be affronted by this
because the fault is yours;
when a woman turns perverse,
someone called Coresma
should be the one to chastise.

If the penances avail   10
you are very well scourged;
it's through Lent that you purge
the heat of all that's carnal.
Don't condemn yourself twice
by returning to your errors,
for now you have revised
your ways, *no one called Coresma*
need a second time chastise.

Quem no mundo quiser ser

TO A GENTLEMAN IN INDIA
WHO WAS LATE WITH A GRACEFUL
SHIRT HE HAS PROMISED HIM.

In this world, whoever aspires
to extraordinary fame,
to descend to particulars,
must always provide the same
gift horse he promises.
And now that your favors
follow the same generous track,
as all the world perceives,
it's high time someone gave
the shirt from off his back.   10

Que diabo há tão danado

SENT BY THE AUTHOR FROM THE PRISON
IN WHICH HE HAD BEEN SEIZED FOR A DEBT
OWED TO MIGUEL RAIZ, NICKNAMED
"DRY-THREADS," TO THE COUNT OF REDONDO,
VICE-ROY, AS HE WAS EMBARKING,
ASKING TO BE SET FREE:

What demon is so ungodly
it doesn't fear the sword-
thrust of the dry-edged blade
of our terrible armed Miguel?
For if indeed his stroke tolls
too loud in this infernal prison
even the devil dreads with reason,
how should I now turn tail?

For the best of reasons I'd flee
if, against him and against the world,   10
I did not have a strong shield
in you alone, Your Excellency.
Therefore, my lord, command,
since I'm sentenced to the galley,
before you yourself put to sea
I should be unconfined.

Vossa senhoria creia

VERSES THAT HEITOR DA SILVEIRA SENT
TO THE SAME COUNT, WINTERING IN GOA:

Your Lordship ought to know
starvation doesn't sustain
talent, as least not such as mine,
but weakens and cuts off the flow.
And whoever thinks the contrary
is as satiated each passing hour

as I'm now pinched with hunger.
But Martha, when you're happy,
who cares about some tear?

Your Lordship, being generous,   10
as your custom is to everyone,
assist me with what alone
gives value to my genius.
Kick-start this muse of mine
that time has made somnolent;
redeem my belly's torment
with that unique medicine
that restores life (and pays the rent).

Help me with the wherewithal,
not of paper, but provender   20
of gold and silver; mere
requisitions are no good at all.
First Lord of the Treasury
strikes me as a suitable berth.
Rescue me, your Lordship, with
some such sovereign remedy
to blunt the sword of death.

Helped by Luís de Camões

In learned books it's reported
great Achilles in his anger
dealt death to Trojan Hector,   30
but now our Lusitanian Heitor's
dying from sheer hunger.
only Your Excellency can prevent
this, given the rare circumstance
and his generous disposition,
by thrusting between the contestants
some appointment's baton.

Viver eu, sendo mortal

ON THIS THEME SENT HIM BY THE VICE-ROY OF INDIA,
LUÍS DE CAMÕES COMPOSED FOR HIM SOME VERSES:

I am so much my mortal foe
that, being unable to expunge
the troubles I was born to,
they put my life in danger.
Would to God it was so!

Being mortal, it's my fate
to be surrounded by trouble;
it's become my nature—
the poison cannot hurt
one who knew it from the cradle.
I am so much my mortal foe
that, so as not to expunge
the troubles I was born to.
I put my life in danger.
Would to God it was so!   10

I see swelling perpetually
troubles unassuaged for
as long as time endures,
and I tire of being watchful
when the troubles never tire.
Should you be also tinged
by the pains that are my theme,
it need not estrange;
to put my life in danger
is for me the finest outcome.   20

Conde, cujo ilustre peito

VERSES SENT TO THE VICE-ROY,
WITH THE THEME ATTACHED:

Count, whose illustrious heart
deserves the appellation "king,"

to whom I know, as a certain thing
will come justly and by right
the Vice-Roy's ermine;
to employ me would bring
you credit, though my stars are loath,
unless it were to give me wings
enabling me to singe
myself in your glory, like the moth.   10

And if, having trimmed it
clumsily, I take up my quill,
it will be to celebrate
your unrivalled merit
that deserves much greater skill.
If my own is to commend
you, it must transcend earth,
becoming eagle-visioned,
not to be blinded
in the sunlight of your worth.   20

The illustrious memory
of your sublime feats of war
has become the world's story,
while in you the glory
of our ancestors is restored.
For your unique spirit,
ready for any act of courage,
baffles all our knowledge
that so immense a heart
could be enclosed in any rib cage.   30

The indulgence that makes tranquil
a heart so uncommon—
such a theme for my quill
would be to shut an ocean
within a shallow pool.
Enough, sir, that you now quicken
your own concerns by employing me;
so doing, you will sharpen

the quill on which some day you'll see
yourself borne up to heaven.   40

So I'll go about extolling
your raising me above the general,
both astonishing the world:
you chopping with your sword,
I with my pain recording.

Se não quereis padecer

INVITATION THAT LUÍS DE CAMÕES
MADE IN INDIA TO CERTAIN GENTLEMEN,
WHOSE NAMES ARE GIVEN HERE.

The first was posted to Vasco Ataide and said:

If you've no wish to tolerate
an hour or two of boredom,
you must do, you know what?
Turn back whence you came,
for there's nothing here to eat.
And even if you care to study
these just-a-little peppery
verses, don't be dismayed,
for the fact is if you run away
you won't get any supper.   10

The second was posted to Francisco
d'Almeida and said:

Heliogabalus made sport of
the guests he invited,
as a matter of make-believe,
for the delicacies he served
came painted on the plates.
Don't fear any such fiction,
for it wouldn't now be novel:
your supper is quite certain,

and it doesn't come as a painting—
it's all in this doggerel.   20

The third was posted to Heitor da Silveira and said:

You can't dine out on a bluff;
however, not to defraud,
for drinking, there's on offer
not Caparica, but a good red
and a thousand goodies to scoff.
Is your snout ravening
over all this ambiguity?
You should remember poetry
serves you ink instead of wine
and paper as a delicacy.   30

The fourth was posted to João Lopes Leitão,
to whom the author added an epigram,
which was sent before on a piece of cloth
he sent to his lady:

Because those who invited you
can't upset your stomach,
in a just cause they exhorted you,
if it was verse that cheated you,
verse should expose the mistake.
You have this test of guile
to reduce all to a rhyme.
Then if you were to see me smile,
don't worry, Senhor, about tricks of style,
for there's nothing to clothe this time.   40

The squib João Lopes Leitão sent in return:

To hell with all the saints (anon.),
I swear with holy heaven in mind,
if they don't supply a supper,
I am no chameleon
that can survive on mere wind.

Senhor, don't let it get you down
that God's putting you to any test;
and if you care to know the rest
you can study on this menu
what delicacies make up the feast.   50

Turning the paper it said as follows:

You have *roasted crumbs* of nothing,
with *zero* as a piquant sauce,
a savory pie of *empty mouthing,*
a saucepan *full of breathing,*
and *boiled toothpicks* as main course.
You have large *slices of smoke,*
and *unplucked blackbirds,*
ill for lack of feeding,
a yawn of wine and garlic
and an excellent *blank pudding.*   60

The fifth and last was posted to
Francisco de Melo and said:

Of a man who held the scepter
of a most marvellous vein,
it was held beyond question
he could metamorphose to meter
the most prosaic Latin.
I want your lordships to lay bets
I have a knack of imagining
beyond anything you ever thought;
and this supper you're about to eat
will be a ballad on the tongue.   70

Sendo os restos envidados

TO JOÃO LOPES LEITÃO, IN INDIA, ON ACCOUNT
OF A PIECE OF CLOTH HE SENT TO HIS LADY
WHICH MADE HER LOOK LIKE A VIRGIN:

> *If your lady gives you*
> *all you ever pursued,*
> *explain: why did you give her*
> *what she's already given you?.*

Having used up every remnant
and been flannelled with a thousand tales,
you should know when the stitching fails
how shoddy was the attachment.
If what she has is what's returned,
you thoroughly deserve her,
because the cloth you gave her
she's dealt you back in kind.

HYMN

Com força desusada

The sun with formidable
power blazes unremittingly
on an island here in the Far East
inhabited by strange people,
where it's only in winter
the green fields are replenished.
By right of bloody conquest
it is we Portuguese
constitute its government.
It is encircled by a current   10
of health-giving ocean water;
on the various plants that exist
here, both cattle and one's eyes feast.

It was decreed by my star
that here the greater portion
of the life I lacked should be set,
and so my sepulcher
when fierce Mars ordains
should be garnished with blood and regret.
If Love should dictate,   20
in exchange for my being dead,
that whatever memory
remained of me, the story
of those marvelous eyes would still be read,
I'd happily barter
life itself with all its laughter.

But this daydream,
arising from ill-fortune,
flatters only to deceive;
fancy should not presume   30
it could encounter in the coffin
what so long eluded it when alive.
I've lost all trace of
my former belief,
arising from disquiet
on reviewing my sad state,
that death would bring relief.
But oh! If my will to live
deserts me, that day I'll survive.

After all I've witnessed,   40
I'm no longer amazed
despair's my best protection.
Someone else caused this;
of this inward fire that blazes
I could never have been the origin.
If the fear of being forgotten
were what most offends,
would to God my peril
should be to me so loyal
that I'd no such fear in mind!   50

Who envisaged such confusion
as hope innocent of suspicion?

He that has something to lose
has good cause to be afraid,
but it's sadder when all's forfeit.
Lady, the fault is yours
that to ensure I'd be dead
it was enough to deny me your sight.
You made certain my plight
was enslavement to false hopes;   60
and what shocks me more
is that I've come not to care
about seeing those hopes eclipsed.
There'll be little gain
in not deserving such sweet pain.

Love then attended me,
mildly and rarely irritable,
whatever he now knows of my sorrow;
there's no greater penalty
for one who's culpable   70
than to deny the pain that's his due.
The comparison holds true
that, as with a patient
whose cure is undone,
the sensible physician
to his every wish consents,
so I'm granted, as indulgence,
hopes, ambition, and this impudence.

Now I come to give
this account of former blessings   80
to this sad life of absence;
whoever could conceive
of such a sin
as to merit this long penitence?
Is it not on your conscience
that an error so trivial

should be so taxed, Lady?
Don't you recognize usury?
But my long, wretched exile
gives you such enjoyment,   90
you'll never agree to end my torment.

Clear and lovely stream
and you, the palm groves
that crown just conquerors,
and keep the peasant on his farm
contented forever
with various fruits from the one trunk;
so time's no token,
in its passing, of any hurt,
and the troubles recorded   100
here find an abode,
while the sun lends the moon its light;
from father to son, it's said truly
to lack a life is not to die.

Song, you will survive this exile,
your voice, unadorned and naked,
until time makes you a mere echo.

❈ ODE ❈

❈ **Aquele único exemplo**

That matchless example
of heroic strength and bravery
who in eternity's temple
deserves to enjoy perpetual day,
Thetis's son, great Achilles, and scourge
for ten years of the unhappy Trojans,

was no less a scholar
in herbs and medical doctrine,

than an expert familiar
with the sublime art of soldiering: 10
so the hands that brought so many to grief
restored an equivalent number to life.

That fierce, indomitable boy
was never one to ignore
the effects on feeble flesh of those rays
emanating from Apollo's tonsure;
if fearful Hector died at his hands,
he knew also how to heal wounds.

In such arts he was tutored
by Chiron, old and learned centaur,   20
as in skill, prudence, and virtue
he came to equal his mentor,
so Telephus, once he had speared
him, could by him alone be cured.

So you, Your Excellency,
most illustrious Count, given
by heaven to reveal to our own day
the exalted heroes of times long gone,
and in whom is copied the memory
of your ancestors' honor and glory,   30

though you have occupied your mind
with troublesome campaigns,
whether Taprobana, so blood-stained,
or Aceh, threatened by the ocean,
or in Cambay, our remote enemy,
all of them trembling at your name,

look kindly on that obscure
knowledge that once Achilles valued;
take care that you favor
the green shoots today displayed   40
as fruits of that Orta, where new
plants flourish even experts don't know;

take care that before many years
pass, some famous Orta produces
in Portuguese meadows
all the various herbs Medea and Circe,
those arrogant witches, never smelt,
despite breaking the rules of the occult,

and regard an ancient, lettered
man, burdened by years   50
and vast experience, instructed
by the muses of the River Ganges,
in the subtle Asclepian rustic
skills of Achilles' master's magic,

the very same that here petitions
your patronage for the mighty tome
even now being published
that will give medicine a new flame,
and will make its way revealing facts
that to the ancients were veiled secrets.   60

In conscience, you cannot refuse
him who petitions you just renown;
though your honor would first choose
hectic battle with Moor and Indian,
aid him who turns death's other cheek
and thus resemble the powerful Greek.

✠ Que novas tristes são, que novo dano

ON THE DEATH OF DOM MIGUEL DE MENESES,
SON OF D. HENRIQUE DE MENESES, GOVERNOR
OF THE HOUSE OF CIVEL, WHO DIED IN INDIA.

What fresh grief, what further harm,
what impending disasters hover,
touching all foreheads with alarm?

I see the monsoon beaches of Goa
seething with an agitated crowd
as flies from mouth to mouth the rumor

Dom Miguel is dead—O cruel sword!—
along with many of that glittering corps
who embarked on that happy, fated armada,

as flaming muskets and that cold spear   10
hurled by that base, unworthy hand
did such injury to our honor.

Shield and breastplate could not withstand,
nor the splendid spirit of his ancestors
with so large a field to defend;

nor to have encircling him in layers
the corpses of his enemies, transpiring
their black souls from their mortal clay;

nor his powerful words, soaring
to animate his wavering companions   20
so they overcome their terror.

But entering on his life's final span,
his limbs to countless debris
hacked, his spirit alone unbroken,

his eyes, supercharged with a fury
that even in death's throes intimidated
the feeble, astonished enemy,

were fixed on heaven as they dedicated
his innocent soul to the supreme immortal
by whom earth and heaven are supported;   30

and asking forgiveness for foibles,
not sins in one of such tender years,
from the most just and merciful,

from the pure snow there drained the roses,
as a lamp begins to expire,
when its oil is done and it weakly splutters,

to the welcoming arms of the heavenly choir
he delivered himself to life eternal,
his reward for his death as a martyr.

Go in peace to everlasting glory, great soul!   40
Go, for such a death by holy decree
is a life given to God, our celestial ruler.

For when some cause, just and worthy,
to do with king or nation or ancestors
requires of us the ultimate charity,

seated among the resplendent stars
we are placed, through heavenly indulgence,
among those heroes destined for glory.

But who will support the perpetual absence
of so dear a lord, such a faithful comrade,   50
and who to such grief bring resistance?

That great soul, the exact similitude
of the greatest of his forebears,
scornful of any commonplace hazard,

treating all with the same gentle manners,
whether his equals or of lesser birth,
pleasing all with his affectionate humor,

that noble spirit, in which our faith
flourished, till the hard event
cut him back to this floral wreath;   60

in his green youth, mature in judgment,
a cheerful smile, a happy, open heart,
secure in an unshakeable temperament,

not preening, nor playing a part,
but genuine, and all by nature,
fitter for heaven than for worldly arts.

Physically, too, his sculptured
elegance, his graceful charm,
in equal measure forceful and shrewd;

his complexion, where roses swarmed   70
those sweet flowers of exhilaration
adorning all cheeks in summer;

all this death's cutting edge, besieging
and toppling all our purposes,
sliced cruelly as it made its incision.

Leave off mourning, lovely Venus,
for the ugly and violent death
of Myrrha's gentle son, Adonis;

and you, Apollo, your sighing for that youth,
darling Hyacinth, beautifully curled,   80
on whose account you give light to the earth;

come and grieve a youth rare in this world,
not wounded by the tusks of a wild boar,
or some other beast, as might be healed,

but who readily, without personal fears,
perished alone at the hands of the enemy,
entrusting his life to irate Mars.

I ask you, Cupid, also to comply:
cease scattering your honeyed poison
to drown glad eyes in melancholy,   90

for today Miguel's glorious vision
is veiled by the impenetrable mantle
of a general law, cruel in application.

You, daughters of Thespis, with sad pastoral
can mitigate the lamentations
of his noble brothers in their sad ordeal;

do not lead them to undermine
their dignity, for, though tears are due,
no tears can compensate this pain.

On the instant, the Muses bring into view   100
rumor's one thousand mouths conveying
to the glittering Tagus the grim news,

and the profound grief, overpowering
in the same instant the greatest hearts,
as if almost beyond reason's bearing;

there, for those afflicted, from the weight
of their grief, ladies will find consolation,
and the men patterns to venerate.

Mild, for sure, would be grief that reason
could rein in, or the distant memory   110
of virtuous heroes of times that are gone,

and though you equate living with glory,
my great Dom Filipe, and you plan
to leave your own mark on history,

I don't admonish you to discipline
your heart in the stoic sophistry,
parading yourself as untouched by passion,

as though our evil nature's the nursery
of fear, hope, sorrow, and delight
as in the old Cynics' philosophy.   120

Inhuman madness!—as Ovid stated
in his verses—and a crass blunder
to ignore the emotions our souls create,

for while only a brute's impervious to wonder,
and such passion makes life acceptable,
it's also wrong to be excessively tender.

If opinion in these bad times troubles
you, and with fears of much worse to come,
they are only the opinions of people.

Unperturbed is the truest wisdom   130
by casual pleasures or the shock
of pain, upsetting the soul's equilibrium,

even before laughter and grief strike,
good sense will already be there to ponder
and is immune to alarm or heartbreak.

And as if observing from a high tower
human pride in all its variety
of ambition, jealousy, and error,

in every case there's one certainty:
that as fevers are to human flesh   140
so emotions are the soul's infirmity.

If you believe this doctrine heathenish,
cast your eyes on our faith that's divine
and sacred, greater than any fetish.

Consider Aaron, who not to profane
his high calling, held his peace
when his sons died, by God's discipline.

It's not enough when kinsmen decease,
their souls delighting in God,
to consider them relieved from distress.   150

We are a holy people, consecrated
to God, who by pagan formulas
must at no time be contaminated.

If it's written of our ancient fathers
they committed their dead to the ground
with public wailing, and nothing further,

it was because those nail-pierced hands
had yet to break down heaven's gates,
cleansing where our ancestors sinned,

and to add luster to those out-of-date   160
pageantries of a pagan sepulcher
with our customary public rites.

That combined courage and despair
of the great captain is your due,
by the laws of sacred Scripture.

I know well there's no corpse in view,
that noble mausoleum being empty
as the vultures and jackals feast on you.

But even this repeats the history
of your great-grandfather, who to save his king   170
exposed himself to the spears of the enemy,

with his own limbs blocking
the passage of the fierce Berbers,
and lacked the tomb that was befitting.

There safely in heaven's bowers
they receive him crowned with victory,
scorning the pangs of the body below.

Interment is what's customary,
whosoever the corpse, but some
who die for God, only the angels bury.   180

What richer or lovelier mausoleum,
what greater pyramid, than the shroud
arriving in the heavenly kingdom!

Missing out on burial is not hard:
wise Diogenes and Theodorus thought
little of what happened after they were dead.

So beautiful, decorous, so complete,
worship whoever achieves like him,
when is heard the sound of the last trumpet!

But oh! what sudden fear consumed 190
your famous courage, you Portuguese?
With what terrors were you unmanned?

What spears, what strokes, what reverses
caused you to do such injury
to the Lusitanian battledress?

Or of the great captain, was it frailty
or negligence? Neither, for his own
flesh bore the barbarian's fury.

Or was it the iron power of the cannon,
its blasts stupefying sea and land, 200
that turned your hearts to stone?

How does it happen you no longer withstand
war's frenzy, with that enviable
scorn for the life-burying fury at your hand?

For king and country, by their simple
sacrifice, your grandfathers left us
land, seas, and their sublime example.

They taught us to despise
all fear: so what makes their posterity
so altered, suddenly, for the worse? 210

Beyond any doubt, no generous heart
can live serenely with dishonor,
whether in the public gaze, or in secret.

Dead Spartans, held in the greatest favor
by the fierce crowd for giving their utmost,
had such epitaphs as this to their valor:

You will say you are buried here, our guest,
dispatched by the fierce enemy, obeying
your fatherland's most sacred behest.

When with icy terror, they were fleeing 220
the Persians, they encountered their women
in the roadway, each exposing her belly:

[275]

"If you are running from the danger that looms,
cowards, come," they said, "hide yourselves
a second time in your mother's womb."

Observe which group had more to boast of:
those who ended dying for their nation,
or those others who shamed their wives.

But you, bright Miguel, who now awaken
from life's short dream, given you are   230
safe and at rest in that fortress of heaven,

your bright and courageous soul secure
in God, and shining along with your veterans,
for each of your wounds is a dazzling star,

your feet measuring heaven's crystalline
floor, stepping on that radiant sphere,
already averting your eyes from what's human,

now contemplating one path or another,
now the vanity of mortals
you have surpassed, being there,   240
but grief will sing out, and be all-powerful.

❈ PART FOUR ❈ *Portugal*

⊞ Correm turvas as águas deste rio

The waters of this river run turbid
as from sky and mountain they cascade;
the flowers in the meadow run to seed,
the valley turns intractable, and frigid.

Summer is gone, its heat spent,
as things follow in their due order;
the excitable Fates here surrender
control of the world, or its derangement.

Time lives out its familiar rhythm.
The world, no; but confusion's rife,   10
as seems due to God's negligence.

Events, opinions, nature, and custom,
make up what appears to us as life,
being in truth no more than appearance.

⊞ Como fizeste, Porcia, tal ferida?

"How come you, Porcia, to be so wounded?
Was it willingly? Or through innocence?"
"It was Love, making the experiment
if he could bear to spill my blood."

"And is your blood not determined
to resist your own destruction?"
"It accustoms me to resignation
since death's terrors are no constraint."

"So why do you now eat hot coals
if you are accustomed to iron?" "To suffer   10
belongs with death. So Love ordains."

"And the pain of iron is impalpable?"
"Yes. The pain you live with is a cipher,
and I don't want any death without pain."

Tal mostra dá de si vossa figura

Such an impact, Sibela, your lovely figure
makes, lighting up your vicinity,
it purifies with its clarity
the very pith and power of nature.

Whoever saw so secure a warrant,
or beauty of such brilliance,
but suffers the more it he seeks defense
against a vision of such refinement?

So to avoid any likely repulse,
I let fancy conquer my reason,   10
my feelings enforcing this relapse.

If such intrepidity insults,
you can make fresh retaliation
on the dregs of my life that escaped.

Aquela que, de pura castidade

She who was driven by extreme chastity
took cruel revenge on her own flesh
for that alteration, violent and rapacious,
to her Roman honor and quality;

her beauty was conquered by her good faith,
and her hopes conquered by her suicide,
and so the memory should forever abide
such love, such innocence, such truth.

From herself, friends, and the world distracted,
she plunged hard steel in her soft bosom,   10
drenching the tyrant's power with her blood.

Unique daring, in a unique act,
bringing a swift end to her human frame,
made eternal Lucretia's record!

Dizei, Senhora, da Beleza ideia

I spoke, Lady, of beauty's ideal form:
in order to make those braids so gilded,
where did you search for the finest gold,
from what hidden mine or seam?

Or Phoebus's dazzling beams for your eyes,
worth an empire's equal in esteem,
and, if you attained divine wisdom,
such skill in enchantment as Medea's?

From what secret oyster shells did you pluck
precious pearls, from which eastern gulf,   10
smiling so sweetly in your discourse?

Given you composed your form to your liking,
I caution you against seeing yourself:
avoid pools, remember Narcissus.

Se a Fortuna inquieta e mal olhada

If giddy, squinting Fortune that mocks
the just laws of providence
had granted me the quiet existence
she so detests, one honest and relaxed,

it might have been that the Muse, inspired
by the light of a flame more ardent and vivid,
had caused the Tagus, in its native bed,
to halt at the sound of the loved lyre.

But since burdensome destiny,
has left my muse slack and dulled,   10
not meriting such high esteem,

your own, unsparing in praising me,
searches for some worthier world
receptive to some higher theme.

De um tão felice engenho, produzido

That from one such marvelous talent flowed
another, greater than the sun ever witnessed,
is to bring up matters of rare taste,
astonishing and due every accolade.

Musaeus was the earliest writer of all,
famous poet and philosopher,
and disciple of that musician-lover
who with his voice alone arrested hell.

The former could shake the silent mountain,
singing a calamity I survived, the lot   10
of the youth of Abydos while swimming.

Now Tasso and our Boscán (next in line)
are esteemed for all their insight
into the secret life of the blind king.

De tão divino acento e voz humana

So divine a dialect in so human a voice,
in such a sweet, exotic style—
compared to this my own works fail,
their rough-hewn methods all too obvious.

But in your writing there starts and flows
something more than the waters of Hippocrene,
and the flowers of Tagus poets will combine
to make the Mantuan imprint jealous.

Meanwhile, far from being misers,
the beautiful daughters of Mnemosyne   10
have given you talents the world loves;

while mine, along with your greater muse,
are unique in their personal overtones,
yours sublime, mine more like envy.

Despois que viu Cibele o corpo humano

Once Sibele had seen the handsome body
of human Attis changed to a green pine,
repenting her vain, angry passion
she bewailed his grievous injury;

and, making her pain account for her error,
she begged of Jupiter the further prize
that over the palm and laurel trees
her pine should forever reign superior.

But the almighty son humored her so
that it climbed till it could touch the stars   10
where heaven's secrets were all displayed.

O happy Pinheiro! and most happy, too,
he who, crowned with leaves in your honor,
sings everlasting verse in your shade.

"Não passes, caminhante!" "Quem me chama?"

"Stop, passer by!" "Who is calling me?"
"Some long-overlooked epitaph
to one who exchanged his finite life
for divine, clear and unfading glory."

"Who is spilling such gentle plaudits?"
"One always ready to spill his blood
in following the enlightened standard
of a captain of Christ, who loves us most."

"Happy end, happy atonement,
made for God and for the world as one: 10
speak out, proclaiming such a holy outcome."

"But will you, in turn, make pronouncement,
his life always gave the clearest sign
of growing to merit such martyrdom."

▨ "Que levas, cruel Morte?' "Um claro dia."

"Death, what are you taking?" "The daylight."
"What hour did you take it?" "As it dawned."
"Do you know what you're taking?" "I'm unconcerned."
"Then who made you do it?" "The Creator."

"Who's enjoying the body?" "The cold earth."
"What became of its Light?" "Benighted."
"What does Portugal say?" "Stop, it's not right,
Dona Maria was beyond my desert."

"Did you kill whom you saw?" "She was dead."
"What does bare Love proclaim?" "She dares not."   10
"Who made her stay silent?" "My caprice."

"What's left at the court?" "A void."
"What's there left to remark?" "Hopeless regret.
It remains only to bewail her grace."

▨ Chorai, ninfas, os fado ponderosos

I wept, nymphs, over Fate's severe
dealings with that paramount loveliness.
Were such gracious, regal eyes
intended only for the sepulcher?

O deceptive worldly vanities!
And what lamentation! That such a figure
lies in the hard earth without splendor,
with hair so lovely, and such a face!

What will become of others when death
could have such power over something so rare   10
it eclipsed the light of the brightest day?

But the world was not worth her breath,
and so on earth she exists no more;
she ascended and takes her mansion in the sky.

Quem jaz no grão sepulcro, que descreve

"Who lies in this grand tomb, such distinguished
emblems carved on the mighty buckler?"
"No one: for here he gives everything back,
though he once could have had all he wished."

"Was he king?" "He did all a king should,
giving due attention to both peace and war;
but so pestilent was the cruel Moor
that at last in the earth he is laid."

"Could it be Alexander?" "On that, no one errs;
he reckoned it better to hold than to gain."   10
"Could it be Hadrian, Rome's great commander?"

"He was more observant of Heaven's laws."
"Is it Numa?" "Numa, no—it is John,
the third of Portugal, who had no second."

Ilustre e dino ramo dos Meneses

Deservedly famous branch of the Meneses,
to whom a wise and generous heaven
(without error) gave as your marriage portion
you should breach the Mohammedans' defenses;

disdaining fortune and its adversities,
you went wherever Fate summoned;
the high Eritrean seas you inflamed
were a beacon to the Portuguese.

You overcame through strength and velour
that insolent pirate who shook Ceylon   10
and Gedrosia with his grim works.

You gave the Arabian seas their color;
so the Red Sea from that time on
became so only with the blood of Turks.

Vós, Ninfas da Gangética espessura

Nymphs of the forests of the Ganges valley,
I sang sweetly in a sonorous strain
of a great captain who defended the sons
of the red dawn against nightfall.

In a tough, dark army were conjoined
the peoples of the gold peninsula
to cast adrift from their dear harbor
those not dependent on fortune.

But a Lion, with a handful of men,
making the fierce rabble seem credulous,   10
conquered and left helpless the attacker.

Then sing, too, Nymphs! For plainly,
more than Leonidas did in Greece,
this noble Leonis accomplished in Malaca.

Que vençais no Oriente tantos Reis

You overcame in the East so many rulers
you gave us our India once again,
eclipsing the original glory won
by those first conquerors of the infidels.

You have overcome immortality's laws
with no more time than you spent in arms.
But it's to win your fatherland in other terms
you take on monsters and chimeras.

In short, beyond the enemies you overcame,
unrivaled in what's achieved by the sword,   10
so your reputation will always remain;

but what will win you the greater name
you overcame, my lord, such ingratitude,
and such envy in a happy reign.

Os reinos e os impérios poderosos

The kingdoms and empires that most matter
in marking their greatness either prevailed
by sheer might and valour in the world
or through their illustrious men of letters.

Greece had her famous Themistocles;
on the Scipios were conferred greatness;
the twelve peers brought glory to France,
and to Spain the warrior Laras and El Cid.

Your forebears gave our Portugal
(today so declined from what she once was)   10
her first freedom and honor.

And in you, great successor and rightful
heir, shines the greatness of the Braganças,
equal to your blood and beyond your years.

Vós outros, que buscais repouso certo

You others who search for peace of mind
in your lives through various exercises,
from whom, while enjoying worldly prizes,
the world's invisible order stays hidden;

dedicate if you wish to such derangement
further hours and blind sacrifices,
as fair chastisement for such ancient vices—
God allows things to happen by accident.

I never fell into that mode of censure
that, blaming Fortune, reckons events   10
are all that exist in a world of well-being.

But great experience is a great danger,
for what to God seems just and evident
seems to mere humans profoundly wrong.

⊠ Verdade, Amor, Razão, Merecimento

Truth, Love, Merit, and Reason
anchor the human soul and protect it,
but Fortune, Accident, Time, and Luck
rule over this world's confusion.

A thousand purposes turn in the mind
without understanding what gave them birth;
yet to know what's greater than life and death
is more than mortals can understand.

Erudite men give lofty reasons:
much better is to have travelled around,   10
for experiences are the truer test.

There are things that happen without credence,
and things credited that never happened,
but best of all is to have faith in Christ.

⊠ SONGS ⊠

⊠ Ved que engaños señorea

ALL THAT'S POSSIBLE IS TRIVIAL:

Note, lady, the deceptions
in our imbecile reasoning
for much that's understood;
of all desired good
once won, little remains.
Whatever good we aspire
to, if attainment seems impossible,
it remains much desired.
But when once gained,
all that's possible is trivial.

Os bons vi sempre passar

ON THE DISHARMONY OF THE WORLD:

I watched the world tasking
good men with adversity,
and, on my further asking,
evil I saw basking
in an ocean of prosperity.
When I tried to question
why goodness was disdained,
I was called bad, and arraigned.
It seems I'm the only one
for whom matters are so ordained.   10

Corre sem vela e sem leme

THE AUTHOR'S LABYRINTH,
QUESTIONING THE AGE:

Rudderless and without sail proceeds
this chaotic age
as a great gale rages,
and the danger no one heeds
is not expressed on any page.

We hold in our hand reins
for what reins cannot control,
given how much more powerful
are envy and ambition,
each with their insidious role.   10

A man of war about to founder
destroys a thousand hopes.
I foresee coming mishaps,
and observe the dangers attending
those unready when all collapses.

Those never on horseback
are now placed in the saddle;
there's no end to their meddling;
like demons, they have the mark
of what desecrates the good.   20

What could not come to pass
if evil is never curbed?
Surely, he'd go deluded
who wishes to be virtuous,
following the wrong road.

For the good, all is confusion
watching the bad prevail;
though they contain
themselves by simulation,
they still end up in jail.   30

For not controlling the helm
in turbulent, angry seas
that could have driven any man off course,
he shouts and complains, it seems,
against the disordered years.

They should have just quittance,
and those who deserve it, pain:
for there should always be correction
and without any mercy,
even when they restrain.   40

In the tempest, should it howl,
or in a calm, he'll lose hope
who fails in seamanship.
It will be pointless to bewail—
the scales cannot be duped.

Those who never labored,
avoiding too much stress,
though they deceive the guileless,
will forfeit heaven's reward
if they do not change their ways.   50

⊞ **A quem darão de Pindo as moradoras**

To whom will the dwellers on Mount Pindus,
as learned as they are lovely,
award their trophies
of winning laurel or fresh myrtle
or glorious palm that never belittles
its sublime state,
nor is overburdened by any weight?

To whom will they bring in their soft laps
roses from vermillion Chloris,
shells from white Doris,   10
flowers of the land, flowers of the sea,
yellow, white, red, and silvery,
with dances and ballads
of the wood nymphs and lovely Nereids?

To whom will they make odes and anthems
in Thebes, Amphion,
in Lesbos, Arion,
if not for you who resurrects
what our poetry most lacks,
honor and glory above all,   20
Lord Dom Manuel of Portugal?

The pattern of souls already departed,
kindly, sublime, regal,
you give benign approval
to my humble, hard-working genius.
I celebrate you as my Maecenas,
and will make your name
sacred, if verse can have such aims.

My peasant song that resuscitates
the honor long buried,   30
the palms already faded

of our Lusitanian warriors,
with your help makes abject
Lethe's law, to which all are subject,
as a treasure for coming years.

I found a stem there on your tree
festooned with honor and glory,
vigorous ivy,
so my own lineage, little regarded,
could attach myself and be supported,   40
and by your means to rise
to the tips of your uttermost boughs.

There were always rival talents
begrudging my fortune;
so however pinioned
I was by the power of fame's wings,
in the same measure by hostile reckoning
the wheel's gravity
brought me back to dire necessity.

But hearts that make their own fortune,   50
worthy to be rulers,
have always been the pillars
of true art: Octavian,
Scipio, Alexander, and Gratian,
each is judged
deathless, as you who adorn our age.

Then, so long as the world relishes
the harmonies of the lyre,
studied and full of cheer,
and while Tagus and Douro kindle   60
hearts fit for Mars and golden Apollo,
your glory will be immortal,
Lord Dom Manuel of Portugal.

❈ **Espirito valeroso, cujo estado**

Worthy spirit, whose condition
may God on high prosper and increase,
guiding the calm and faithful nation
in the ways of happiness and peace,
you whom the most poverty-stricken
find invariably loving and courteous,
I beg you to hear me, my only motive
being zeal in your service through God's love.

Do not be affronted by my nerve
in raising with you a strange affair;   10
it was through tears I myself was moved
to come before you, as now I venture;
and if, in turn, you wish to have
my loyal service in any matter,
my name, right arm, possessions, and my muse,
they are much, my lord, and all yours.

The one making this offer will swear
how much I have longed to be of service
because, given your interest, such favor
would greatly benefit my verse;   20
and with your influence as my cover,
having some claim to noble status,
what I lack I know you will supplement,
for I'm not short of energy and talent.

Beyond this, my lord, and quite apart
from what's due to reason as my guide,
I bring you energy, talent, and art,
sent by heaven's influence to your side;
to you both Apollo and Mars impart
their riches, seeing them better applied,   30
as I come with a voice, tearful and frail,
to sing of an unhappy lady now in jail.

In approaching you, it's my principle
to put my trust in your name, my lord,
for whoever has faith in you prevails,
this being a means of serving God.
For this He entrusts to you the scales
where justice is duly heard and weighed:
hear then the petition of one in misery,
to whom fate has shown little courtesy.   40

Hear, then, of wretched Lady Catherine
in her helpless and desperate strait,
for whom there is no prescription
to soften her harsh and cruel fate;
for if her tender age was a burden,
her life reduced to an empty caveat,
her due penalty should be lenient,
for her fears will keep her compliant.

Take care, my lord—this is a poor girl,
whose poverty wins her no respect,   50
and whose years were too few to avail
in knowing to flee what is incorrect;
take care how noble blood entitles,
and the church to which she is subject;
what could be born of such proceedings
but a vast and cruel foreboding?

Surely, with clear and pressing logic,
the unhappy girl has good reason,
for if no one safeguards or protects
in the flower of her youth a sad orphan,   60
cruel Fortune, always meanly cryptic,
to ensure her long and sad decline
delivers her honor and pure chastity
into the hands of cruel necessity.

I know well she is hardly free from blame,
if only for forgetting her noble descent,
but let the punishment fit the crime,
not the banishment that's threatened.

If it's to *there*, beyond, it's a maxim
how viciously she will be maligned,
motivating the rude navigators
to become licentious butchers.

Beware, my lord, the risks that assail
an unfortunate and nubile minor
if a friend in need, or her virtue, fail
to come in defense of her honor.
You don't want, my lord, the world to rail,
"Ah, what cruelty, what merciless rigor,"
as already they are muttering in abuse,
great ignorance being their great excuse.

Nothing's more certain than that the captain,
the pilot, the master, the common sailor
will commit their customary, shabby sin
with all that come within their power.
Name me, my lord, just one who refrains
from such a morsel in such an hour,
and I'll admit what's written here is a lie,
and take whatever chastisement you apply.

Today, alas, no St. John in the wilderness
is so loved by heaven for his chastity,
nor exists anyone who in this business
of brute misconduct is not guilty,
no one so firm as Jerome, alas,
who, well aware of his body's frailty,
stone in hand, struck himself, adding the wish,
"Don't come near me, enemy flesh!"

It was her kinsmen's fault, neglectful
on seeing her homeless and without defense
at a time when the richest and most powerful,
fearing God and fleeing his pestilence
for their estates or somewhere habitable
where heaven would show more beneficence,
they abandoned her alone in this city
struggling with vicious necessity.

70

80

90

100

Whoever existed who would not have sinned,
trapped in such extremes of misery?
What Artemis would not have resigned,
what Roman Sempronia, what Valery?
And what of Lucretia so questioned,
would she not yield to vile reality?   110
What of Theban Timóquia, or lovely Sarah?
Would Ulysses's wife sell herself dearer?

Who, caught up in the final breath
of so turbulent and shocking a battle,
assisting sad, relentless death
in his harsh and savage ritual;
what nymph, alas, sharing Vesta's faith
in the potency of being virginal,
would not yield herself to the nearest stranger
so as not to die at the hands of hunger?   120

Ah, worthy spirit, the case is this,
to show mercy to a weak ewe, given
it won't be your pardon, but Christ's,
since He counsels us to forgive.
So in heaven on high, where God lists
a thoughtful ear, you will be loved;
reminding Him how he was abandoned
as father to the poor, and their friend.

Therefore, take note, my lord, of the need
to cut circumstance with a sharp wire,   130
for not cutting it opens the road
to the lust of the rude mariner.
And if, as I say, it is divided,
using knowledge in applying the law,
your greatness will be much extolled,
as the true product of your royal blood.

Consider, my lord, this is the lone girl
of an absent husband, his little one,
forsaken, and to this day very small,
far from home, unprotected and forlorn.   140

Drink, my lord, of mercy's phial;
care is your greatest attribution.
And if this moves you, I dare swear
all she petitions will be conceded her.

⊠ HYMN ⊠

⊠ **Vinde cá, meu tão certo secretário**

Come, my trusty writing desk,
always at hand for scribbling protests,
and paper for my pen to unburden its heart!
Madness we call it that simply existing
involves implacable and grotesque
fate, deaf to tears and all entreaty.
On a huge fire, we toss a little water;
and it sets a vocal torment ablaze
that should have no place in memory.
      We proclaim a fallen history   10
to God, the world, people, and to the breeze
in which I have confided many times
to as little purpose as my present chatter;
but I was born to commit blunders
and that this should be one is no wonder,
and though I am far from amending matters,
if I have erred in this I am not to blame.
I took refuge in a single axiom:
to speak is to err, freely, without censure.
Unhappy the man whose comforts are so meager!   20

I was long ago undeceived that protesting
could bring redress. But whoever suffers
is bound to complain if the pain is great.
So I did! But the cry that could offer
relief is itself feeble and exhausted,
and it is not through weeping that pain abates.

Who will provide, then, what dissipates
endless tears and infinite sighs,
proportionate to the soul's torment?
        But who could, at a given moment,   30
measure suffering with groans and tears?
In the end, I declared to that which taught
anger, grief, and their memory,
there is another pain, harsher and more obdurate.
Come and hear me, those who are desperate,
but scatter all who inhabit some tower
of ivory, with Hope as your passport,
because you reckon Love and Fate
have empowered you to comprehend,
and measure whatever grief they send.   40

When I emerged from the maternal tomb,
new to the world, unlucky stars
at once seized me for their own;
despite my free will, they did not choose
I should know good fortune's thousand forms
and I followed the worst by compulsion.
And so that a suitable desolation
should match my years, when I opened
my eyes as an infant, tenderly,
        they arranged that, diligently,   50
a blind child should open a wound.
My infant tears were already stirring
with amorous complaint.
The whimpering sounds I made in my cot
were already like sighs of regret.
Fate's compliance, as I was weaned,
was such, for example, that if the airs
that lulled me were of love's despair,
I would soon be sleeping naturally,
so attuned was I to melancholy.   60

My wet nurse was a wild beast, as destiny
scorned a mere woman should take
such a role for me, and was fulfilled.

I was so nurtured as to suck
amorous poison while yet a baby,
so at a greater age I would willingly
drink, and through habit it would not kill me.
Soon afterwards, I saw the likeness and trope
of that human beast, so exotic,
        so delicate and so toxic,   70
that suckled me at the breasts of hope,
of which later still I saw the original,
who, for all my imbecile conceits,
bore the absolute and paramount blame.
It seemed she had a human form
but irradiated some divine spirit.
It wore such a trembling profile
as if proudly anticipating the evil
in prospect; the shade was a creature
so vivid, it surpassed all the power of nature.   80

What fresh experiments in agony
had Love projected, that were not
merely tried on me, but executed!
Implacable hardships, as hot
appetite that empowers fancy,
confounded Love's very aim,
to see itself vexed and maimed;
here were fantastic shadows, conjured up
in presumptuous dreams;
        that happiness supreme   90
that is merely a painted utopia;
but the torment of being scorned,
as fantasies had driven me mad,
threw those deceptions into confusion;
how to prophesy, and know for certain
all was true as was prophesied,
and then recant it as being confounded;
giving to things seen a different end,
and concluding looking for reasons
where reasoning makes very little sense.   100

I don't know how I knowingly passed
under the influence of those rays flowing
subtly from her, through her eyes!
Little by little, they emerged all-powerful,
much as the dawn's veil of mist
is dispelled by the subtle wit of sunrise.
At length, her pure and lucid gaze
that leaves behind as inadequate
the normal tenets of loveliness,
        her sweet and piteous 110
shift of the eyes, suspending hearts,
became magic herbs that heaven
forced me to drink; and down the years
transformed me into another being,
so content with what I was seeing
that my very torments proved liars;
I placed the veil before my vision
disguising the harm that burgeoned—
so I grew, as one smothered
by the very means by which I matured. 120

For who could portray one's missing life,
forever displeased with what one was seeing,
and that far removed from where one was;
to talk not knowing what one was saying,
going no idea where and, without relief,
sighing without knowing of the cause?
For when that condition traumatized
me, and pain brewed in the waters of Tartarus
burst on my world to hurt supremely,
        then often I became 130
anger incarnate transformed to sorrows;
now in the fury of angry grief, I want
and I don't want to cease being love-sick,
to look to some other, out of sheer
revenge at my never-to-be-fulfilled desire,
though I'd suffer the more from such trickery;
but now, this grief-laden lament

for my former, sweet, pure torment
has power to convert such raving
into sorrowful tears of love.   140

What lonely excuses I sought in myself,
as gentle Love would not tolerate
blame in the one beloved, and how loved!
In the end, they were drugs to counterfeit
torment's fears, that instructed life
how to carry on while being deceived.
One part of such a life was lived
so that, if I knew a little contentment—
short-lived, imperfect, fearful, ingenuous—
          it could only be a source   150
of long-lasting and most bitter torment.
This enduring career of sadness,
these steps uselessly taken,
were quenching those ardent passions
that had had a place in my heart's caution,
in favor of amorous ways of thinking,
the source of my natural tenderness,
which, from a long habit of bitterness
no human power could allay,
were changed to a taste for melancholy.   160

After this style, my life was changed;
not by me, but by destiny's angry hand,
from which my course could in no way differ.
It made me abandon my native land,
crossing the wide ocean, amid dangers
that often threatened my very life,
at times subjected to the lawless fury
of Mars, who fixed me at once with his stare
so I should see and pluck his bitter yield
          (on my personal shield   170
you will see painted pernicious fire);
at times a traveler, free to wander,
seeing nations, languages, and customs,
various constellations, different types,

ordained to pursue with diligent steps
you, unjust Fortune, that consumes
the years, buoying up in the mind
hope with all the glitter of diamond
that once from the hand it tumbles,
becomes the fragile glass it most resembles.   180

My humanity failed me; in my first
danger, I saw the friendly people
as hostile; and in my second,
the land I had set foot in seemed lethal
as to breathe the very air was refused,
while time and the world were what in the end
I missed, with their tough and profound
secrets; being born, living, and throughout
life losing all that the world lends it,
              not being able to end it,   190
though it was often already forfeit!
In the end, Fortune had no ordeals,
nor dangers, nor dubious decisions,
injustices of the kind that old abuses
in the misrule of the world imposed
on other, more powerful men,
that I did not match, tied to the pillar
of my wretchedness, as the galling
persecution of a thousand separate harms
targeted me with their powerful arms.   200

I do not reckon these harms as one who,
after surviving some dreadful hurricane,
relives the event in a happy port;
for even now unsteady Fortune
will make me suffer some enormous blow,
such that I fear where to place my feet.
From the evil to come I do not retreat,
nor do I pretend dying would be good,
a matter for me beneath human sophistry;
              I lean, ultimately,   210
on the sovereign providence of God;

what I think and see, I sometimes treat
as consolation for so much injury.
But when my human eyes attend
to what happens, and cannot understand
without remembering years gone by,
the water I then drink, the bread I eat,
are sad tears I never defeat
without elaborating in my fantasy
wholly invented images of joy.   220

So that if it were possible to turn
time back, in the manner of memory,
to the vestiges of my earliest being
and, weaving afresh the old story
of my sweet follies, I should again
regard the sweet flowers of my spring
and recall the endless longing
that was then my greatest satisfaction,
seeing companionship, so light and easy,
        that, with another key,   230
opened my fresh imagination—
meadows, excursions, marvels,
beauty, the eyes, the tenderness,
grace, and gentleness, the ceremony,
the unfeigned friendship that shuns
all low, worldly, impure purpose
that I never knew with another individual . . .
Ah! Vain memories! How do you control
me, my feeble heart, that I can't discipline
these yearnings that are also in vain?   240

No more, song, no more; I could speak
effortlessly for a thousand years. And if your lot
is to be widely blamed, and heavily,
the sea's water, as they like to say,
can't be contained in a small pot.
Nor do I sing for courtesy's sake,
with a taste for praising, but to make

pure truths known about my former times.
Would to God that they were mere dreams!

◼ **Depois que Magalhães teve tecida**

After Pêro de Magalhães had composed
his brief history to elucidate
the little-known land of Santa Cruz,

wondering to whom it should be dedicated,
or through whose patronage he could defend
his work from any Zoilus who might sneer at it,

this matter occupying his lively mind,
a refreshing sleep overtook him, just before
the sun bringing the bright day dawned.

In his dream, Mars appears, kitted out for war,   10
brandishing an indignant lance,
intended to terrify anyone who saw,

and stating in a voice, deep and ominous,
"It is not appropriate to dedicate to anyone
a work that could turn out to be famous,

except one whose name and fame are known
throughout the world for his martial deeds,
earning him deathless approbation."

At this pronouncement, Apollo, who guides
the sun's celestial chariot, also appears,   20
addressing him as he pronounced these words:

"Magalhães, no matter how Mars
makes you tremble with his terrors, you must
let me be first among your mentors.

"Some wise authority that Thalia trusts
with her comedy, along with my own science,
should be the one to promote your Brazilian digest.

"It's appropriate writing should find its defense
in wisdom, for a battle's uproar
is the very antithesis of eloquence."   30

So he spoke, and striking with rare
skill his golden lyre, he off-
set the power of the god of war.

But Mercury, who spent much of his life
adjudicating quarrels, most of them dubious,
with his customary serpent-twined staff,

was resolved on pacifying the dangerous
disagreement of the hostile gods
with arguments both rational and courteous.

"We all know about ancient heroes," he said,   40
"and those of the present day who weathered
grave Belona's most fearful odds,

"but have also regularly brought together
arms and eloquence, given the muses
have accompanied countless captains to war.

"Alexander and Caesar, however confused
their battlefields, always found time to enquire,
while in strategy science has its uses.

"In the one hand books, in the other steel and fire;
the one guides and instructs, the other bruises;   50
but knowledge and a mighty arm both conquer.

"Therefore, Apollo, if you wish to choose
some man of whose qualities to be proud,
while you expect palms and glory, mighty Mars,

"I will name you a hero, visibly endowed
with wisdom and courage in a steady heart:
it is Don Leonis, universally envied.

"As they recognized in him a fine recruit,
all nine Muses took him in their arms,
suckling him in his earliest cot.   60

"They taught all the arts along with wisdom,
implanting a heavenly disposition
through the moral virtues that adorn him.

"Thereafter, he took a soldier's station
in the distant Orient, made amiable
from the first by his vocation.

"There he gave clear proofs of his noble
descent, of Christian magnanimity
and steadiness in his self-control.

"Afterwards, a captain in his maturity,   70
governor of the peninsula of Malacca,
his arm atoned for the rampart's insufficiency,

"for when he saw encircling and ready to attack
all the army of Aceh, conniving
with foreign allies, being on the wrack,

"he alone, in your very image, Mars, contrived
to punish them in such manner the defeated
were content to escape with their lives.

"The kingdom's defenses being now complete,
he was elected governor for a second   80
term, serving with yet greater credit;

"the memories persisting, among friends
of a truly lenient governor, among
enemies of his victory's deep wound,

"the former with genuine love longing
for his quick restitution, the latter
cold with fear of him and trembling.

"Contemplate how they will be scattered
by his arm, should he return once more,
and throughout the Indian Ocean lose caste!   90

"For it's fitting no one should ignore
the favor of the gods on high Olympus
and their help in pursuing this war.

"So, in this matter to whom to address
Magalhães' book, it's beyond doubt
Don Leonis, gods, should be your choice."

So Mercury pronounced; and without
disagreement, from that pleasant sleep, Mars
and Apollo made their joint exit.

Magalhães awoke, and on the instant offered   100
you, famous Sir, all his combined art
and science in a division of labor.

It has a lucid style and a curious wit,
and deserves you should do him honor
with an ungrudging hand and a loving spirit.

A bright genius can remain obscure
if he fails to find some generous backer;
so defend him with all your power
like that feeble rampart at Malacca.

⊞ ECLOGUE ⊞

⊞ A Rústica contenda desueda

Alieuto   *Agrário*

That time-honored rural contest
between the Muses of the woods and the beaches,
sung melodiously by mutual specialists

whose unfamiliar sounds reached
and astonished the mountain's white cattle
and the river lampreys in their stony reaches,

it's my ambition once again to make vital,
such as moved trees and the shepherds' reeds,
as forest creatures suspended their rituals,

not ignoring the fishermen's serenades   10
pacifying the ocean's restless waves
while the fish swimming mutely overheard.

And if, amid rough work, blind Love
occupies himself by inflaming the soul
where calm and tranquility have their haven,

Rumor's voice finds it yet more remarkable
that on the undulating sea amid cold winds
his purple passion lights its purple coal.

You, Sir, branch of a tree whose fronds
already spread their leafy shade   20
over all Lusitania's cattle and lands,

and whose Sacred Cross already ventured
to cast its strong and ample nets
in the furthest seas man ever surveyed;

you, whose gallantry so utterly bests
all praise, in however divine a style,
the fount of Parnassus is driven to thirst;

I heard you elevate my feeble
song, so inspiring its harmonies
you made its making worthwhile.   30

If now, bending your ear in courtesy,
you don't hear the sound of battle trumpets
that the world burnished by you owes,

if, though your royal ancestors crumpled
the defenses of Mauritania's kings,
you don't hear exalted, soaring numbers,

if pastoral flutes have no skill in painting
the battlefield of Toro, sown
with arms and strong men of good breeding,

inspired by a matchless young man   40
against all Spain's indomitable father,
against fate's injustice and vain fortune,

a prince whose strength, spirit, and culture
made iron Mars descend from Olympus
to make him a companion of the fifth sphere;

if they can't devise the smallest praise
of your wise heart and statesman's demeanor
to give you, illustrious ruler, repose;

a full-blooded heart, which made Apollo retire
from the sacred mountain, while the sisterly nine   50
said it affected them as in a mirror,

their skill being only to sing the mundane
contest of Alieuto and simple Agrario,
one dressed in scales, the other in sheepskin;

you'll hear, serene duke, a sweet delivery,
novel to us, but devised on another shore
by one who was merely the Muses' secretary;

the fisherman Sanazzaro, whose vernacular
calmed storms in the Gulf of Naples,
the sonorous waves providing his meter.   60

Following this sound of such potential,
and blending it with the ancient Mantuan,
we forge a new style and fresh marvels.

Agrario in a rage abandoned the mountain,
where only the power of thought
could support the weight of being human,

intoxicated enough to forget
himself, his cattle, and meager flock
after such a vision of tender delight;

through horrid brambles he hacks   70
his way across the boulders of the summit,
fleeing, in short, all human contact.

Before his eyes the smiling eyes of white
Dinamene appear, giving life
by her gestures alone to the valleys and heights.

Now he laughs to himself, as he weaves
in fantasy some imaginary pleasure;
now he speaks, now he mutely grieves.

So it would be if a tender heifer
that has scoured the mountains and the wood   80
hunting for her broad-horned partner

should fling herself down, exhausted,
in the lush greenery beside an inlet
as swiftly the evening shadows crowd,

and not even nightfall bids her mate
remember to return, as he is bound,
to her, abandoned by her consort;

so Agrario came to where he discerned
the vast, heaving ocean as it hissed
on a cold beach of glistening sand.   90

As this perplexing sea drew his eyes
he heard, from far off, played by a skilled
but invisible hand, a new strain of verse,

and being by this unfamiliar sound compelled,
he turned to where it was loudest, ready
to listen and converse and be thrilled.

He had taken only a few strides
when, in a small cave in a cliff-face
that the sea had little by little eroded,

he found a fisherman seated motionless   100
on a rock, who with gentle, skillful strokes
was making the tranquil sea rejoice.

He was a youth plainly of vigorous stock,
tall for a fisherman, and known
personally to all the ocean-going folk.

Alieuto is his name, and his passion
the beautiful nymph Lemnoria,
she who gives dignity to the ocean.

Night and day he casts his nets for her,
for her he scorns the advancing rollers,   110
both heat and hail endures for her.

With her name, woven in soft numbers,
he has pacified a thousand gales,
softening the very boulders,

and now, in a terse and fluent style,
it is his name that instructs the echoes
in a strain other than the pastoral;

at which the astonished Agrario, still engrossed
partially in dreams of his own passion,
was spell-bound, hearing the different measures.   120

But Alieuto, noting this interruption
by one who herds the music of the gods,
and glancing up with a calm expression,

said, "Cowman of the pastures and woods,
what brings you to these sandy beaches
where lovely Amphitrite alone presides?

"What cause, shepherd, makes you approach
this vile and scaly land of ours,
quitting your fresh myrtles and tall beeches?

"For if the sea you observe has abandoned its wars   130
and its waves are spreading on the sand,
assuaged by my grief's salt tears,

"you'll soon see Aeolus unbridle the winds,
whipping the waves to such a pitch
that Neptune himself feels threatened."

Agrario replies, "O mellifluous, bewitched
fisherman, I'm not here to watch your lagoon
change mood as the winds sigh or screech;

"I was drifting, quenching with reason's
aid the flames of an old desire,   140
but deaf, abstracted, without vision,

"until aroused by the sheer euphoria
of your angelic harmonies, in praise
of your perilous Lemnoria.

"But if seeing me here surprises
you, I am also shaken by this new style
with which you bridle the raucous seas,

"and though I approve and applaud, it's my will,
as no more than a feeble mimic,
to test it against my woodland pastoral.   150

"And you, being plainly a master of music,
can judge if there's indeed clear water
between the maritime and the bucolic."

"I have no objection," said Alieuto,
"but before I'm transported, I'm well aware
your assurance alone will emerge the better.

"But so you should know we fishermen bear
towards shepherds no envious rivalry
in that sound the whole world must desire,

"take the harp in your hand, for I observe   160
creatures that dwell in the transparent depths
gathering to hear of our rustic loves.

"You can seem them on the beach, palpable
to human view in their multicolored shells,
with the sea between them, rippling.

"Secure from the fury of the gales,
there are little swirls in the pleasant river
where the fresh water meets with the saline.

"This concave boulder you see covered
with crabs will give us cool and quiet   170
lodging from the sun's fever.

"All induces, then, peace of mind and invites
us to song, at which dumb fish
are leaping in the open air to take note."

So those rustic poets prepare to clash,
contrasting in their livelihoods,
but in their talents subtle and accomplished.

And already there are vast crowds
surrounding them to listen and make
to the winner the appropriate rewards,   180

as straightaway the harps are struck;
Agrario commenced, and the fishermen
all wondered at the rich music;
then in response, Alieuto took his turn.

Agrario

You Centaurs of the highest passes,
Dryads, long-lived Fawns, and Satyrs,
you gods of the woods and bright Parnassus,
or of those trees where you spend long years,
if you bend a little your sacred faces
to our rustic, all-too-human verses,   190
either award me a laurel crown
or hang my harp on the nearest pine.

Alieuto

You watery deities of the ocean,
cerulean Tritons, and Palaemon with Proteus,
and you Nereids of the salt I sail on,
undaunted by the gale's furies,
if I never deny, on my oar's fin,
wriggling congers for your rich altars,
don't vouchsafe any other should usurp
your sea-going singer with his harp.   200

Agrario

He once turned shepherd, blond Apollo,
who drives and steers the chariot of the sun;
the river Anphrisus heard his harp of gold
as he played there on his own invention.
Io was a cow, Jupiter a bull;
gentle ewes guarded handsome Adonis
by the cold river; and Neptune himself
was once found changed to a bull calf.

Alieuto

Glaucus was a fisherman, now in turn
a sea-god, and Proteus herded seals.   210
Ocean-born, too, was the goddess who governs
amorous pleasure, which predictably fails.
If once a bull, he was also a dolphin,
that god the oceans adore; and recall
that young fishermen were the ones to deliver
that baffling riddle to the poet Homer.

Agrario

Lovely Dinamene, if once I stole
sweet Philomene's naked fledglings
from their nest, and berries from the myrtle—
all for you, wild one! I went gathering   220
flowers, and if you found so acceptable
those mottled strawberries I would bring,
why not bestow on wretched Agrario
one glance from those eyes so free with sorrow?

Alieuto

For whom do I bring hook-shaped prawns,
fresh and wriggling in water-pots;
for whom do I dig the exposed dunes,
red clams and white whelks my harvest;
for whom, diving in remote oceans

do I tear branched coral with my fists,   230
if not for the beautiful Lemnoria,
one smile from whom is my ultimate cure?

Agrario

Whoever saw winter, raw and wind-blown,
dressed in deep snow-drifts, at its most odious,
obscuring the bright face of heaven;
while the flooding river uproots trees,
a hell of thunder, lightning, and rain,
showing the world its most dreaded face;
such is envy, in one who comes to believe
some other is profiting from all his love.   240

Alieuto

Should anyone survive a strident
storm at its height, with fire and clangor,
with mountainous waves pursuant,
dreadful to see, dreadful to hear,
the force released by smashed elements
crushing this revolving sphere;
so appears the appropriate trope
for that sudden seeing that kills all hope.

Agrario

My bright Dinamene, spring days
that paint and clothe the charming meadow,   250
and, smiling, lend color to those eyes
that repeat on earth heaven's rainbows;
the scents, the roses, the green ivy
with all their pleasant rural glow,
all to my eyes are not half so lovely
as yours that outshine rose and lily.

Alieuto

The little shells of the beach giving up
the colors of first light in the east;
the Sirens' song that lulls to sleep;
mother-of-pearl inside the oyster;   260
to sail oceans full of hope
with a gentle breeze in a cool siesta,
cannot, my nymph, so fully please me
as to see you, some hour, happy to see me.

Agrario

The goddess Minerva, who first appeared
in virginal form in that Libyan lake
whose name she adopted, so much revered,
has eyes that are sky-blue, or much like;
greenish-blue they are; but one empowered
to be crowned queen of all that's rustic   270
has eyes like the meadow grass in color.
Who says they are not far lovelier?

Alieuto

Sea-gods, forgive me; but you, Venus,
by whom the marbled sea was pregnant,
the living, heavenly light of your eyes
has acquired, through love's vices, a squint—
"cross-eyed," we call it; but a simple shepherdess,
tranquil, and more than the day lucent,
draw mine from yours, there's no denying,
and the upshot is, I am blind.   280

So sang the two adepts, from the sea shore
and the mountain, to the fishermen
and the shepherds, and then they sang no more;

and each group gave its poet a crown
of lovely and appropriate materials,
which the nymphs had procured and woven;

for Agrario, roses and myrtles;
for Alieuto, a chain of spiral whelks,
along with lustrous, crimson shells.

The fish protruding at the brink,   290
their heads on the sand, were bemused;
the musical dolphins were drunk.

The shepherds from the hills chose
the old song as without parallel;
to claim otherwise wronged the Muses.

The fishermen thought their rival
poet had just the same sonorous flutes
as were heard in the old Mantuan pastoral.

But now the one-time shepherd to Admetus
was plunging his chariot in the salt ocean,   300
extinguishing the last, brief, purple glints,
the day concluding, like the competition.

▥ SONG ▥

▥ Sóbolos rios que vão

By the rivers that flow through
Babylon I found myself,
there I sat down and wept
at the memory of Zion,
and all I experienced there.
At this a fresh river streamed
copiously from my eyes
as everything stood in contrast—
Babylon, the dreadful present,
and Zion, the time past.   10

Images of happier days
were brought before my mind,

and memories from other times
rose up so vividly
as if they had never faded.
Awakening there each dawn,
my face bathed in water,
I saw my morning dreams
dissolve, as the past
became pain, not pleasure.   20

There I saw that all the harm
was brought about by change,
and change by the passing years—
I saw how swiftly time
cheated the best endeavors.
There I saw what little room
existed for the greater good,
how swiftly evil descended,
and how sad the outcome
of those trusting to hazard.   30

Those of the very highest merit,
in a better understanding,
became the most accursed;
I saw the good inherit
evil, and from evil worse.
I watched enormous effort
spent in purchasing regret.
I saw not one contented mind,
and I watch myself scattering
sad words to the wind.   40

Full as rivers are the tears
with which I bathe this paper;
and cruel indeed appears
all the sad confusion
and varied grief of Babylon.
Like a man who,
returning from war
after fearing for his life,

will hang up his armor
on the walls of the temple: 50

in the same way, recording
all that time had despoiled,
out of my gathered sadness
I hung upon the willows
the pipes I once sang to.
That cheerful instrument
of my former life, I quit,
saying, music, my first love,
as sacred monument
I surrender you to this grove.   60

My flute that, when fingered,
coaxed the very mountains
to come skipping in your track,
while rivers in their sliding
on the instant turned back;
tigers could not attend to you
without becoming tamed,
while sheep in their clover
gorging themselves, when they
heard your notes, abstained.   70

No more with gentle melody
along the flowering riverbank
will you coax thorns into roses;
nor will you dam the flow,
least of all from my eyes.
No more will you charm forests,
or be gifted to call
fresh springs in your wake,
powerless to control
the cacophony of fate.   80

Be an offering to fame
guarding forever over you,
my flute, my mistress;
for as life advances,

its pleasures are never the same.
The tender adolescent finds
congenial pursuits,
but growing a little older
soon abandons as trifles
those outmoded delights.   90

The style that today's the vogue
tomorrow is mere foppery;
so mutability drives us
from hope to hope,
and from desire to desire.
But in such a febrile existence,
what can be relied on?
O the frailty of human breath,
which even as life continues
rehearses our death!   100

But moving on in this forest
from youth's tuneful refuge,
the young never contemplate
what will be the work of age,
what the power of fate.
Given age, time, and the shock
of time passing so rapidly,
nothing weighs heavier with me
than, abandoning the song,
the necessity of moving on.   110

But, in sadness and discontent,
in pleasure and satisfaction,
in sun or storm or winter snows,
tendré presente á los ojos
por quiem muero tan contento.
My pipes and flute, my dearest
possessions, I bequeath
to the willow that grows there,
to remain as the trophy
of the one who conquered me.   120

But thoughts of the passion
that once held me captive
put to me the question:
what of the songs
I used to sing in Zion?
What was the point of singing
of a people so renowned?
Why did I not continue,
for it was always help in enduring
whatever work was at hand.   130

The cheerful traveler sings
on the arduous track
through the dense, gloomy forest;
and the timorous, after dark,
with a song conquers his trembling.
The prisoner sings to himself,
while tapping the iron bars;
so, too, the happy harvester,
and through singing, the workers
are less fatigued by their task.   140

What will they say, I responded,
that, overwhelmed as I am,
my heart consumed with grief,
I am so foreign to myself
as to sing in an alien land?
How can anyone sing
whose heart's awash with tears?
Though there may be some worker
who sings to be less weary,
I am beyond comforting.   150

What seems neither right
nor in any way fitting
is that, just to calm my heart,
I should raise in Babylon
the anthems of Zion.
Or that when the heavy weight

of past regret enfeebles
my health, that vital fortress,
that before dying of sadness
I should sing to mitigate it.   160

If our tenuous thoughts
are composed of mere sadness,
I have no fear of torment;
to die of pure regret—
what could be greater happiness?
Nor will I sing to my flute
what I've endured and endure;
still less will I write,
because my pen will tire
and my pain never quit.   170

For if a life so circumscribed
is expended in a foreign land,
and if Love should so ordain it,
it's only right my quill
should weary of transcribing pain.
If, however, in recording
my heartfelt agony,
my quill soon falters,
it doesn't tire of soaring
at the glad thought of Zion.   180

Land of such happy fortune,
if through some perversion
of my soul you should change,
let my pen be sentenced
to perpetual oblivion.
I would rather see the pain
of my exile sculpted
in stone or obdurate iron
then my error's sentence
would be carried out unheard.   190

And if I seek to sing
while still subject to Babylon,

without remembering you, Jerusalem,
let my voice, as I begin,
turn to ice in my ribs.
Let my tongue cleave
to my palate, forfeiting
you, if at any time
while I am yet alive
I deny you or forget you.   200

But you, O land of glory,
if I never glimpsed your essence,
how do you recall me in my absence?
With you I have no history,
except in reminiscence.
For the soul is a *tabula rasa*
that, inscribed with doctrine,
so fully imagines heaven
that it flees its individual house
and climbs to its divine home.   210

So the soul does not yearn
for the land where it was born
in the flesh, but for heaven,
for that holy city
from which it first descended.
And those fleshly traits
that alter at every moment
are not worth thinking of;
it is the beam of perfect beauty
that alone deserves our love.   220

For the eyes and the light that kindles
the passions to which we are subject,
not the sun but the candle,
are the shadows of that idea
which in God is made perfect,
while what holds me prisoner
are those powerful affections
that captivate our hearts,

mere sophists that direct me
not in the right roads but false ones.   230

These hold inexorable power,
compelling me, like one raving,
to sing, to the sound of destruction,
not anthems of divine love
but ballads of profane desire
Yet I, purified by a sacred
ray, in a Babylon of sorrow,
of shock and confusion,
how should I sing the song
that belongs only to the Lord?   240

Such a blessing is divinely due
to grace that confers wholeness,
ordaining that life changes,
and so I, committed to evil ways,
take a step toward virtue,
and make love, which is natural
and confers such delight,
soar from the shadow to the real,
from the beauty of the individual
to beauty in general.   250

So let it remain suspended,
the flute I played formerly,
O Jerusalem the sacred,
while I take up the golden lyre
to sing solely of you—
not as a prisoner chained
in infernal Babylon,
but delivered from wrongdoing,
and raised above it toward you,
my natural fatherland.   260

And if I must still resign myself
to this earthly lottery,
so exacting and oppressive,
much is already blotted out

from the book of humankind.
And so now as I take in hand
my sacred lyre, well-attuned
to a higher invention,
may I silence this madness,
may I sing the vision of peace.   270

Hear me, shepherd and king,
re-echo the holy mode,
moving the world to astonishment,
as to all I formerly sang amiss
I now sing the Palinode.
To you alone I wish to journey,
Lord and great Captain
of the high keep of Zion,
to which I cannot hope to ascend
unless you take my hand.   280

That unique day of praise
that I endow the lyre with a voice
to celebrate Jerusalem,
I will remind you to chastise
the wretched sons of Edom.
Those that are drenched crimson
in the innocent blood of the poor,
arrogant in their power,
I will tread them down
so they know they are only human.   290

And the force of those powerful
passions that attend me,
inflaming my heart and imagination,
that breach the defenses
of my inborn free will;
those evil, destructive spirits
that rush with their war-cries
to scale me, determined
in their mindless fury
to raze me to the ground;   300

I will demolish and expose them,
leaving them fearful and weak, for
neither through them may we come
to you, nor without you tear
ourselves from them.
My frailty will not suffice
to build my own defenses
if you, my sacred Captain,
here within this fortress
do not provide the garrison.   310

And you, Babylonian whore,
the flesh that bewitches,
source of all wretchedness,
rising up a thousand times
against whoever masters you;
happy alone that man can be
who, with the help of heaven,
prevails against you,
and returns to you the harm
you formerly did to him;   320

who, with rigid self-control,
flogs himself regularly,
whose spirit, stripped of vices,
marks on his flesh the scars
the flesh first made on his soul;
and happy is the man who takes
his latest daydreams
and stifles them at birth,
so as not to see them culminate
in serious, compounding crimes;   330

who dashes them instantly
on the stone of holy zeal,
casting them down

on that rock ordained to be
the chief cornerstone;
who, when his mind is seduced
by carnal obscenities,
turns his thoughts immediately
to that sacred body
that was hung upon the cross;   340

who, from his contentment
with this world of the visible
(so far as for man this is possible),
proceeds in his understanding
to the world of the ideal.
There he will encounter happiness,
complete in everything, and perfect,
its sweet harmony
that lacks nothing in particulars,
nor satiates with excess.   350

There will he find mystery
in its most profound epitome,
and, triumphing over nature,
condemn as merely idle
the great pageant of the world.
O you, happy dwelling,
my only native land,
if merely imagining you
so enlarges understanding, what
in heaven will my arrival do?   360

And happy is he who departs
for you, excellent city,
justly and in penitence,
and after such ascension
rests there eternally.

⊠ Arde por Galateia branca e loura

He burned for Galateia with her golden hair,
poor Sereno, fisherman, fettered
to a penniless death by his cruel star.

Other fishermen had cast their nets
in the Tagus; he alone was flinging
to the heedless winds this complaint:

"When, beautiful nymph, will there spring
the day you pinpoint an exact cause
for our insane and useless quarrelling?

"Don't you see how my soul wearies,   10
hanging on your lips for a single smile
or some gentle harvest from your blue eyes?

"If my ardor recalls some past trouble,
Galateia, that has left its imprint,
what can you lose by this removal?

"I gave you my soul; you purloined it;
I don't ask for it back; just give me instead
one glance from eyes so indifferent.

"If this seems excessive, and my stars forbid
so blessed and prosperous a harbor,   20
I award you the wings Love forfeited.

"What more, lovely nymph, can I offer,
though the sea should scatter pearls
the length of this happy, gracious shore?

"The waves subside, the wind's anger fails;
only my torment knows no rest;
the heart burns vainly, its sighs no avail.

"At daybreak comes the blind mist
over the luxuriant hills of Arrabida,
as the sun's rays are effaced.   30

"I see other, lovelier rays appear,
stealing grace and color from the sky;
they leave my sightless eyes still sadder.

"How often the waves have reared at my sighs!
How many times, in my mourning,
have they halted with grief to hear me!

"If raising my voice, reinforced by pain,
to the sound of my oar plashing the water,
I sing of my heartache to the distant moon,

"as the tender dolphins overhear;   40
the night is peaceful, the sea still—
Galateia alone swims off with laughter.

"You find strange, perhaps, this feeble
net ringing the sea, my boat at the wind's mercy,
and a poor fisherman here propelled?

"Before the sun revolves once in the sky
it could well improve my fortune,
as happens to others in the tumbling sea.

"Beauty's fair price is not that golden
dust the Tagus deposits on its sands,   50
but a devotion that is evergreen.

"Turn your eyes, lovely nymph, to that strand;
you'll see written in the sand *Galateia*,
well above where the sea's fury extends,

"and unaffected by winds or the still air.
I wrote it three days since, and tethered
Love to guard it from any alien power.

"He with his own hands helped to gather
this yield for you alone, shell
by red shell, stringing them together.   60

[329]

"I picked you a branch of soft coral;
even before I surfaced, I knew
your soft mouth was my all in all.
Happy some day it should be so!"

▦ SESTINA ▦

▦ Foge-me pouco a pouco a curta vida

Little by little it ebbs, this life,
if by any chance I am still alive;
my brief time passes before my eyes.
I mourn the past in whatever I say;
as each day passes, step by step
my youth deserts me—what persists is pain.

And what a bitter variety of pain,
that not for an hour in so long a life
could I give evil so much as a side step!
Surely, I'm better dead than alive?   10
Why complain, at last? What's more to say,
having failed to be cheated by my own eyes?

Those lovely, gentle, and lucid eyes,
whose absence caused me as much pain
as her not understanding whatever I say,
if, at the end of so long a short life,
you should keep the burning ray alive,
blessings will attend my every step.

But first I'm aware the ultimate step
must advance to close these sad eyes   20
Love opened to those by which I live.
Pen and ink must bear witness to the pain
in writing of so troublesome a life,
the little I lived through, and the more I say.

O, I know not why I write or what I say!
If contemplating yet another step
I envisage a sad version of life
that places no value on such eyes,
I cannot conceive how such pain
could find a pen to declare I'm alive.   30

In my heart, the embers are still alive;
if they found no relief in what I say,
they would now have made ashes of my pain,
but beyond this grief I overstep—
I'm softened by the tears of those eyes
that, though life is fleeting, keep me alive.

I am dying alive,
in death I live;
I see without eyes,
tongueless I speak;   40
they march in goose step,
glory and pain.

❖ NOTES TO THE POEMS ❖

PART ONE: *Before Africa*

25, "Eu cantarei do amor tão docemente": a version of Petrarch's "Io canterei d'amor si novamente."

26, "Tanto de meu estado me acho incerto": a version of Petrarch's "Pace non trovo, e non ò da far guerra."

26, "Amor é um fogo que arde sem se ver": another version of Petrarch's "Io canterei d'amor si novamente."

27, "O fogo que na branda cera ardia": compare the song "Aquele rosto que traz," p. 50, describing a similar incident in which a lady's face is scorched by a candle flame, and naming her in the epigraph as Dona Guiomar de Blasfé.

31, "Num jardim adornado de verdure": in line 14, the play is on the words "violante" and "viola antes."

34, "O culto divino se celebrava": traditionally read as describing Camões's first sight of Dona Catarina de Ataíde, in the Chagas Church in Lisbon, on the model of Petrarch's first glimpse of Laura in his sonnet "Era il giorno ch'al sol si scoloraro."

38, "Senhora, se eu alcançasse": in line 21, Camões puns on "pena," meaning both "quill"—hence a pen—and "pain." This complex pun occurs routinely when he is "writing" of "suffering" and his poetry "soars."

39, "Este tempo vão": Sá de Miranda, Andrade Caminha, Frei Augusto da Cruz, Leitão de Andrade, and D. Francisco de Portugal, Camões's near-contemporaries, all have poems glossing the same song.

41, "Nos seus olhos belos": one of the freshest and most charming of Camões's Vilancetes, a courtly poem in a pastoral style.

42, "Dotou em vós Natureza": the first of a series addressed to "the girl with green eyes" in an age when blue eyes were considered most beautiful. The language is playful and teasing, suggesting she was very young.

47, "Eles verdes são": green eyes again, with a running pun on "verdes" (adj., green) and "verdes" (derived from "ver," to see)

49, "Quem põe suas confianças": here, as elsewhere, Camões puns on "menina," meaning both "young girl" and "pupil of the eye."

50, "Aquele rosto que traz": see note on "O fogo que na branda cera ardia," above.

56, "Pues me distes tal herida": this and the two following songs, "Desque uma vez mire" and "Tiempo perdido es aquel," are from the Spanish.

57, "Aquele mover dos olhos excelente": published as Elegy IV in *Rimas* 1595, though its tone is not elegiac. The sonnet "Um mover d'olhos, brando e piadoso," p. 98, is similar in theme.

59, "Já a roxa manhã clara": Camões's ten Hymns (*Canções*), eight of which are collected here, are his most elaborately sculptured poems. Formally, with their long stanzas and lines of varying length, they owe a debt to Petrarch's *Canzoniere*.

61, "Fermosa fera humana": an ode, loosely modeled on the Roman poets Catullus and Propertius, with deliberate echoes of Horace and Ovid, coldly warning his "Circe" that she should not play fast and loose with love. The list of classical examples to illustrate a theme is one of Camões's favorite devices.

line 7: Circe: the sorceress who turns Odysseus's men to swine in book 10 of the Odyssey.

37: Flora: Pompey's mistress, "weeping for her captain" after his defeat and death at the battle of Pharsalus in Thessaly.

44: Sappho: the Greek poetess, born in Lesbos. One of many legends declares that for love of Phaon, who repulsed her, she threw herself from the rock of Leucas, off the coast of Epirus. Phaon had been granted youth and beauty by Aphrodite when he carried her, disguised as an old woman, in his boat without demanding payment.

64, "As doces cantilenas que cantavam": Camões's early eclogues have an air of extended poetic exercises, displaying his intricate knowledge of Ovid's *Metamorphoses*, but with no larger purpose than to amuse friends at court and, perhaps, win patronage. It's possible some of the details refer to people and events obscure to modern readers; for instance, the nymphs mentioned in lines 103–6 might be attempts to flatter certain ladies at the court of the infanta Dona Maria.

Dedication: Dom António de Noronha is also dedicatee of the elegy "Aquela que de amor descomedido," p. 86, while the eclogue "Que grande variedade vão fazendo," p. 199, was composed partly in response to his death in Africa. No one knows for sure who he was, other than a trusted friend, and a young courtier in a position to improve Camões's circumstances.

line 14: Pegasus: the horse that with a stamp of its hoof struck open the fountain of Hippocrene, sacred to the Muses, on Mount Helicon.

16: Parnassus: a high mountain north of Delphi, associated with the worship of Apollo and the Muses.

26: Procne avenged her sister Philomela after she had been raped by Tereus, her husband and king of Thrace. The women were transformed into a swallow and a nightingale, respectively.

28: Galateia: one of Camões's favorite nymphs, borrowed from Theocritus. She is still present in "Arde por Galateia, branca e loura," p. 328, one of his final poems.

30: Tityrus: a shepherd in Virgil's pastorals.

100: Dinamene and Efire: recurring nymphs in Camões's poems. For Dinamene, see the introduction, p. 16. Efire is the nymph pursued by Leonard in canto 9: 75–82, of The Lusíads.

103: Syrinx and Nise: further recurring nymphs. Syrinx was pursued by Pan and changed to a reed to escape him, giving her name to Pan's pipe of seven reeds. Nise, perhaps an anagram of Ines, is elsewhere a shepherdess. See also the sonnets "O raio cristalino s'estendia" and "Apartava-se Nise de Montano," p. 166.

106: Daliana and Belisa: perhaps referring to ladies-in-waiting at Dona Maria's court.

127: Cyprian Cupid: Cyprus is one of the islands where Venus, Cupid's mother, was said to have been born.

174: Eurydice: died from snakebite when fleeing Aristaeus.

176: Hespere: one of the three Hesperides, living in the far western orchard that Earth gave to Hera.

256: Arachne: challenged Athene to a contest in weaving, her tapestry depicting the love affairs of the gods.

301: Alpheus: a river god who pursued Arethusa under the sea to Syracuse, mixing his waters with hers when she was turned by Artemis into a fountain.

304: Acis: a youth loved by the nymph Galateia, loved in turn by Polyphemus, who crushed him under a boulder, creating the Acis River in Sicily.

309–11: Egeria and Numa: Numa, loved by Egeria, a goddess of fountains, succeeded Romulus as king of Rome.

312: Byblis: fell in love with her brother and, fleeing to avoid incest, became a river watering the meadows.

320–24: Leteia and Oleno: Leteia believed herself more beautiful than any goddess and was punished, along with her husband, Oleno, by being turned into boulders on Mount Ida. See also the sonnet "Em fermosa Leteia se confia," p. 168.

324: Iphis: hanged himself for love of the nymph Anaxarete. Venus avenged him by turning her into a block of marble.

326: "the lovely nymph": Echo, punished by Hera (Juno) with the loss of her voice for entertaining her with stories while Zeus's concubines made their escape.

330: Daphnis: Sicilian shepherd, legendary inventor of pastoral verse, blinded by the nymph Chloë for infidelity, but continued to love her and was turned to stone.

340–47: Pyramus and Thisbe: Babylonian lovers, forbidden by their parents to marry. Arranging to meet by the tomb of Ninus, Thisbe arrived first and was attacked by a lion, taking refuge in a cave. Pyramus, finding her blood-stained veil, assumed she was dead. Mutual suicides ensued, their combined blood watering a mulberry tree, whose berries, hitherto white, have since been red.

348: Sabeya: in Arabia, where Myrrha, after committing incest with her father, Cinyras̀, and giving birth to Adonis, was turned into the fragrant shrub of the same name.

352–55: The references are to Daphne, turned to a laurel, and Cyper-esso, turned into a Cypress, both to escape Apollo who afterward watered both trees with his tears.

356–71: Attis, punished, perhaps for infidelity to Sibele, perhaps for violating his vow of chastity, by being turned into a pine tree. In another version of the myth, Attis castrates himself out of devotion to Sibele. See also the sonnet "Despois que viu Cibele o corpo humano," p. 283.

372–85: The references are to feasting in honor of Bacchus on Mount Lycaeus in Arcadia, sacred to Pan, and to Lotus, who, after her seduction by Priapus, god of the Hellespont, was turned into the flower that bears her name.

386: A further reference to Syrinx (see note to l. 103, above).

388–95: Phyllis: hanged herself in despair at Demofonte's long absence and was turned into an almond tree, which he embraced when at last he returned.

396: Jacinto: loved by Apollo but equally by Zepherus, god of the west wind, who killed her through jealousy. Apollo turned her into a daisy.

400: The reference is to Adonis, loved by Venus and killed by a boar, the drops of his blood sprouting anemones.

404: Clicie: loved Apollo, was forced to suffer his infidelities, and became a sunflower, her face turning constantly to the sun's course.

428: See note to l. 26, above.

436–41: The references are to Coronis, whom Pallas Athene rejected for talking too much and who became a crow, and her successor Nictimene, who committed incest with her father and became an owl.

442: Scila: daughter of Nico, king of Thebes, who betrayed her father to his greatest enemy and became a skylark.

444: Picus: rejected Circe's love and was turned by her into a woodpecker.

446: Esacus: drowned himself for love.

448–54: "two most constant lovers": Alcyone: daughter of Aeolus, god of the winds, and wife of Ceyx, whose drowned body she found on the beach. Both became kingfishers.

472–75: Atalanta and Hippomenes used Sibele's temple as a refuge for love-making and for this desecration were turned into lions.

476–83: A single stanza deploys three myths: that of Io, loved by Jupiter and turned into a cow to protect her from Juno's wrath; of Calisto, turned by Juno into a bear as punishment for her affair with Jupiter, and by Jupiter into the Great Bear constellation; and to Actaeon, the hunter, who witnessed Diana bathing and was turned by her into a stag and subsequently devoured by his own hunting dogs. The two subsequent stanzas describe his fate. See also canto 2, 35 and canto 9, 26, of *The Lusíads*.

80, "O Sulmonense Ovídio, desterrado": the first of Camões's poems of exile, and the first to turn for inspiration from Ovid's *Metamorphoses* to his *Tristia* and *Black Sea Letters*. Ovid, born in Sulmona in the Abruzzi, was exiled by Augustus Caesar in AD 8 to Tomis on the Black Sea, on account of what he calls an "error," never adequately explained. Camões seems to have felt his own exile to Ceuta was equally inadvertent (see ll. 34–35: "I find it strange / I've done no wrong").

line 42: See note to "As doces cantilenas que cantavam," l. 26, above.

58–63: This perhaps refers to a type of curved boat, driven by oars or a single sail, once seen at Punhete, a small town on the Tagus, where Camões may previously have been exiled. See the introduction, p. 4.

79–81: Gates of Tartarus: the doors of the underworld, entered by crossing the River Lethe, river of forgetfulness.

82: Tantalus: condemned to suffer eternal hunger and thirst, with food and water visible but beyond reach. Tycius, a giant who insulted Latona, Apollo's mother, was condemned, like Prometheus, to have his liver eternally eaten by a vulture.

83, "A Instabilidade da Fortuna": the first of Camões's mature hymns, reflecting once again on his punishment for "an error" in love (l. 11).

lines 33–48: The stanza expands on the myth of Tantalus. See note to "O Sulmonense Ovídio, desterrado," l. 82, above.

49–64: The stanza develops the myth of Ixion, who tried to seduce Hera and was punished by being bound to an eternally revolving wheel.

65–80: The lines parallel the previous two stanzas but with reference to the myth of Tycius.

81–96: The fourth of these adapted myths is the story of Sisyphus, who chained Death, preventing him claiming anyone until Ares released him, and who for other misdeeds was condemned eternally to push a boulder to the top of a hill, only to watch it roll down again.

115: Death sentences at the time were accompanied by a proclamation explaining the reasons for the judgment.

86, "Aquela que de amore descomedido". For D. António de Noronha, see note to "As doces cantilenas que cantavam," dedication, above.

line 1: Echo: see note to "As doces cantilenas que cantavam," l. 326, above.

2–3: Aphrodite punished Narcissus for his cruelty by making him die of love for his own reflection in a fountain.

46–57: Heracles: the labors of Heracles included establishing the Pillars that bear his name on either side of the Straits of Gibraltar; stealing the apple of the Hesperides by killing Ladon, the serpent entrusted with guarding it; and slaying the giant Antaeus, who drew strength from touching his mother, Earth. All three myths are plausibly said to have taken place in north Africa.

124–25: Salmoneus, son of Aeolus, rivaled Zeus, driving a bronze chariot and hurling fake thunderbolts; he was imprisoned in Tartarus. Belo, otherwise called Danaus, whose fifty daughters married the fifty sons of Aegyptus and, with the single exception of Hypermnestra, stabbed their husbands on their wedding night.

PART TWO: *Before India*

93, "Transforma-se o amador na cousa amada": one of the most philosophically dense of Camões's poems, and one of the toughest to translate given that clarity feels like simplification. It is sufficient to note that the terms of reference are Platonic and Aristotelian.

96, "O cisne, quando sente ser chegada":

line 14: Translates to "your false faith and my own love," a quotation from Juan Boscán.

97, "Suspiros inflamados, que cantais":

    line 4: Lethe: see note to "O Sulmonense Ovídio, desterrado," ll. 79–81, above.

97, "Fiou-se o coração, de muito isento":

    lines 9–10: Hippolytus, son of Theseus. Phaedra, Theseus's wife, fell in love with him and, when rebuffed, hanged herself, leaving a note denouncing him as her seducer. Banished, he died in a riding accident, Theseus learning the truth too late.

98, "Um mover d' olhos, brando e piadoso":

    line 13: Circe: the sorceress in book 10 of the Odyssey. The sonnet's conclusion echoes Petrarch's "Grazie ch'a pochi il ciel largo destina."

101, "Num tão alto lugar, de tanto preço":

    line 14: The line, meaning "a good death honors an entire life," is quoted from Petrarch's "Ben mi credea passar mio tempo omai."

103, "Diana prateada, esclarecia": Diana, the moon-goddess, illumined by Phoebus, the sun. The sonnet plays subtly with this paradox.

106, "Sustenta meu viver ua esperança":

    line 10: Camões puns once more on "pena," meaning, as noted above, both "suffering" and "a quill pen."

106, "Que modo tão sutil da natureza": in sixteenth-century Portugal, girls would take their convent vows as early as their twelfth birthday.

107, "Pues lágrimas tratáis, mis ojos triste": one of a handful of poems by Camões written in Spanish.

112, "Se derivais da verdade": Camões offers mock derivations of "citim" (which he writes in l. 2 as "sitim"), and "amarelo" (ll. 41–44) from "amarei-lo" ("I'll love you").

121, "Da lindeza vossa": the device refers to a phrase, in this case "Miraguarda" ("gaze and wonder") that would be written on a knight's shield at a tournament. Camões reverses the meaning.

122, "Pois a tantas perdições": the pen / pain pun once again.

123, "Despois de sempre sofrer": the theme is by Francisco de Morais, author of *Palmeira de Inglaterra*, who served with the family of D. António de Noronha, to whom several of Camões's poems are dedicated and who was probably a mutual friend.

125, "Despues que Amor me formó": from the Spanish. The theme is from Boscán.

127, "Se vos quereis embarcar":

    line 10: Povos, a village on the Tagus, near Vila Franca.

131, "Cum real de amor":

    line 13: Tronco, the Lisbon prison where Camões himself was incarcerated.

135, "Mande-me Amor que Cante Docemente":

> line 22: The sun enters Taurus on April 22, heralding spring and the return of the swallows, For Procne, see note to "As doces cantilenas que cantavam," l. 26, above.

138, "Pode um desejo imenso": the most celebrated of Camões's odes, a platonic (in every sense) celebration of the transcendent beauty of the loved woman.

> lines 68–70: The references are to Italian renaissance poetry, especially Dante (Beatrice) and Petrarch (Laura).

> 82: Betis: the River Guardalquivir. The line refers indirectly to Spanish and Roman poets, of whom the Tagus (Portugal) is a little envious.

141, "Quem pode ser no mundo tão quieto": dedicated once again to D. António de Noronha, and possibly written during Camões's imprisonment in the Tronco jail.

> line 18: Momus: in Greek mythology the personification of fault-finding.

> 25: Democritus: Greek philosopher b. 460 BC, a contemporary of Socrates.

> 57–64: Diogenes: 4th century BC Greek philosopher known for his unkempt lifestyle and his contempt for knowledge and morality. An anecdote has him trampling his dirty feet over the mosaic floor of Plato's house.

> 110: Cynic: refers again to Diogenes (about whom see the previous note), who scorned burial rituals.

> 129–52: Thrasyllus: Athenian naval officer, tried and executed after losing the battle of Arginusae (406 BC). Crito was his brother.

> 193–200: Petrarch's Laura is assumed to have been named for the laurel into which Daphne, fleeing Apollo, was transformed, the reward for poetic merit. The crystalline river is the Sorga, near where Laura is said to have lived. The other poets named are Jacopo Sanazzaro and Garcilaso de la Vega (see the introduction, p. 8).

148, "O Poeta Simónides, falando": Simonides (more usually, Semonides, 544–467 BC) was a Greek poet whose verses were so memorable they functioned as mnemonics. On this poem, see the introduction, p. 9.

> line 1: Themosticles: 524–480 BC, Athenian statesman and commander.

> 38: Pythagoras: Greek philosopher b. 580 BC, taught, among much else, the doctrine of the transmigration of souls.

> 45: Alecto: one of the Furies, avengers of crimes against kinship.

> 50: Hircania: territory north of the Caspian Sea.

> 56: Lethe: see note to "O Sulmonense Ovídio, desterrado," ll. 79–81, above.

> 67–141: Camões describes his voyage to India in 1553, anticipating the fuller account of Vasco da Gama's voyage in canto 5 of The Lusíads.

67–70: Aeolus: god of the winds, which were kept in a bag; Zephyr, the gentle west wind; Neptune, the sea god.

74–78: Galateia, etc.: See the introduction, p. 9, and notes to "As doces cantilenas que cantavam," lines 28 and 100–103, above.

93 Tethys: originally one of the Titans, wife of Oceanus, here making her first appearance in Camões's poetry, but destined to become (blended with Thetis, mother of Achilles) one of the presiding goddesses of *The Lusíads*.

95–96: The alluvial sands of the Tagus contain tiny fragments of gold dust.

112: "new star": the Southern Cross. Camões's knowledge of constellations was exact and detailed, and alien skies caused him more unease than alien lands or peoples.

121: Boreas and Notus: the north and south winds, respectively.

149–65: Camões's first expedition in Goa was against the Sultan of Chembe, under Vice-Roy Afonso de Noronha. See the introduction, p. 4.

162: Styx: one of the rivers of the underworld.

181–82: Paros marble: from the island of Paros in the Aegean. Corinth was famous for its dried fruits.

190: Tityrus and Silenus: shepherds in Virgil's eclogues. According to the myth, Justice (Astraea) lived on earth during the Golden Age, but fled to heaven with its demise.

203: primum mobile: in the Ptolemaic system, the original force driving the whole universe.

213: Rhadamanthus: son of Zeus and Europa, who became judge of the dead and ruler of the underworld.

PART THREE: *India and Beyond*

158, "Em flor vos arrancou, de então crecida": in memory of D. António de Noronha. Camões heard of his death at Ceuta shortly after arriving in India. The sonnet was enclosed with his letter from Goa, with the comment "I'm sending you (it) as a sign of how much it upset me." See the introduction, p. 20n, and the eclogue "Que grande variedade vão fazendo," p. 199.

161, "No mundo poucos anos, e cansados": commemorating a Portuguese youth, born in Alenquer, died at sea off Abyssinia. One manuscript names him as Pêro Moniz.

162, "Senhor João Lopes, o meu baixo estado": João Lopes Leitão was a friend of Camões's in Goa. He is one of the recipients of the invitation to the feast in "Se não quereis padecer," p. 260.

163, "Seguia aquele fogo, que o guiava": Leander, a youth of Abydos, swam nightly across the Hellespont to his lover, Hero, the priestess of Aphrodite. When he drowned, she flung herself into the sea.

164, "Por sua Ninfa, Céfalo deixava": This, and the succeeding sonnet "Sentindo-se tomada a bela esposa," are based on the myth of Cephalus, married to Procris, but loved by Aurora, goddess of the dawn. When Cephalus refused her, Aurora arranged for him to attempt to seduce Procris, disguised as a certain Pteleon, offering her a gold crown. Finding his wife succumb so easily, he became Aurora's lover. Procris was subsequently seduced by King Minos of Crete, but Cephalus, who loved her despite everything, went in pursuit and they were reconciled.

165, "Os vestidos Elisa revolvia": Elisa is Dido, queen of Carthage; her love for Aeneas, his abandonment of her, and her subsequent suicide together constitute the theme of book 4 of Virgil's *Aeneid*.

165, "Ferido sem ter cura perecia": Telephus, king of the Mysians, was wounded by Achilles en route to Troy. The oracle advised only the rust of Achilles' sword could cure him.

168, "Em fermosa Leteia se confia": Leteia believed herself more beautiful than any goddess and was punished, along with her husband, Oleno, by their being turned into boulders on Mount Ida. See note to "As doces cantilenas que cantavam," ll. 320–24, above.

169, "Enquanto Febo os montes acendia": line 14: refers to Venus caught with her lover Mars in a net woven by Vulcan, her husband.

170, "O filho de Latona esclarecido": Apollo's first feat was to seize Delphi as his shrine, killing the resident python. He had various lovers, but with the presiding nymph of the River Peneus in Thessaly he got nowhere.

172, "Cara minha inimiga, em cuja mão": on this and the subsequent five sonnets, see the introduction, p. 16. See also "Alma minha gentil, que te partiste", p. 222.

181, "Vêm-se rosas e boninas": Graça de Morais lived in Goa.

190, "Por cousa tão pouca": several stories have attached themselves to this song, probably apocryphal, but one of great popularity in India.

192, "Junto um seco, fero e estéril monte": Camões sailed with D. Fernando de Meneses's expedition to the Red Sea late in 1554. See the introduction, p. 4.

line 8: Arabia Felix: one of the three-fold divisions of Arabia (see canto 4, 63 of *The Lusíads*).

12: Abbasiya: Abyssinia.

13: Ptolemy is said to have founded a city there, named for his wife, Berenice.

18: compare canto 10, 97 of *The Lusíads*. Camões knew this part of the world intimately.

196, "Aquele moço fero": this ode has close affinities with "Aquela cativa," p. 253.

line 1: Achilles: son of Thetis, raised by the wise centaur Chiron, who educated several Greek heroes.

5: Achilles was dipped in the River Styx to make him impregnable. His weak point thereafter was the heel by which his mother held him.

22: "the gentle slave": probably Briseis, the girl confiscated by Agamemnon in book I of the *Iliad*, and the cause of Achilles' prolonged sulk in his tent.

26: Pelias: Achilles's spear.

30: "eyeless": the reference is to blind Cupid.

33: "one": the subject shifts to Camões himself.

61: "Jewish king": Solomon, to please his wives, raised altars to Ashtoreth and Molech, among others. See 1 Kings 11:5–7.

66–80: Aristotle: this accusation was leveled by Diogenes Laertius (AD200–250), unreliable Greek author of *The Lives and Opinions of Eminent Philosophers*.

199, "Que grande variedade vão fazendo": D. António de Noronha, dedicatee of several of Camões earlier poems, was killed in the attack on Ceuta in 1553 (see the sonnet "Em flor vos arrancou, de então crecida," p. 158). D. João, prince of Portugal and father of the future king Sebastian, died in January 1554. Camões's letter from Goa (see the introduction, p. 5) mentions this poem, "which seems to me better than every eclogue I've written."

69–70: Ceuta: enclave in Morocco, captured by Portugal in 1415. Hidaspe is the river Jhelum, now in West Pakistan, where Alexander the Great defeated King Porus.

85–96: the lines describe the national disaster of the temporary loss of Ceuta to the Moroccans in 1553, when the whole garrison was massacred, including D. António. From here to l. 284, the poem is a sustained lament for Camões's lost friend.

187: Oreads: nymphs of the mountains.

243: Euryalus: see the great battle scene at 10:176–502 of the *Aeneid*.

259: Marfida: perhaps stands for D. Margarida da Silva, daughter of D. Garcia da Silva, the lady D. António is said to have loved. She was a niece of the D. Francisco de Almeida whom Camões invited to his feast in "Se não quereis padecer," p. 260.

285: the second part of the eclogue turns to the death of D. João, mourned by his widow D. Joana, daughter of the emperor Charles V.

345: "One": the shepherds encounter the widow weeping by her husband's open tomb.

364: Taprobana: identified with Ceylon in canto 10, 51 of *The Lusíads*.

365: "this little one": the infant Sebastian, born weeks after his father's death.

371: Ampelusa: north Africa, where the giant Atlas was turned to stone (the Atlas Mountains) by gazing at Medusa.

385: Aonia: is an anagram for Joana, who sings in Castilian Spanish, her native tongue.

421: Citerian: from Cyprus.

212, "Naquele tempo brando": the ode reworks Ovid's account in book 11 of *Metamorphoses* of the rape of Thetis by Peleus, king of Phthia.

line 10: Notus: the south wind.

18: Clicie: see note to "As doces cantilenas que cantavam," l. 404, above.

20: "heavenly twins": the sun enters the constellation Gemini in May.

85–90: Thetis was fated to bear a son mightier than his father, so Zeus avoided her, permitting Peleus's rape. See note to "Aquele moço fero," l. 5, above.

219, "Sete anos de pastor Jacob servia": based on the account in Genesis 29:15–30.

222, "Alma minha gentil, que te partiste": according to Diogo de Couto, in *Decada* VIII, this sonnet was addressed to Camões's Chinese lover, whom he called Dinamene, and who was drowned off the Mekong Delta. See the introduction, p. 16, and the series of sonnets on pp. 172–173.

224, "Em prisões baixas fui um tempo atado": Camões was jailed at least three times, once in Lisbon's Tronco prison and twice in Goa.

line 6: "lambs and heifers": animals used in sacrificial rituals.

228, "Quem fosse acompanhando juntamente": possibly written in prison.

229, "Cantando estava um dia bem seguro":

line 7: "two wolves": these appear to signify two disasters, though in a life of so many disasters it is hard to know which two Camões has in mind—perhaps his dismissal from his post in Macão and the drowning of Dinamene?

234, "Cá nesta Babilonia, donde mana": this, and the sonnet that follows, "Na ribeira do Eufrates assentado," with their bitter identification of Goa with Babylon, draw much of their imagery from Psalm 137. See "Sóbolos rios que vão," p. 317, which develops the theme further.

237, "O dia em que eu nasci, moura e pereça": this sonnet is based on Job 3:1–9.

239, "Querendo escrever um dia": another of Camões's catalogue poems, but drawing this time not on Ovid's *Metamorphoses* but on examples drawn from his own travels.

lines 9, 15, 19–20: "quill": here again, Camões utilizes the "pen/pain" pun.

43–45: "mountain dwellers": perhaps a vegetarian Hindu sect whose followers covered their mouths with a veil to avoid breathing in small insects. Compare canto 7, 19 of *The Lusíads*.

51: "a tree": various plants have been mooted, such as Nicotiana (tobacco plant) or Oenothera (evening primrose), but none properly fits Camões's description.

61: Mithridates: king of Pontus circa 115 BC, who protected himself against being poisoned by taking small doses to build up his resistance.

71: "the royal disease": jaundice.

92: Pygmalion: king of Cyprus who carved a statue of Galateia, and was permitted by Venus to bring her to life and marry her.

121–125: "andorinha": meaning both "swallow" and the plant chelidomium (greater celandine), which swallows are said to use to open the eyes of their chicks, which are blind at birth.

131–35: "unknown river": in canto 10, 134 of *The Lusíads*, Camões locates this river in Java.

141–45: "silent eel": the electric eel, *Electrophorus electricus*, found in the Amazon and Orinoco rivers.

182: The bird ("camão" in the text) is the alqueimão or galinha sultana (*Porphyria porphyria*), called variously in English the purple gallinule or purple swamp hen. The legend is the theme of Number 97 of the *Book of Emblems* by the Italian Andreas Alciatus, 1492–1550.

198: harpies: mythological birds with the faces of women. In the legend of Phineus, they were sent by Helios (the sun) to defile his food after he blinded his children by his first wife.

251, "Perdigão, que o pensamento": based on an old folksong, perhaps a tongue-twister (playing on "perdigão," partridge, and "perder," to lose).

253, "Aquela cativa": see the introduction, p. 14, and compare "Aquele moço fero," p. 196.

254, "Quererdes profano amor": the poem involves a sustained pun on Coresma, the name of the wronged husband, and Quaresma, meaning Lent.

256, "Vossa Senhoria creia": Heitor da Silveira was one of the friends invited to Camões's feast in "Se não quereis padecer," p. 260. The first three stanzas are said to be his, with Camões adding the fourth.

258, "Viver eu, sendo mortal": composed on a theme sent him by Vice-Roy D. Francisco Coutinho, which is taken to imply a mild rebuke.

258, "Conde, cujo ilustre peito": addressed once again to Vice-Roy D. Francisco Coutinho and appealing for employment.

260, "Se não quereis padecer": as his English translator, I find Camões a much wittier poet than many Portuguese commentators believe him to be. But

it is rare to find him in so light-hearted a mood as here, and further anno-
tation would be ridiculous.

263, "Com força desusada": see the introduction, p. 12.

266, "Aquele único exemplo": the first of Camões's poems to be published, by way
of a preface to Garcia de Orta's *Colóquiodos Simples e Drogas da India* (Goa,
1563), a pioneering study of medicinal plants. The ode takes the form of an
appeal to Vice-Roy D. Francisco Coutinho to offer the author his patronage.

line 20: Chiron: see note to "Aquele moço fero," l. 1, above.

23: "Telephus": see the sonnet "Ferido sem ter cura perecia," p. 165.

34–36: Taprobana: see note to "Que grande variedade vão fazendo," l.
364, above. The Aceh people threatened Malucca. See also "Vós, Ninfas da
Gangética espessura," p. 286. Cambay is Gujerat in India.

41: Orta: the author's name, but also a pun on "horta" ("kitchen garden").

46: Medea and Circe: mythological sorceresses.

53: Asclepius: the god of medicine.

269, "Que novas tristes são, que novo dano".

epigraph: no one knows for sure which member of the Menses family,
several of whom served in Goa, is celebrated in this elegy, or which battle
led to his death.

78: Myrrha: see note to "As doces cantilenas que cantavam," l. 348,
above. Venus loved Adonis, who was killed by a wild boar.

79–80: Hyacinth: loved by Apollo, but Zepherus, who was jealous, blew
a quoit with which the two were playing, striking Hyacinth on the head
and killing him. From his blood sprang the flower that bears his name.

94: Thespis: pre-Homeric poet, credited with being the first to intro-
duce an actor into his performances. His "daughters" are the Muses.

113: D. Filipe: D. Miguel's brother.

120: "the old Cynic": for Diogenes, see note to "Quem pode ser no
mundo tão quieto," ll. 57–64.

121–22: Ovid: born in Sulmo.

145: Aaron: see Leviticus 10:1–3.

169–74: "great-grandfather": D. Duarte de Meneses, killed at Ceuta cov-
ering the retreat of King Afonso V. His mausoleum at Santarem contained
just one of his teeth.

185: Diogenes: see note to "Quem pode ser no mundo tão quieto," ll.
57–64, above. Theodorus, a Byzantine philosopher.

220–25: Camões is quoting from Justine, *History* 1, chap. 4.

PART FOUR: *Portugal*

279, "Como fizeste, Porcia, tal ferida?": Porcia, wife of Brutus and an ardent re-
publican, proved her worthiness to join the conspiracy against Caesar by

stabbing her arm. After Brutus's defeat and suicide, she killed herself by swallowing coals.

280, "Tal mostra dá de si vossa figura":

line 1: Sibela is probably an anagram of Isabel.

280, "Aquela que, de pura castidade": Lucretia, raped by King Tarquin's son, told her husband and stabbed herself. The incident led to the expulsion of the Tarquins from Rome.

281, "Dizei, Senhora, da Beleza ideia":

line 8: Medea: see note to "Aquele único exemplo," l. 46, above.

14: Narcissus: see note to "Aquela que de amore descomedido," ll. 1–2, above.

282, "De um tão felice engenho, produzido": published for the first time in 1668 with the epigraph, "To D. Simão da Silveira, in reply to one of his with the same rhymes, sending it him to enquire who was the first poet to make sonnets." A sonnet with the same rhymes is an agreeable compliment, but the theme is the rise of poetry in general.

line 5: Musaeus: legendary pre-Homeric poet, said to be Orpheus's pupil.

7–8: "musician-lover": Musaeus, about whom see previous note.

11: "youth of Abydos": see "Seguia aquele fogo, que o guiava," p. 163.

12: Bernardo Tasso: Italian poet, whose *Gerusalemme Liberata* appeared in 1575, becoming a late influence on Camões; Juan Boscán: the Spanish poet, a long-standing favourite of the poet's.

14: "the blind king": Cupid.

282, "De tão divino acento e voz humana": like the previous sonnet, sent in response to one addressed to him and employing the same rhyme scheme.

line 6: Hippocrene: the Muses' fountain.

8: "the Mantuan": Virgil.

10: Mnemosyne: the mother of the Muses, associated with memory.

283, "Despois que viu Cibele o corpo humano": see note to "As doces cantilenas que cantavam," ll. 356–71, above.

line 12: some editions, including Costa Pimpão's, capitalize Pinheiro, suggesting Camões is referring to D. António Pinheiro, Bishop of Miranda, who in 1574 had the temerity to criticize King Sebastian for his military adventures.

283, "'Não passes, caminhante!' 'Quem me chama?'": commemorating an unknown hero, possibly D. Gonçalo da Silveira, the missionary killed in 1561 at the court of Monomotapa, as described in canto 10, 93 of *The Lusíads*.

284, "'Que levas, cruel Morte?'": as with the sonnet that follows, this commemorates a lady not conclusively identified.

285, "Quem jaz no grão sepulcro, que descreve": a funeral elegy for King Jõao III, who died in 1557, but was reburied 1572 in the chapel of the Jerónimos Monastery at Belém.

> line 9: Alexander the Great.
>
> 11: Hadrian: Roman emperor, AD 117–138.
>
> 13: see note to "As doces cantilenas que cantavam," ll. 309–11, above.

285, "Ilustre e dino ramo dos Meneses": in praise of D. Francisco de Meneses, son of the Vice-Roy D. Afonso de Noronha, who led the Red Sea expedition of 1554 against the Turkish fleet, in which Camões participated. See the introduction, p. 4.

> line 11: Gedrosia: now West Pakistan.

286, "Vós, Ninfas da Gangética espessura": the only sonnet published in Camões's lifetime, it commemorates D. Léonis Pereira, who defended Malacca in 1558 against the King of Aceh. It appeared in Pêro de Magalhães Gândava's *Historia da Provincia de Santa Cruz* (1576). See also "Depois que Magalhães teve tecida," p. 304.

> line 13: Leonides: king of Sparta, and commander of the Greeks at Thermopylae.

286, "Que vençais no Oriente tantos Reis": addressed to D. Luís de Ataide, Vice-Roy from 1568–71, and reappointed in 1577.

287, "Os reinos e os impérios poderosos": in praise of the heir to the Duke of Bragança. The most likely candidate is D. Teodósio, sent by his father at the age of ten to join King Sebastian's disastrous expedition to Morocco in 1578. Captured at Alcacer Kebir, he returned to Portugal in 1580 in the retinue of Philip II.

> lines 5–8: the heroes listed are Themistocles, the Athenian statesman and commander; the two Roman Scipios, father and son, named Africanus Major and Minor; and the Spanish heroes, Rodrigo Diaz de Biva (El Cid) and the seven "Infantes de Lara," celebrated in the several collections of the Romanceros.

288, "Ved que engaños señorea": from the Spanish.

289, "Corre sem vela e sem leme": a labyrinth—that is, a poem—that might be read in sequence from start to finish, or in reverse, from the last line to the first; or by taking the first lines of each in sequence followed by the second lines, et cetera; or by reading lines 1, 3, 5, 7, and 9 followed by lines 2, 4, 6, 8, and 10, and so on. Obviously it makes impossible demands on the translator and I have given here only the literal meaning.

291, "A quem darão de Pindo as moradoras": praises addressed to D. Manel de Portugal, son of the Count of Vimioso, and a poet much influenced by Italian models, as Camões's style reflects.

> line 1: Mount Pindus: another home of the Muses.

4–8: The laurel for poetry, the myrtle for love, and the palm for victory in battle.

9: Choris: wife of Zepherus, the west wind, presiding over flowers.

10: Doris: a sea-nymph, one of the Nereids.

16–17: Amphion: legendary musician of ancient Thebes, credited with charming the very stones; Arion, legendary poet from Lesbos.

26: Maecenas: patron of Virgil, Horace, and Propertius. It has been suggested that D. Manuel facilitated the publication of *The Lusiads*.

53–54: four distinguished figures who all valued and protected poets.

293, "Espirito valeroso, cujo estado": a plea for leniency in the case of a certain D. Caterina, a young lady of noble birth, imprisoned for adultery while her husband was absent in India. Those involved, and the outcome of the case, are not known.

69: *"there"*: Camões envisages her preyed on by sailors en route to banishment in India.

89: St. John: see Matthew 3:1–6.

93: Jerome: Christian saint, writer, diplomat, and hermit (342–420).

97–101: During the plague years of the 1570s, many wealthy families left Lisbon for their estates.

105–12: these examples of chastity are: Artemis (the goddess Diana); Sempronia and Valeria (references unknown); Lucretia, (see also "Aquela que, de pura castidade," p. 280); Timóquia (reference unknown); Sarah (wife of Abraham); and Penelope (wife of Odysseus).

116: Vesta: goddess of chastity.

297, "Vinde cá, meu tão certo secretário": see the introduction, p. 18.

51: "a blind child": Cupid.

128: Tartarus: part of the underworld reserved for those who committed crimes on earth.

304, "Depois que Magalhães teve tecida": an appeal to D. Léonis Pereira, twice governor of Malacca, to lend his patronage to Pêro de Magalhães Gândava's *Historia da Provincia de Santa Cruz* (1576). See also "Vós, Ninfas da Gangética espessura," p. 286. Both poems were included in the book.

line 3: Santa Cruz: Brazil.

6: Zoilus: fourth-century BC Greek critic, who filled nine books with detailed criticisms of Homer.

25: Thalia: muse of comedy.

34: Mercury: messenger of the gods, skilled in arbitration.

42: Belona: goddess of war.

74: "army of Aceh": the indigenous people of Malacca.

307, "A Rústica contenda desueda": a poetic contest in contrasting styles between Agrário the shepherd, in love with Dinamene, and Alieuto the fisherman, in love with Lemnoria, as also between the traditional pastoral eclogue and the new "piscatorial" eclogue invented by the Italian Jacobo Sanazzaro (1458–1530).

line 13: "blind love": again, Cupid.

19: "you": the Duke of Aveiro, grandson of King João II. The next ten tercets praise the dynasty as much as the individual.

22–24: referring to Portugal's voyages to India and Brazil.

27: "fount of Parnassus": shorthand for the source of poetry itself.

34–36: "royal ancestors": Kings João I, Duarte, Afonso V, and João II all campaigned in north Africa.

38: Toro: site of the battle in 1476 between Afonso V and Ferdinand of Spain. Afonso was only saved from defeat by the intervention of his son, the future João II. See canto 4, 57–59 of *The Lusíads*.

62: "ancient Mantuan": again, Virgil.

126: Amphitrite: wife of Poseidon, god of the sea.

194–95: Tritons: mermen; Palaemon, a sea-god; Proteus, another sea-god and the herder of seals.

201: Apollo: the sun god, as punishment for killing the Cyclops, was condemned to serve Admetus for a year in the guise of a shepherd beside the river Anphrisus.

205: Io: raped by Jupiter and turned into a cow to hide her from Juno's anger. Jupiter himself became a bull to seduce Europa.

209: Claucus: a fisherman, became immortal through eating magic herbs; Proteus: see note to ll. 194–95, above.

211: "the goddess": Venus.

213: "a dolphin": Neptune became a dolphin to seduce the sea-nymph Melanto.

215: the reference is to an anecdote in Ravísio Textor's *Officina* about a group of fishermen who encountered Homer on the beach and teased him with the riddle, "We freed what we caught, and we brought what we couldn't catch." Apparently, they had only been bathing.

299: see note to l. 201, above.

317, "Sóbolos rios que vão": a sustained meditation on Psalm 137, continuing the theme of the sonnets "Cá nesta Babilónia, donde mana" and "Na ribeira do Eufrates assentado," p. 234 and p. 235, respectively. For the first two hundred lines, Zion represents past happiness and Babylon the misery of exile. From line 201 to the end, however, Zion represents future happiness in heaven, and Babylon life on earth. The contrast is paralleled by Camões's avowal to abandon "ballads of profane desire" and sing instead their palinode, "anthems of divine love" (ll. 234–35).

114–15: the lines are by Juan Boscán—"She will be present to my eyes / for whom I die contentedly."

201: the poem's turning point, with Camões at his most Platonic.

328, "Arde por Galateia branca e loura": another piscatorial eclogue.

29: Arrabida: the mountain range south of Lisbon, dominating the Setubal Peninsula.

330, "Foge-me pouco a pouco a curta vida": a sestina, a form comprising six six-line stanzas. Instead of rhyme, the same line-endings appear in each stanza, but in shifting order following a strict pattern, and are emphasized in the shorter lines of the final stanza.

❊ SUGGESTED FURTHER READING ❊

Editions of Camões's Lyrics

Luís de Camões: Obras Completas, com prefácio e notas do Prof. Hernâni Cidade. 1971. Redondilhas e Sonetos. 1985. Géneros Líricos Maiores. Lisboa: Sá da Costa.

Rimas, ed. Álvaro J. De Costa Pimpão, com apresentação de Aníbal Pinto de Castro. 1994. Coimbra: Almedina.

Lírica de Camões, 5 vols, 1985–2001. ed. Leodegário A. de Azevedo Filho. Lisboa: Imprensa Nacional: Casa de Moeda.

Lírica Completa, 3 vols. 1986–2002. ed. Maria de Lurdes Saraiva. Lisboa: Imprensa Nacional: Casa de Moeda.

Translations

Seventy Sonnets of Camoens, trans. J. J. Aubertin. 1881. London: Kegan and Paul.

Camoens: the Lyricks, Englished by Sir Richard F. Burton. 2 vols. 1884. London: Bernard Quaritch.

Camões: Some Poems, trans. Jonathan Griffin, with essays by Jorge de Sena and Helder Macedo. 1976. London: Menard.

Camões: Epic and Lyric, ed. L. C. Taylor and trans. Keith Bosley, illus. Lima de Freitas. 1990. Manchester: Carcanet.

113 Galician-Portuguese Troubadour Poems, in Galician-Portuguese and English, trans. Richard Zenith. 1995. Manchester: Carcanet.

The Lusíads. Luís Vaz de Camões, trans. with an introduction and notes by Landeg White. 2001 [1997]. Oxford: Oxford University Press.

Luís de Camões: Selected Sonnets, ed. and trans. William Baer. 2005. Chicago: University of Chicago Press.

Background and General Studies

NOTE: among the best general essays on Portuguese early literary history, and on Camões as traveling soldier and poet, are those of Aubertin, Burton, Helder Macedo, de Sena, and Zenith in the introductions and appended essays to the translations listed above. The introduction to António Salgado Junior, *Luís Vaz de Camões: Obras Completas*, série Portuguesa 7, 1963 (Rio de Janeiro: Biblioteca Luso-Brasileira) questions the legends surrounding Camões's life, many of which are reinstated in José Hermano Saraiva, *Vida Ignorada de Camões* (Lisboa: Europa-America, 1978).

Storck, Wilhelm. 1890. *Luís de Camoens Leben*. Paderborn, Germany: Schöningh. Trans. from the German by Carolina Michaelis de Vasconcelos. 1897. *Vida e Obras de Luís de Camões*. Lisboa: Academia das Ciências.

Bell, Aubrey F. G. 1923. *Luís de Camões*. London: Oxford University Press.

Boxer, C. R. 1969. *The Portuguese Seaborne Empire*. London: Hutchinson. Pearson, M. N. 1988. *The Portuguese in India*. Cambridge: Cambridge University Press.

Birmingham, David. 1993. *A Concise History of Portugal*. Cambridge: Cambridge University Press.

Chandeigne, Michel. 1990. ed., Lisbonne *Hors les Murs: 1415–1580; l'invention du monde par les navigateurs portugais*. Paris: Éditions Autrement. Trans. and ed. Carlos Araújo. *Lisboa e os descobrimentos: 1415–1580: a invenção do mundo pelos navegadores portugueses*. 1990. Lisboa: Terramar.

Marques, Alfredo Pinheiro. 1991. *A Cartografia Portuguesa e a Construção do Mundo*. Lisboa: Imprensa Nacional: Casa da Moeda.

Costa Ramalho, Américo da. 1992. *Camões no seu Tempo e no Nosso*. Coimbra: Almedina.

Saraiva, António José. 1997, *Luís de Camões*, rev. by Manuel Joaquim Vieira. Lisboa: Gradiva.

On Camões's Lyric Poetry

Sena, Jorge de. 1969. *Os Sonetos de Camões e o soneto quinhenista peninsular*. Lisboa: Portugália.

Macedo, Helder. 1980. *Camões e a Viagem Iniciática*. Lisboa: Morães:

———. 1998. "Love as Knowledge: the Lyric Poetry of Camões." *Portuguese Studies* 14:51–64.

Earle, T. F. 1987. "Autobiografia e retórica n uma canção de Camões." *Arquivos do Central Cultural Português* 233:507–21.

Fraga, Maria do Ceu. 1989. *Camões: um bucolismo intranquilo*. Coimbra: Almedina.

————. 2003. Os *Géneros Maiores na Poesia Lírica de Camões*. Coimbra: Centro de Estudos Camonianos.

Aguiar e Silva, Vitor Manuel de. 1999. Camões: *Labirintos e Fascínios*. Lisboa: Cotovia.

Recommended Especially

"Post-Imperial Camões." *Portuguese Literary and Cultural Studies* 9 (2003), Center for Portuguese Studies and Culture (University of Massachusetts/ Dartmouth), which contains the following excellent essays on the lyrics:

Vendler, Helen. "Camões the Sonneteer," 17–37;

Tamen, Miguel. "Second Attempt," 39–48;

Marnoto, Rita. " 'Bárbara Escrava' ": canon, beauty, and color—an embarrassing contradiction," 49–61;

Macedo, Helder. "Conceptual Oppositions in the Poetry of Camões," 63–77.

On the cover picture, see Soares de Azevedo, Maria Antonieta, 'Uma nova e preciosa espécie iconográfica quinhentista de Camões' in *Panorama* IV Série, n.º 42–43, Setembro 1972, pps. 96–103.

I once sang, and now hear me lamenting
231
I passed on earth a few weary years   161
I saw Cupid when tiny   50
I spoke, Lady, of beauty's ideal form   281
I, to gain the laurel   250
It's a matter for history   181
It's high time my confidence   217
It's the fashionable art   245
I was singing, happy as the day was long
229
It was to my advantage   40
I watched the world tasking   289
I wept, nymphs, over Fate's severe   284

Lady, after long enduring   123
Lady, if I could contrive   38
Lady of strange perfection   107
Lay down some law, Lady, for wooing
you   95
Leander followed the fire that steered
163
Leteia put her faith in beauty   168
Life, I abandon you! In such a demise
162
Little by little it ebbs, this life   330
Love commanded me to sing   135
Love is a fire that burns invisibly   26
Lovely presence, modeled on angels   32
Love, not knowing any cure   183
Lovers change themselves into the thing
93
Love, that stamps on the soul a human
brow   35
Love, wishing to secrete you   180
Love, whose providence   180

Meadows full of pleasure   185
Memorial to the good times, carved in
flowers   237
Memories, you recall my happy times
232
Misfortunes, seeing that you plot against
223

Modest and maidenly behavior   53
Mottled dawn was spreading her crystal
166
My dearest enemy, in whose hand   172
My errors, ill fortune, and ardent love
230
My heart had always set such store   97
My jealous heart   116
My lady, if it is Fortune's will   160
My Lord João Lopes, my low degree
162

Naiads, you who dwell in the rivers   37
Never in past enjoyments   249
Nise was parted from Montano   166
None of us could allay   43
No pleasure in living memory   177
Note, Lady, the deceptions   288
Nymphs of the forests of the Ganges
valley   286

Observe what a harsh judgment   182
O, how it drags me along year by year
218
Old thoughts that now, newly minted
219
On account of his nymph, Cephalus
broke up   164
On a place so exalted, of such credit
101
Once Cupid had fashioned me   125
Once Sibele had seen the handsome
body   283
One hope sustains my whole existence
106
On her head she bears her water pot
187
On seeing you, what's visible   181
Out of desperation I laid to rest   231
Over something so trite   190
Ovid, born in Sulmo and banished   80

Pardon now, Lady, and from your heart
all   100

George Seferis: Collected Poems (1924–1955), translated, edited, and introduced by Edmund Keeley and Philip Sherrard

Collected Poems of Lucio Piccolo, translated and edited by Brian Swann and Ruth Feldman

C. P. Cavafy: Selected Poems, translated by Edmund Keeley and Philip Sherrard and edited by George Savidis

Benny Andersen: Selected Poems, translated by Alexander Taylor

Selected Poetry of Andrea Zanzotto, edited and translated by Ruth Feldman and Brian Swann

Poems of René Char, translated and annotated by Mary Ann Caws and Jonathan Griffin

Selected Poems of Tudor Arghezi, translated by Michael Impey and Brian Swann

"The Survivor" and Other Poems, by Tadeusz Rózewicz, translated and introduced by Magnus J. Krynski and Robert A. Maguire

"Harsh World" and Other Poems, by Angel González, tr by Donald D. Walsh

Ritsos in Parentheses, translated and introduced by Edmund Keeley

Salamander: Selected Poems of Robert Marteau, translated by Anne Winters

Angelos Sikelianos: Selected Poems, translated and introduced by Edmund Keeley and Philip Sherrard

Dante's "Rime", translated by Patrick S. Diehl

Selected Later Poems of Marie Luise Kaschnitz, translated by Lisel Mueller

Osip Mandelstam's "Stone", translated and introduced by Robert Tracy

The Dawn Is Always New: Selected Poetry of Rocco Scotellaro, translated by Ruth Feldman and Brian Swann

Sounds, Feelings, Thoughts: Seventy Poems by Wislawa Szymborska, translated and introduced by Magnus J. Krynski and Robert A. Maguire

The Man I Pretend To Be: "The Colloquies" and Selected Poems of Guido Gozzano, translated and edited by Michael Palma, with an introductory essay by Eugenio Montale

D'Après Tout: Poems by Jean Follain, translated by Heather McHugh

Songs of Something Else: Selected Poems of Gunnar Ekelöf, translated by Leonard Nathan and James Larson

The Little Treasury of One Hundred People, One Poem Each, compiled by Fujiwara No Sadaie and translated by Tom Galt

The Ellipse: Selected Poems of Leonardo Sinisgalli, translated by W. S. Di Piero

The Difficult Days by Robert Sosa, translated by Jim Lindsey

Hymns and Fragments by Friedrich Hölderlin, translated and introduced by Richard Sieburth

The Silence Afterwards: Selected Poems of Rolf Jacobson, translated and edited by Roger Greenwald

Rilke: Between Roots, selected poems rendered from the German by Rika Lesser

In The Storm of Roses: Selected Poems by Ingeborg Bachmann, translated, edited, and introduced by Mark Anderson

Birds and Other Relations: Selected Poetry of Dezso Tandori, translated by Bruce Berlind

Brocade River Poems: Selected Works of the Tang Dynasty Courtesan Xue Tao, translated and introduced by Jeanne Larsen

The True Subject: Selected Poems of Faiz Ahmed Faiz, translated by Naomi Lazard

My Name on the Wind: Selected Poems of Diego Valeri, translated by Michael Palma

Aeschylus: The Suppliants, translated by Peter Burian

Foamy Sky: The Major Poems of Miklós Radnóti, selected and translated by Zsuzsanna Ozváth and Frederick Turner

La Fontaine's Bawdy: Of Libertines, Louts, and Lechers, translated by Norman R. Shapiro

A Child Is Not a Knife: Selected Poems of Göran Sonnevi, translated and edited by Rika Lesser

George Seferis: Collected Poems, Revised Edition, translated, edited, and introduced by Edmund Keeley and Philip Sherrard

C. P. Cavafy: Collected Poems, Revised Edition, translated and introduced by Edmund Keeley and Philip Sherrard and edited by George Savidis

Selected Poems of Shmuel HaNagid, translated from the Hebrew by Peter Cole

The Late Poems of Meng Chiao, translated by David Hinton

Leopardi: Selected Poems, translated by Eamon Grennan

Through Naked Branches: Selected Poems of Tarjei Vesaas, translated and edited by Roger Greenwald

The Complete Odes and Satires of Horace, translated with introduction and notes by Sidney Alexander

Selected Poems of Solomon Ibn Gabirol, translated by Peter Cole

Puerilities: Erotic Epigrams of The Greek Anthology, translated by Daryl Hine

Night Journey, by María Negroni, tr by Anne Twitty

The Poetess Counts to 100 and Bows Out, by Ana Enriqueta Terán, translated by Marcel Smith

Nothing Is Lost: Selected Poems by Edvard Kocbek, translated by Michael Scammell and Veno Taufer, and introduced by Michael Scammell

The Complete Elegies of Sextus Propertius, translated with introduction and notes by Vincent Katz

Knowing the East, by Paul Claudel, translated with introduction and notes by James Lawler

Enough to Say It's Far: Selected Poems of Pak Chaesam, translated by David R. McCann and Jiwon Shin

In Hora Mortis / Under the Iron of the Moon: Poems, by Thomas Bernhard, translated by James Reidel

The Greener Meadow: Selected Poems, by Luciano Erba, translated by Peter Robinson

The Dream of the Poem: Hebrew Poetry from Muslim and Christian Spain, 950–1492, translated, edited, and introduced by Peter Cole

The Collected Lyric Poems of Luís de Camões, translated by Landeg White